Freedom of Religion and Constitutional Law

This book investigates the intersection of religion and modern law. It explores how secular courts encounter the religious or mythical question which is disavowed by modern institutions. It questions the private-public dichotomy of liberal constitutionalism which relegates religion to the private sphere. It argues that in ex-colonial societies like India which are foundationally and diversely religious, the courts need to work through and engage with the difficulties and complexities posed by their continual encounter with the question of religion rather than re-affirming the myth of separation of law and myth, state and religion. This work demonstrates that any other approach leads to its repression and resultant reemergence in various forms. Such an approach of working through religious categories will be effective in the struggle against religious fanaticism that has seen a resurgence in contemporary times.

The book will be a valuable resource for students and academics working in law, religious studies, history and political science.

Amit Bindal is Professor at Jindal Global Law School, O.P. Jindal Global University, India.

ICLARS Series on Law and Religion

The *ICLARS Series on Law and Religion* is a new series designed to provide a forum for the rapidly expanding field of research in law and religion. The series is published in association with the International Consortium for Law and Religion Studies, an international network of scholars and experts of law and religion founded in 2007 with the aim of providing a place where information, data and opinions can easily be exchanged among members and made available to the broader scientific community. The series aims to become a primary source for students and scholars while presenting authors with a valuable means to reach a wide and growing readership.

Series Editors:

Silvio Ferrari, University of Milan, Italy, Russell Sandberg, Cardiff University, UK, Pieter Coertzen, University of Stellenbosch, South Africa, W. Cole Durham, Jr., Brigham Young University, USA, and Tahir Mahmood, Amity International University, India

Other titles in this series:

Fundamental Rights, Religion and Human Dignity
A Constitutional Journey
Edited by Javier Martínez-Torrón and Li-ann Thio

Secularism and Freedom of Religion in Italy
Religious Symbols in the Public Space
Maria Cristina Ivaldi

The Jewish Legal Tradition
Edited by Ari Mermelstein, Suzanne Last Stone, and Yair Lorberbaum

Freedom of Religion and Constitutional Law
Traversing Myth and Modernity in India
Amit Bindal

For more information about this series, please visit: www.routledge.com/ICLARS-Series-on-Law-and-Religion/book-series/ICLARS

Freedom of Religion and Constitutional Law

Traversing Myth and Modernity in India

Amit Bindal

Routledge
Taylor & Francis Group
LONDON AND NEW YORK

First published 2025
by Routledge
4 Park Square, Milton Park, Abingdon, Oxon OX14 4RN

and by Routledge
605 Third Avenue, New York, NY 10158

Routledge is an imprint of the Taylor & Francis Group, an informa business

British Library Cataloguing-in-Publication Data
A catalogue record for this book is available from the British Library

Library of Congress Cataloging-in-Publication Data
Names: Bindal, Amit, author.
Title: Freedom of religion and constitutional law : traversing myth and modernity in India / Amit Bindal.
Description: Abingdon, Oxon [UK] ; New York, NY : Routledge, 2025. | Series: Iclars series on law and religion | Includes bibliographical references and index.
Identifiers: LCCN 2025003504 (print) | LCCN 2025003505 (ebook) | ISBN 9781032463469 (hardback) | ISBN 9781032504551 (paperback) | ISBN 9781003398561 (ebook)
Subjects: LCSH: Freedom of religion—India. | Religious law and legislation—India. | Constitutional law—India. | Civilization, Modern.
Classification: LCC KNS2116 .B56 2025 (print) | LCC KNS2116 (ebook) | DDC 342.5408/52—dc23/eng/20250128
LC record available at https://lccn.loc.gov/2025003504
LC ebook record available at https://lccn.loc.gov/2025003505

ISBN: 978-1-032-46346-9 (hbk)
ISBN: 978-1-032-50455-1 (pbk)
ISBN: 978-1-003-39856-1 (ebk)

DOI: 10.4324/9781003398561

Typeset in Galliard
by Apex CoVantage, LLC

For Latika

Contents

	Acknowledgements	*viii*
	Introduction	1
1	Interpreting the Free Exercise Clause: Reflections on the Doctrine of Essential Religious Practices	33
2	Constitutionalism and the Sacred Cow: Secular Mythology of the Indian Supreme Court	71
3	Religion and Elections: Legal Interpretation of Hinduism as Religion	100
4	Mythology as/and History in Indian Courtrooms: The Ayodhya Dispute	129
5	In Lieu of a Conclusion	166
6	Epilogue	181
	Author Index	*187*
	Thematic Index	*189*

Acknowledgements

This book owes its genesis as a doctoral dissertation under the guidance of eminent historian Prachi Deshpande. More than exploring the intersection of myth, modernity and law, the thesis was an effort to make my writing meaningful to a historian's eye. Prof. Deshpande not only rendered a keen eye on reading my multiple drafts but also lent her ears to my flights of imagination traversing from psychoanalysis to critical theory. However, to her, the eye is always more acute than the ears. I recall, after giving me careful hearing in her cosy office space, her remark: 'Can you write all this down what you are saying quite passionately. Then only I can comment.' This was both an encouragement and indictment which I now, and only now, consider as a must for every doctoral student. Her dissection of my written drafts with nuanced and detailed comments made it possible for my flights of fancy to be grounded and turned into a manuscript. I am grateful to her for being super wise as a supervisor. If this book is readable to a non-law audience, the credit goes to her and her insistence on cutting the legal jargon to make sense to a reader untrained in law.

Another parallel event which made me think of publishing the manuscript as a book is my teaching of an elective course titled 'Law and Religion' at Jindal Global Law School of OP Jindal Global University (JGU). I offered many courses at JGU but got stuck with this one. It was repeated almost compulsively every semester. I think that I found the ears to my ramblings in my students. This is not simply a formal statement but a sincere acknowledgement that classroom as a space and keen and receptive students encouraged me to write this book.

This book deserves special mention of some individuals who were after my life to ensure that my dissertation should have an afterlife as a book. They are Latika Vashist, Rakesh Ankit, Shiv Visvanathan and Ashley Tellis. At times individually and at other times conspiratorially they made me fight my own lethargy for writing, which surprisingly matches my enthusiasm for classroom lectures!

Latika Vashist has carefully read this draft and never shied away from fighting with me for my incredibly indiscernible prose. This has been certainly traumatic to both of us in ways which cannot be mentioned. Nevertheless, this makes me learn the unlearnable message of William Blake that 'opposition is true friendship'. I hope still to learn how opposition is *love*. Sigmund Freud writes that 'opposition is not necessarily enmity; it is merely misused and made an occasion for enmity'. She has been the Freud and Blake in female form at once for this book, adhering to the rigour of writing and encouraging my mytho-poetic fantasies. Rakesh Ankit has been a gentler friend (perhaps because he is the historian who still does not understand the legal writing of mine) to insist incessantly. My conversations with Shiv Visvanathan convinced me that the overlaps between science, myth, magic and law cannot be sidestepped. Coming from a historian of sciences, this re-instated my own convictions. Ashley Tellis's encouragement was in the form of repeated conviction that my work has things to say which must be said. He is as sympathetic to my work as he is acerbic to me. He never misses reminding me of my flaws when we meet in person. Thus, I must believe him on both counts.

To this list of insisting voices, I must add the persistence of my once student and now colleague, Jibraan Mansoor. He was the only student who found my doctoral dissertation with his own effort and fully read it in his student days. As a colleague he has never missed an opportunity to press me about the book or even announce to the students to exacerbate my embarrassment.

I owe a debt to various other colleagues who have added to my thinking about law and religion in their conversations, patient listening or encouragement and providing me with necessary readings. They include Sabarish Suresh, Rituraj Singh Chauhan, Avantika Tiwari, Payal Mangla, and Harshit Rai. I must mention the warm and affectionate support which I received from my colleagues Raunaq Jaiswal, in his warm home with delicious food and soulful music, and Gayatri Virmani for having conversations during a semester when we were without any office in post-Covid times.

My gratitude is due to our Vice Chancellor C. Raj Kumar and Executive Dean S. Sreejith for providing a conducive atmosphere to the faculty members to write and research and their encouragement to write widely.

I want to thank my teaching assistants for the elective course on Law and Religion with whom I discussed ideas which somehow found a place in writing this book: Niharika Mishra, Vijetha Ravi, Sneha Jayakumar, Ananya Tyagi, Marushka Kenia, Shivam Kataria and others. It is not possible to enlist many students who raised questions and participated in the classroom, making many ideas take shape for this book. But they are the reasons for me to write an academic book. Niharika Mishra in her faculty avatar as tirelessly toiled to assist me in the last moments before sending this book to press. I must mention this without thanking her.

Lastly, I feel that traversing through myth is not possible with the flight of imagination, or the madness. One of my colleagues noted the lack of *madness* in my writing despite its conspicuous presence in lectures. I am still convinced that I could not bring the *madness* into the written word in writing this book. This after all is only one half of the story for 'law *and* religion' with emphasis on law, social science and judgments. The other perhaps must more accurately attend to the phenomenon of religion – the imagination, ecstasy, flight and the art of the impossible. For this, I must fight with my resistance to writing.

If I succeed, then, the madness perhaps will be written in another monograph. I must acknowledge that I see the possibility of the other half in my *play* with six-year-old Kabir Kaivalya, who is teaching me the impossible possibility of not distinguishing play from work. I hope I learn from him the wonder of existing and it should not be the other way round.

*

[A shorter version of Chapter 2 was published as 'Constitutionalism and the sacred cow: the secular mythology of the Indian Supreme Court', 23(1) *Oxford University Commonwealth Law Journal* 93–116 (2023). Chapter 3 in a shorter form appeared as 'Political Hinduism in the Courts of Law: Religious Speech and Struggle for Democracy in India' 9 *Indon. J. Int'l & Comp. L.* 153 (2022). A part of Chapter 4 was published as 'Complete Justice? Silences and erasures in the Ayodhya judgment' 11(1) *Journal of Indian law and Society* 48–71 (2020)].

Introduction

Religion has made an emphatic resurgence in the latter half of the twentieth century in India and in the global arena.[1] In contemporary times, the law has become an instrument to confer legitimacy on the decisions taken by the political class. It is not only religious minorities that seek protection through the law, but majoritarian forces that ardently seek the legal stamp for their proposals, actions and policies in the sphere of religion.[2] Nevertheless, religion remains the 'other' of modern law. It is premised on faith, belief or myth in contrast to the self-understanding of modern law as an episteme of reason, proof and empiricism, the hallmarks of the Western Enlightenment tradition. One of the reasons for this study's close focus on law's encounter with religious claims is that it is in this encounter that the contrast between the two appears stark. I focus, therefore, on the Indian Supreme Court's interpretations of the free exercise of religion clauses,[3] the directive principle exhorting the State for protection of the cow and its legal construction, the construal of religious appeals by political parties during elections and finally the dispute of the Babri Masjid-Ram janambhumi in Ayodhya.

Modern law and religion are perceived as two opposing ends of a spectrum. One is associated with democratic participation and is a harbinger of reason and modernity; the other is seen as a 'pre-modern' relic governed by hierarchy, myth and unreason. Despite these dominant conceptions, there exists a wide scholarship that contests this division and shows how Western

1 See generally Jose Casanova, ***Public Religions in the Modern World*** 1–39 (University of Chicago Press, Chicago, 1994). For a comprehensive overview of how in the secular age being religious is one of the options available to a person and is not a default identity, see Charles Taylor, *A Secular Age* (Harvard University Press, Cambridge, MA, 2007).

2 I will take two instances of the majoritarian Hindu Right seeking and celebrating the ratification of the judiciary. Justification by the Supreme Court that the appeal of 'Hindutva' is unrelated to religion to 'Hinduism' is a way of life is discussed in Chapter 3, and the verdict of the Apex Court in the Babri Masjid-Ram janambhumi dispute which settled the title claim in favour of the Hindu parties in Chapter 4.

3 Specifically, Articles 25 and 26 of the Constitution of India together provide the fundamental right to religious freedom.

DOI: 10.4324/9781003398561-1

secularism was never really separate from religion.[4] Ran Hirschl's suggestion aptly captures the essence of the relationship between modern constitutional law and religion:

> constitutionalism and religion often fail to get along well with each other not because they are so different – although in many respects they no doubt are – but because they are so similar, each with its own constitutive texts, elevated moral aspirations, interpretive institutions, and, at times, less-than-reverent motivations.[5]

Taking these provocations forward, this book is a study of the intersection of modern law with religion through a close look at the Indian Supreme Court discourse.

Legal historiography in ex-colonial societies faces a unique hurdle because of the transplantation of an alien legal system. Modern law, conceived as a gift from the West to the rest of the world, locates itself in opposition to its colonised 'other'. The inquiry into the origins of modern law, in other words, needs to account for the fact that its identity and legitimacy is premised on a 'lack' in non-Western societies: it represents rational, systemic, coherent and modern orderliness as against the despotic, savage, status-oriented, pre-modern and mythic rules of the colonised.[6] Peter Fitzpatrick remarks that 'modern law emerges, in a negative exaltation, as universal in opposition to the particular, as unified in opposition to the diverse, as omnicompetent in contrast to the incompetent, and as controlling of what has to be controlled.'[7] Modernity in itself is a laden term which can refer to a specific historical time period as well as an attitude or a state of mind.[8] As an attitude of mind, which is how this study employs the term, modernity is linked to the Western enlightenment tradition with a singular aim of 'the dissolution of myths and the substitution of knowledge for fancy.'[9] As Horkheimer and Adorno mention: 'In the enlightened world, mythology has entered into the profane. In its blank purity, the reality which has been cleansed of demons and their conceptual descendants assumes the numinous character which the ancient world attributed to demons.'[10]

4 Graeme Smith, *A Short History of Secularism* (I.B. Tauris, London, 2008).

5 Ran Hirschl, *Constitutional Theocracy* 207 (Harvard University Press, Cambridge, MA, 2010).

6 See Upendra Baxi, 'The Rule of Law in India' 4(4) *Sur-International Journal of Human Rights* 7–25 (2007).

7 Peter Fitzpatrick, *The Mythology of Modern Law* 10 (Routledge, London and New York, 1992).

8 See Sionaidh Douglas-Scott, *Law after Modernity* 7 (Hart Publishing, 2013).

9 Max Horkheimer and Theodor W. Adorno, *The Dialectic of Enlightenment: Philosophical Fragments* 3 (Trans. by Edmund Jephcott, Stanford University Press, 2002). For a critical review of how the Western enlightenment orchestrated secularisation, reducing the sphere of religion in the public sphere, see Jose Casanova, *Public Religions in the Modern World* (University of Chicago Press, Chicago, 1994), Ch. 1.

10 Horkheimer and Adorno, note 9 at 28.

The three terms in the title of this book – *Law, Myth and Modernity* – are thus central for unpacking the contemporary functioning of the modern legal system, especially in a country like India, where law continues to be central to the idea and substantiation of modernity. Here, myth is to be understood as the 'other' of law, in the sense that it is constitutive of all that marks unreason: irrationality, religion, faith and non-modernity. However, without endorsing such a law-myth binary, I approach law as an emancipatory force requiring an imagination which is neither premised on the progressive erasure of the mythic in the march towards modernity, nor any elevation of the mythic in opposition to modernity in the romanticisation of 'pre-modern' societies. I seek instead to underline that 'law' and 'myth' are intersecting and constantly impacting each other. Modern law emphasises its ability to carry out the project of modernity by constructing its own mythical status – as something above religion, faith or irrationality and therefore above reproach. This is mythical because it rests ultimately on a belief. These two ways – disavowal of the irrational and a faith in laws' insular positivism – is how I employ the term secular mythology in this book.

In the four chapters of this book, I focus principally on the judgments of the Apex Court of India, the Supreme Court,[11] with references to various High Court decisions wherever necessary. My focus on the Supreme Court is guided by two reasons. One, the pronouncements of the Apex Court become binding law for all judicial and civil authorities in India.[12] Two, many cases pertaining to the free exercise of religion clause originate directly in the Supreme Court, as the Indian Constitution vests the Court with original jurisdiction in cases where the violation of fundamental rights is in question.[13] The choice of judicial verdicts as the major archive for this study is premised on the assumption that legal interpretation provides a glimpse into the tradition of 'living law.' Here, I understand law as not merely constituted and inscribed in notifications, rules, statutes, codes or the Constitution, but as something protean which reformulates itself continually when confronted with new situations that arise with changing times. Critically engaging with this aspect of the law is the motivation for undertaking this work. Fitzpatrick explains this dimension of the law succinctly:[14]

> For there to be a rule of law, for law to rule, it itself must have determinant force. Yet if it were merely or fixedly determinant, if it were not

11 After independence from the British rule in 1947 and before the commencement of the Constitution in 1950, the highest judicial organ in India was the Federal Court. With the coming into force of the Constitution, the Supreme Court became the highest judicial body. For a recent historical account of this interim period, see Rakesh Ankit, *India in the Interim: The 1947–1951 Nehru Government* (Cambridge University Press, New Delhi, 2024).

12 Article 141, The Constitution of India.

13 Article 32, The Constitution of India.

14 Peter Fitzpatrick, *Modernism and the Grounds of Law* 16 (Cambridge University Press, New York, 2001). This quoted passage reminds one of the emphases which Jacques Derrida places on the importance of judicial decision as a break or 'cut' inaugurating an altogether new

> responsive, it would cease being able to rule a situation which had inexorably changed around it . . . The legal decision is ever responsive. It can neither be rendered beforehand nor sustained simply in terms of some empirical reality or simply in terms of a previous decision.

This *responsiveness* of law is ingrained in the legal process and is best captured through a study of legal interpretive techniques. The mythology of modern law refutes this uncertainty and contingency by foregrounding determinacy, fixity, certainty and clarity. In doing so, it presents itself as a self-contained and an autonomous system uninfluenced by history or politics. It is this self-image of the modern law, which is a hallmark of all positivist legal thinking, that forms one of its many 'myths.' An exposé and exposition of this mythic self-enclosure of the law by foregrounding the historical and political processes that shape legal interpretation is another task pursued through this book.

Following Fitzpatrick, I see law's uncertainty as the potential to respond to the unknown, or yet to be known, which forms the subject matter of legal interpretation. By acknowledging this uncertainty as inherent in the legal process, modern law can dispel its insularity to learn about its limitations from, and be in conversation with, other disciplines.[15] I will try to establish how legal reasoning elides historical specificity to present itself as eternal, universal and unaffected by historical contingencies. Foregrounding these contexts in different chapters helps us see how such claims to universality obscure the self-representational myths that underlie legal reasoning. This move is also mindful of the drawback in existing historical scholarship on law in avoiding 'the questions of doctrinal development' in preference to 'statutes as definitive expressions of the law.'[16]

I will focus on interpretive techniques and doctrinal methods linked with judicial interpretation, excavating the contradictions in the process of legal interpretation while engaging with judicial discourse, and suggest that this contradiction is ingrained in the legal process. This will hopefully provide the necessary corrective to the lawyers' habit, via the black-letter-legal-tradition,

---

response. See Jacques Derrida, 'Force of Law: "The Mystical Foundation of Authority"' in Drucilla Cornell, Michel Rosenfeld, David Carlson (eds.), *Deconstruction and the Possibility of Justice* 3–67 (Routledge, New York, 1992). But Derrida's notion of 'decision' is loaded with a multiplicity of judicial, political and theological meanings which, I think, require a comparative study of this essay with his work on the Biblical story of Abraham's decision to sacrifice Isaac. See Jacques Derrida, *The Gift of Death* (Trans. by David Willis, University of Chicago Press, Chicago, 1995). This is immensely fruitful but beyond the scope of this work, and I leave this for a future study. I will stay with the idea of judicial decision as a form of response to the changing historical times, which is how Fitzpatrick uses the term.

15 The Critical Legal Studies (CLS) inaugurated an alternative jurisprudence to this positivist understanding of law. However, it ventured into the other extreme of indifference to the legal doctrine or posited law which led to its failure. See Peter Goodrich, 'The Empty Tomb: Post-Critical Legal Hermeneutics' 10 *Nevada Law Journal* 607 (2010).

16 Michael R. Anderson and Sumit Guha, *Changing Concepts of Rights and Justice in South Asia* 2 (Oxford University Press, Oxford, 1998).

which tends 'to approach the history of case law with an eye for doctrinal coherence rather than subtle contradiction or social context.'[17] However, this does not mean that the political or historical context is the final determinant of law and law is merely an instrument in the hands of political progression. Political history undoubtedly *conditions* the legal reason, but it is never *determinative* of it.

Quentin Skinner has developed the theory of historical method with his fundamental assumption that it is the textual context that is essential in order to find out the nature of the 'intervention' that the author proposes.[18] This context includes the biographical details or the 'actual conduct' of the writer, information with respect to the social surrounding, the political environment and for Skinner, the literary culture of the times.[19] In one way the Skinnerian framework is useful to counter the tradition of legal positivism which sees the law as all about text, bereft of any context. However, there are limitations of (t)his approach as well. First, such an approach would make it difficult to capture the intertextual developments within the legal precedents over a long period of time. Second, in elevating the context as everything there is a danger of discounting the textual as merely determined by the historical circumstances. Jonardon Ganeri alerts us to the danger of the Skinnerian approach as running the risk of turning 'moderate contextualism into an extreme form of social constructivism.'[20] Third, due to the predominance of legal positivism, there is little available biographical scholarship on Indian Supreme Court judges.[21] Therefore, to fully understand the ideological underpinnings of the judicial discourse one must study, following Ganeri, the 'intertextual contexts' of the living, organic and ever-changing body of law. This methodology helps to trace interpretive patterns *within* the text of judgments as they interpret legal provisions. This approach of 'moderate contextualism' is what I have adopted to read legal cases.

There are multiple registers and roles of the category of myth understood as the antithesis of law: it can be deployed both within *and* against the law. Section I of this introduction provides a synoptic review of the category of myth as critique of modern law. Section II clarifies the way in which this book understands the category and evaluates the politics of modern law as a tool of social justice and its emancipatory possibilities. In Section III, I outline the colonial encounter that contributed to the emergence of modern law and the politics of codification of the laws both by the British colonial authorities in

17 *Ibid.*

18 Quentin Skinner, *Visions of Politics: Regarding Method*, vol. I (Cambridge University Press, Cambridge, 2002).

19 *Id.* at 122–127.

20 Jonardon Ganeri, *The Lost Age of Reason: Philosophy in Early Modern India 1450–1700* 68 (Oxford University Press, New Delhi, 2011).

21 One notable exception to this is George H. Gadbois Jr., *Judges of the Supreme Court of India (1950–1989)* (Oxford University Press, New Delhi, 2011).

India and the process of codification in Britain. Section IV takes a glimpse at the Subaltern Studies project in its effort to foreground the suppressed dimensions of the legal discourse in general and judicial vocabulary in particular. Section V provides a historical background of the 'free exercise clauses' of the Indian Constitution from the late eighteenth to the mid-nineteenth century with the Queen's proclamation and how it shaped the religious freedom clause in independent India. Finally, Section VI provides an overview of the chapters.

I. Myth as a Critique of Modernity and Modern Law

One of the most moving accounts of the modern law encountering myth literally in an adversarial battle can be found in Peter Goodrich's study of *Languages of Law*.[22] He narrates an event from 1985, when the traditional inhabitants of the Lyell Island in Canada – Haida Indians – had to withstand an American corporation which acquired a logging license from the government of British Columbia (Canada). The license was granted without any consultation with the inhabitants. The logging was foisted on the inhabitants and their traditional economy, which was based on woodcraft and fishing, and it invited vehement opposition. The American company obtained a court injunction against any interference. The Haida Indians (Haida) decided to appear before the court without any legal assistance in their persistence to speak for themselves. This impediment of language/s, or the necessity of speech to be translated into an idiom which is not one's own, captured poignantly by Derrida in *Force of Law*, applies with all force to the plight of the Haida:[23]

> I must speak in a language that is not my own because that will be more just . . . it is more just to speak language of the majority, especially when, through hospitality, it grants a foreigner the right to speak. It's hard to say if the law we are referring to here is . . . the law of the strongest, or the equitable law of democracy. And whether it depends on justice or law (droit) . . . because it has been imposed on me as a sort of obligation or condition by a sort of symbolic force or law in a situation I do not control.

The inhabitants appeared in their full 'ceremonial dress' with eighteen elders. The dress or insignia of the modern law is also part of 'myth' and not simply tradition.[24] Goodrich describes this as a clash of two mythologies as 'the

22 Peter Goodrich, *Languages of Law: From Logics of Memory to Nomadic Masks* (Weidenfeld and Nicolson, London, 1990).

23 Derrida, 'Force of Law', note 14 at 4–5.

24 Another variation of this style of argument can be found in Gary Watt, *Dress, Law and Naked Truth: A Cultural Study of Fashion and Form* (Bloomsbury Academic, New Delhi, 2013). For a critical review, see, Jeanne Schroeder, 'Always True to You in My Fashion' 27(3) *Law and Literature* 1–15 (2015).

judge's robes can be contrasted [with] the button blankets of the defendants.'[25] Haida furnished the argument of sacred origins using the vocabulary of rights:

> They had a right "to stand on the islands" and to act as caretakers from that moment at the dawn of time when the first Indians had emerged, according to Haida legend, from a clamshell carried by a raven and dropped on the sands of the islands.[26]

This language could not be heard by the judges. Nor did the totem poles, art forms, masks or poetry and songs qualify as relevant for the court.[27] Though the judge permitted Haida to bring their stories, legends and tradition to the courtroom, none of it met the acceptable standards of legal evidence. This 'limited hospitality' was granted because 'Haida had no other arena available to them, he had been prepared to listen and generously recommended that a record of the evidence presented should be kept for posterity.'[28] Goodrich points to the remark of the judge that he cannot do much as judges cannot enter the domain of policymaking. This 'washing of hands', for Goodrich, is an instance of annulment and annihilation of non-legal vocabulary in the courtroom. More importantly, he argues, this refusal to countenance the 'other' is not merely because of the impossibility of admitting the other language. This refusal, he says, is a necessity to stay in *denial* of the other as it might put into question the identity of modern law itself:[29]

> The court would not compare mythologies, *it refused even to countenance the question of the 'other'*, because to do so would raise questions of its 'self', of the social and mystic construction of its own body, its social role and actions, its own clothes.

For Goodrich, the modern law is in and of itself a mythology. Or mythology is its disavowed self which it refuses to acknowledge. Both Haida and the modern law have their own mythic structures. But modern law consistently denies its 'mystical construction' and presents itself in opposition to myth. Such denial of the 'other', he argues, is intrinsic to modern law. Haida is the most profound illustration of the structure and *habitual logic* of the common law, 'one which throughout its history has systematically obliterated difference

25 Goodrich, note 22 at 181.

26 *Id.* at 182.

27 Throughout this book, I have used 'Court' with a capital C when the word is used as a pronoun, or short form for specifically the Supreme Court or the High Court. When I have used it as a common noun (*viz*, 'the courts were called in to determine the matter' or 'she took them to court' or 'the courts were involved in') or while referring to the subordinate courts, I have used it with a small c, 'court'.

28 Goodrich, note 22 at 182.

29 *Ibid.* (emphasis in the original; internal references omitted).

in all its manifestations, in all its discourses.'[30] This mythology of modern law is recognised in Goodrich's work in the emblems, wigs and gown and architectural visuality inherent in modern law.[31] He does not venture into any deeper resemblance of modern law with its supposed other. Nevertheless, through the Haida narrative, he broaches the question of legal deafness, another ear of law needed for its other – which is not a far cry but buried within the law. In the next section, I will examine the fragility in the binary opposition between myth and modern law in the work of Fitzpatrick, who questions the discursive structure of modern law as possessing a mythical dimension.

Myth in Modernity

Fitzpatrick argues that the Western enlightenment tradition defines itself in opposition to myth. But despite efforts to erase the mythic dimension, myth has been incorporated in the foundational precepts of modernity. He argues that the 'transcendental' dimension of the mythic worldview is only substituted and not annulled in modernity: 'The profane is swept up into a sacred . . . as a project and a progression towards that resolution. For the perfection of beginnings in pre-modern myth is substituted the perfection of ending.'[32] This formulation insists on the reversal of transcendence, or displacement of mythic into the 'fantastic stories devised in the names of reason and history at the cost, or denigration, of the non-western "other"'.[33] This is explained by an illustration of elevation of 'property' as a transcendental object in Western modernity which is both particular and universal, at once:[34]

> As an 'external', reified object, it is suffused with the palpable and the specific. Yet it is also elevated in terms no less extensive than those attributed to the transcendence of myth. It is, to summarize various formulations of Enlightenment, the foundation of civilization, the very motor-force of the origin and development of society, the provocation to self-consciousness and the modality of appropriating nature.

What is given a deified status as a universal category is 'a particular form of Occidental property.'[35] The geographical locations lacking this notion of property 'can only be its precursors or [evidence of] savagery.'[36] Law becomes the

30 *Id.* at 184.
31 See Peter Goodrich, *Legal Emblems and the Art of Law: Obiter Dipicta as the Vision of Law* (Cambridge University Press, New York, 2014).
32 Fitzpatrick, note 7 at 36.
33 *Id.* at 46, 48.
34 *Id.* at 50.
35 *Ibid.*
36 *Ibid.*

transcendental (despite its materiality) and a universal system in its perfection, completeness and rational coherence. This marks the dawn of the discourse of modern law:[37]

> The sovereign is no longer God's earthly representative and is now the autonomous and self sufficient source of law. Law, once it was processed by Kant, is no longer tied to any extraneous order, now deriving its force and origin purely from its intrinsic being. Yet, despite all this, law does not or cannot assume merely terrestrial dimensions. It continues to bear the characters of God. But it does this now in a mundane world.

This 'autonomous' and 'self-sustaining' character of the law likens it to its divine counterpart. The omnipresence and omnipotence of the law is reflected in its claim to do *anything*, if not *everything*.[38] The Kantian reference in the previous passage is noteworthy as Immanuel Kant emphasised the 'systematic unity' in order to distinguish a 'system' from an aggregate of rules.[39] This Kantian idea would take its highest sophistication in the writings of German jurist Hans Kelsen as an exemplar of twentieth-century 'language of faith' of self-sustaining, autonomous and 'pure theory' of law.[40]

II. Varying Visions of Law as a Social Justice Instrument

In the previous section, I argued that mythology is paradoxically exemplified in the very institution of modern law. An immediate fallout of this line of argument would be to question the character and relevance of the law. I must clarify that my purpose is *not* a mere exploration of the violence suffused in legal interpretation or majoritarian reaffirmation in legal pronouncements. Throughout this study, by heightening the repressions and contradictions of modern law, I argue for its emancipatory potential.

In an anthology of essays on law and violence, Latika Vashist and Jyoti D. Sood describe two predominant ways of thinking about law as 'return or reject proposals.'[41] The predominant legal theorisation operates in two mutually conflicting suggestions. The *return proposal* harps on reinstating more rule of law that seems to be lacking in the contemporary times. This proposition, emblematic of the Black letter law tradition, emphasises 'the predominant view of law as a clear, certain and objective set of rules and principles, neutral in origin

37 *Id.* at 55. For a discussion of law as modern myth, see Fitzpatrick, *Id.* at 55–57.

38 *Id.* at 57. 'Some areas are supposed to remain characteristically apart, notably a "private" domain of the subject.'

39 Immanuel Kant, *Critique of Pure Reason* (1887), cited in Peter Goodrich, *Legal Discourse: Studies in Linguistics, Rhetoric and Legal Analysis* 38 (Palgrave Macmillan, UK, 1987).

40 For a critical review of Kelsen's work as a narrative of faith, see Goodrich, note 39 at 35–44.

41 Latika Vashist and Jyoti D. Sood, *Rethinking Law and Violence* (Oxford University Press, New Delhi, 2020).

and uniform in application.'[42] Vashist and Sood point to the linear trajectory of progressive history, emblematic of the discourse of modernity, in the return proposals. On the contrary, the *reject proposal* (which unites post-modernists, post-colonialists and relativists) emphasises law's 'foundational and originary linkages with violence resulting in an impossibility of achieving and securing justice through law.'[43] Such a rejection of law is full of 'scholarly despair and hopelessness with law and legal institutions, often culminat[ing] in proposals of *exceeding* or *transcending* the law to achieve justice.'[44] Despite their seeming opposition, the two proposals align, although for altogether distinct reasons, in their conceptualisation of law as '*inadequate* and *lacking* in its response to violence . . . The law is either too meek to counter injustice or inherently unjust.'[45]

This perspective of theorising law advocates for a constant vigilance against the liberal seduction of principles of cosmopolitan constitutionalism, or the fashionable notions of transformative constitutionalism,[46] which simply demand 'more *faith* in the principles of rights-based frameworks.' It also cautions against a wholesale rejection of the law as immanently violent or a bourgeoisie tool of oppression. Instead, what is advocated is what I described here as the potential which is inchoate but present in the law. Vashist and Sood describe this potentiality as an 'ambivalence' which, 'following Freud, is the simultaneous and co-equal presence of contradictory feelings or tendencies with respect to an object.'[47] They describe the category of contradiction or uncertainty as not necessarily in need of resolution or finality but an open-ended possibility aligning justice with constant struggle. In their words:[48]

> The contradictions of law instead of being seen as weaknesses should be viewed as its strength for these contradictions keep it alive – protean, transient, never so settled or certain, always questioning and in process of change.

What is encouraged is not a celebration but an acknowledgement of contradictions or inadequacies of the law. This perspective is pertinent to appreciate the 'living law,' as law is a system of language and much of interpretation is about the construction of meaning. This reminder that the possibility originates in the very moment of failure serves as a beacon light of this book.

The Marxist analysis of legal complexities in Indian legal scholarship finds an expression in the early work of Upendra Baxi. In his *Marx, Law and Justice* (1993), he outlines two forms of denial of the law in the Marxist tradition: the

42 *Id.* at xv.
43 *Ibid.*
44 *Ibid.* (emphasis added).
45 *Ibid.* (emphasis in the original).
46 See Gautam Bhatia, *Transformative Constitutionalism: A Radical Biography in Nine Acts* (Harper Collins, 2019).
47 *Id.* at xiv.
48 *Id.* at xviii.

instrumentalist and the materialist approach.[49] The instrumentalist approach characterises law as an 'instrument' of the bourgeoisie to perpetuate class oppression.[50] Taken to its ulterior logic, law deserves rejection as it serves as a smokescreen to hide and legitimise injustice. Such a view, for Baxi, is a form of 'vulgar instrumentalism' as it never specifies what it is precisely to say that whatever is called the 'law' is necessarily an instrument of the ruling classes.[51] It paints the 'ruling classes' as monolithic and thus fails to explain the special provisions for the vulnerable sections in the Constitution and welfare legislations. It also remains unsuccessful at appreciating the changing interpretations given to laws in each decade even though, Baxi argues, there has been no 'notable change in the class origins of Indian Supreme Court and High Court justices in the last four decades.'[52] He stresses that the sweeping generalisations miss the nuanced understanding of both the *ruling classes* and the *law*:[53]

> [S]uch an approach *ascribes a degree of permanence* to the ruling classes in the human history and endows them not just with a *lack of heterogeneity* but with, as it were, a *collective unconscious* unerringly and omnisciently pursuing its own interests. This is a wholly unilluminating manner of reading legal history.

This critique raises a second question about the extent to which law is affected by the social structure which is class-dominated. This question is dealt with in the critique of what Baxi calls the materialist approach. This approach considers the law as an entity of the *superstructure* to be determined by the *economic base*. Simply put, the law is determined by the economic modes of production and social relations: '[i]f so, the law cannot be of much relevance in understanding and promotion of social change since it is not an autonomous social force.'[54] Through a careful reading of the passage from Marx's *Preface to Contribution of Political Economy*, Baxi outlines the possible alternative readings, arguing that the economic base does not 'determine' but merely 'conditions' the superstructure.[55] In his reading of Marx in *Capital Volume III* and *Grundrisse*, Baxi argues that Marx has indicated that there exists 'a dialectical

49 Upendra Baxi, *Marx, Law and Justice* (N.M. Tripathi (P) Ltd., Bombay, 1993).
50 On this register, the discourse of rights or law in its 'universal' application masks the inequality of the social.
51 Baxi, note 49 at 16.
52 *Id.* at 17 (internal citations omitted).
53 *Ibid.* (emphasis added).
54 *Id.* at 32.
55 The relevant passage in Karl Marx's *Capital Vol. I* is the following: 'The sum total of . . . relations of production constitutes the economic structure of the society, the real foundation, *on which rises a legal and political superstructure and to which correspond definite forms of social consciousness*. The mode of production of material life *conditions* the social, political and intellectual life process in general. It is not the consciousness of men that determines their being, but on the contrary, their social being that *determines* their consciousness.' Cited in Baxi, *Id.* at 31–32.

relationship between the law as superstructure and the economic system.'[56] He reiterates this point in the conclusion to the chapter, that 'while the material base conditions law as superstructure, the law too influences the base.'[57] This points towards a *relative autonomy* of the law, despite its embeddedness in the social order ridden with class antagonism, which certainly affects it but does not determine it wholly. In his suggestion that the conditioning is mutual, Baxi is arguing for a more radical thesis of questioning the very *topological metaphor* of 'superstructure' and 'base' for the colonised societies (which he argues were well-known to Marx and Engels). He suggests that the experience of colonialism is ridden with 'extra-ordinary inversions' for Indian and other colonial societies. He asserts:[58]

> The legal system introduced by the British imported bourgeoisie relations of property . . . 'the legal system and property relations actually hindered the development of capitalist relations in agriculture, given the context of colonialism.' The base neither 'determined', nor 'conditioned,' the superstructure of colonial law in India. (But if it did, it was the 'metropolitan' base of the English society!) Marx who wrote extensively concerning the British rule in India was deeply aware of this inversion.

He finds a possibility of interrogating the 'seductive simplicity of the topological metaphor' and an alternative explanation, which is marred by a 'rapid reading of Marx' which betrays 'anything Marx and Engels themselves said.'[59] The neglect of this work in Indian legal scholarship and the vanishing scholarship on Marx, especially in legal academia, has not compelled Marxist scholarship to take up this provocation. For my purpose, this reading remains important as it outlines a possibility of relevance and significance of law despite the predominantly dismissive attitude towards it in classical Marxism. Baxi convincingly argues for a foundational and central role of the law. In doing so, he distinguishes himself from those left-leaning intellectuals who are suspicious of the law as a site of emancipatory politics.[60] Baxi's approach also has its limits, as in his later works he appears to be insufficiently critical of *Hindutva judgments* (Chapter 3) and more specifically his reading of the *Ayodhya Judgment*.[61] His appreciation of the *Ayodhya Judgment*, for instance, based on abjuration of what is present, discounts any 'conditioning' of the judiciary by the Hindu

56 *Id.* at 40.
57 *Id.* at 47.
58 *Id.* at 32.
59 *Ibid.*
60 See Nivedita Menon, *Recovering Subversion: Feminist Politics Beyond Law* (University of Illinois Press, 2004).
61 Upendra Baxi, 'Award of Five Acres for Masjid in Ayodhya is an Effort to do Complete Justice' *The Indian Express* (Nov. 12, 2019); Upendra Baxi, 'Ayodhya Verdict Must Be Seen Dispassionately from the Prism of Law, Constitutionalism' *Outlook* (Nov. 14, 2019).

majoritarian sentiment. Contra such denial, I argue for a more robust and critical reading of the workings of the judicial processes which entails exploring 'possibilities' in failure while remaining alert to the *internal resistances* within the system to such possibilities. In the next section, I will map the historical trajectory of the colonial legal history linked to my research questions. This will help in understanding the unique status of law in colonised societies as well as the meaning of 'modernity' in this book.

III. Religion, Law and Colonial Modernity

Jonardon Ganeri argues that in the history of philosophy, modernity is conceptualised in two mutually opposite ways. The predominant version defines modernity as a total rejection of ancient knowledge. Modernity makes a fresh beginning by entirely purging itself of the past. The second approach views it not as rejection but as what Ganeri describes as a 'profound reorientation' of the ancient past. In this study, I prefer the latter view as it helps in an understanding of modernity as a continuum where the traces of the past are ever present. He argues that the predominant view 'radically simplifies the ways in which the moderns drew upon the ancients.'[62] He shows that Indian philosophy witnessed its own 'modernity' but it remained neglected in the history of ideas. He expounds the historical diversity of the Indian tradition vis-à-vis European tradition,[63] the dialogic relationship between Hindu and Arabic traditions,[64] and philosophical debates and opposition between the positions of scholarly conservativism (in favour of ancient knowledge) and radical revision.[65] These aspects of his work, however, are beyond the scope of this work.

The reason for a discussion of this dimension of Indian philosophy serves an important backdrop in thinking about the Indian judges' incessant preoccupation with the theological. The interpretation of scriptures to rediscover new meaning(s) for contemporary times is not alien to ancient Hindu philosophy. This may not be understood as an advocacy for judges to act as theologians. But certainly, my argument in Chapter 1 with respect to the essential practices test is that any self-righteous plea for disengagement of secular courts with theological questions without any reference to ancient Indian or colonial history negates this historical context of colonial

62 Ganeri, note 20 at 2.

63 *Id.* at 6–7.

64 Ganeri's finest analysis appears in his excavation of Dārā Shukoh, the elder son of Shāh Jahān. Shukoh encouraged scholars from Varanasi to translate 52 Upanishadas in Persian. This inaugurated the tradition of interpreting the Qurān through Hindu Upanishadas. The premise of the project was to see Upanishadas as a commentary on the Qurān, which eventually became the basis of his execution for heresy by his younger brother, Aurangzeb, in 1659. See Ganeri, note 20 at 22–30.

65 For a discussion on Raghunātha Śiromani (1460–1560) as pioneer of path-breaking work on 'new reason' in the town of Navadvīpa in Bengal, see Daya Krishna, 'Raghunātha the Rebel' in *Indian Philosophy: A New Approach* 174–180 (Sri Satguru Publications, Delhi, 1997).

modernity in general and legal codification in particular. However, in the interaction of the legal/modern with theological/scriptural/ancient, it is important to acknowledge the difficulty in any attempt to look for origins of Indian legal tradition. Most of what we describe as pre-colonial/indigenous law of India originated in the search of the colonisers to learn about and apply the 'Indian law' to 'Indians' (which is a new colonial category). It thus needs to be clarified at the outset that my search here is ***not*** for origins (as that would already be 'modern') but for what may have been lost or occluded in the trajectory followed by the modern law. It is this 'anti-search' that we must undertake for the legal traditions and systems that existed prior to and during British rule.

Classical Hindu Law

Robert Lingat's *Classical Law of India* (1973) presents an analysis of the intersection between theological and legal categories in ancient India. The work explores the simultaneous presence of spiritual salvation and the moral code of duty in the notion of *dharma*.[66] *Dharma* was both a social and religious category, defying any clear demarcation. *Shastra* is the name given to early Indian treatises relating to forms of conduct desirable for the Hindus. Lingat explains how the *Dharmashastras* were not codes of law as understood by the Europeans. Instead, they were integrally linked to the tradition of interpretation (*mimamsa*) which interpreted, validated and bridged the gap when customary law came into conflict with the *Dharmashastras*. It was a juristic device to align the textual edicts with the unwritten customary law.[67] An illustration of the indirect manifestation of the textual and the people's law is visible in the following instance. Despite the *shastric* prescription condemning the marriage of a *dvija* (twice-born or upper-caste) and a *sudra* (a term used for a lower caste undertaking menial work), there were categorical 'rules for a share of paternal estate for a son of Brahmin, *ksatriya* [warrior upper caste], or *vaisvaya* [trading caste] born of female *sudra*!'[68]

Lingat explains the co-relation between the textual and customary, but he takes a conclusive position on classical Hindu law as reflecting prominence of *authority* and absence of *legality* (positive law made by a sovereign State). By contrast,

66 Lingat writes that *dharma* was 'essentially rule of *interdependence*, founded on the hierarchy corresponding to the nature of things and necessary for the maintenance of social order' and to deviate from *dharma* was 'to violate one's salvation'. Robert Lingat, *The Classical Law of India* 211 (translated from the French with additions by J. Duncan M. Derrett, University of California Press, Berkeley, 1973). Also see Upendra Baxi, *Towards a Sociology of Indian Laws* 5–10 (Satvahan, New Delhi, 1986).

67 *Shastric* law had predominant 'transcendental character,' whereas custom as a source of law was entirely a 'social phenomenon.' But Lingat warns the reader against neat categorical separation as at times the *Shastric* law included the customary law. Lingat, note 66 at 176–177.

68 Baxi, note 66 at 8.

Western law was based on legality and clear statutory rules. This conclusion reinforces the stereotypical understanding of colonial societies.[69] It also presupposes that the positive law of the Western style is the normative standard to validate a legal system. Such conclusions are indicative of the problems in reframing the historicity of the ancient Hindu laws on the register of Western legality.[70]

Colonial State and Formations of Its Juridical Forms

Warren Hastings brought about a major transformation in eighteenth-century juridical administration. His Judicial Plan of 1772 replaced the existing indigenous dispute settlement system in Bengal with the English court system. While there was an admiration for the ancient Indian past, East India Company was reluctant to endow indigenous adjudication the status of 'law'. The representation of Indian rulers as 'despotic and lawless' formed the basis of the consolidation of British rule in India. The predominant view about India of the eighteenth century under the Mughal rule was marked by the dominance of arbitrary whims of the monarch as well as the absence of any laws/codes in the form of governance. This representation served a dual purpose. One, it led to vilification of existing systems of law and order to establish the British as superior administrators. Two, the notion of times of 'crises' or *exceptional* situations demanding extraordinary measures served as justification for better governance. The colonial subjectivity of the natives was discursively invented: lacking any civilised sense of governance and requiring a paternalistic guardian. Bernard Cohn describes this as 'the ideological infrastructure of British rule in India.'[71] This provided a justification for paternal authority of the British as benevolent:[72]

> As benevolent despots, the British were to appear in several forms – as 'platonic-guardians,' as patriarchs habitually addressed by the simple folk as *ma-bap* (mother and father), as authoritarian rationalist utilitarians, and in *times of crisis* as the not-so-benevolent *Old Testament avengers.*

The colonial sovereign in his decision-making capacity, during crisis, dawns an authority of God-like sovereign performing the miraculous task of civilizing the 'heathens' from darkness to the light of law and order. The notion of

69 It also simplifies the complex dimension of the Western law. See Costas Douzinas and R. Warrington, *Justice Miscarried: Ethics Aesthetics and the Law* 25–92 (Edinburgh University Press, 1994).

70 Baxi underlines Lingat's limitations in perceiving forms of Indian positive law by pointing out that 'even at the level of history of ideas, one might relate to Lingat his own criticism of the classical commentators: like them, he too pays very little attention to Arthashastra. The latter contains, at any rate normatively, the science of positive law.' Baxi, note 66 at 10.

71 Bernard S. Cohn, *Colonialism and Its Forms of Knowledge: The British in India* 65 (Princeton University Press, 1996).

72 *Ibid.* (internal citations omitted, emphasis added).

crisis had created circumstances that were exceptional. The exception elicited a sovereign who could decide upon that exception.[73]

A counter model to ***despotism*** was proposed by Warren Hastings: India as the ***theocratic*** State. Hastings opposed the 1772–73 Parliamentary Committee's recommendation of introducing British laws and institutions to ameliorate despotic governance in India. A declaration on August 15, 1772, by the East India Company under the 'provision of plan for the Administration of Justice' under Hastings declared that the civil courts should 'administer Islamic law to Muslims and the law of the 'Shaster (*Dharmashastra)* to Hindus.'[74] This was in accordance with the principle of non-interference in the 'personal laws' – a peculiarly colonial term – of the Indians.[75] Hastings persuaded a group of Bengali Brahmins to cooperate with the British in developing Anglo-Indian legal codes. The Hindu laws were primarily drawn out from the *Shastras* and the Muslims from the *Quran*.

Many scholars were not trained in Sanskrit although they were well versed in Persian. This led to the difficulty in translation of the codes from Sanskrit to English. The issue was resolved as the texts were first translated into Persian and from that into English. Eventually in 1776, *A Code of Gentoo Laws* was brought into existence, translated by N.B. Halhed. This served as an important instrument for the beginning of Indic studies and elicited many translations. Sir William Jones (1746–94), the well-known scholar of Persian and Arabic from Oxford and the founder of the Asiatic Society of Bengal, studied Sanskrit and undertook the task of codification of the Hindu and Mohammadan laws in line with the Justinian Code. By the end of his life, he succeeded in translating both Hindu and Mohammadan law from Sanskrit and Arabic, respectively. It was only after his death in 1798 that the final English translation was completed by H.T. Colebrook and published as *The Digest of Hindu Law on Contracts and*

73 This formulation finds a notable elaboration in the work of controversial German jurist Carl Schmitt. He famously remarked that '[s]overeign is he who decides on the state of exception.' See Carl Schmitt, *Political Theology: Four Chapters on the Concept of Sovereignty* (University of Chicago Press, 2005). The connection between theology and exceptional times is captured exquisitely in Schmitt's work. The 'exception in jurisprudence,' Schmitt argues, 'is analogous to the miracle in theology.' As a jurist trained in the Catholic tradition, Schmitt is quite explicit in his likening of concepts of politics as transformed theological precepts. For him, it is unsurprising that the modern law would become the mythmaker of modernity as its structure is deeply embedded in mythology. *Id.* at 36.

74 Ganeri, note 20 at 59.

75 This initial protection of 'personal laws' had been reiterated in the nineteenth century in the Royal Proclamation of the Queen in 1858: 'We declare it to be our royal will and pleasure, that none be in anywise favoured . . . by reason of their religious faith or observances . . . And we do strictly charge and enjoin all those who may be in authority under us, that they abstain from all interference with the religious belief, or worship.' Cited in Terence Thomas, 'The Impact of Other Religious' in Gerald Parsons (ed.), *Religion in Victorian Britain (II Controversies)* 280, 287 (Manchester University Press, 1989).

Successions in Calcutta.[76] Cohn captures the paradoxical nature of the colonial enterprise in his assessment that '[w]hat had started with Warren Hastings and Sir William Jones as a search for the "ancient Indian constitution" ended up with what they had so much wanted to avoid – with English law as the law of India.'[77]

Ganeri argues that the collation and compilation of important texts and commentaries in the late eighteenth century was 'still another modernism,' but something that was in line with Indian modernity of rediscovering the meaning of the ancient texts for changing circumstances. From the legal standpoint, to appreciate the seventeenth-century classical codes requires an understanding of the interpretations rendered by the colonial law courts to these codes. The adjudication process under these new codes required the assistance of native priests who could expound the meaning of the Hindu and Muslim codes. This led to the practice of adjudication including Hindu and Muslim priestly scholars helping the British judges to interpret the codes. However, the British officers were not without suspicion about these theocratic scholars aiding the judicial process. The suspicion of these native officials (*pandits* and *maulvis*) soon gave way to the colonial judges as interpreters of the indigenous texts. Kunal Parker's article dwells on this understudied dimension of colonial adjudication and the interpretive techniques of the Anglo-Indian courts during this time.[78] For Parker, this historical episode exposes a 'momentous process of controlling sacred legal texts through translation, from which the textual Orientalist tradition of British India descends.'[79] He reveals that in a private letter to Charles Chapman (Commander-in-Chief of the British army), William Jones cast doubt on the trustworthiness of the native officials: 'I can no longer bear to be at the mercy of our pundits . . . who deal out Hindu law as they please, and make it at reasonable rates, when they cannot find it readymade.'[80] This inaugurated the surreptitious introduction of the principles of English common law to adjudicate the claims of 'personal laws' of the natives. This inaugurated and cemented the process of judges taking up the role of theologians via modern law, which I will show in this book is continuing in post-independence India. Parker remarks that the 'undocumented process of judicial legislation . . . has escaped the scrutiny of contemporary historians

76 Cohn points out how Jones convinced then-governor-general Cornwallis by formally writing to him in March 1778 for government funding for his project. Cohn, note 71 at 70.

77 *Id.* at 75. William Jones, who followed Hastings, had no illusions that the notion of liberty and liberation may be extended to the natives. Cohn notes: 'it appears that Jones believed that even though manners, habits, dispositions, and prejudices were not fixed or immutable, the Hindus of India had usages that were fixed from time immemorial. Unlike British with their case law . . . the Hindus . . . lived a timeless existence, which in turn meant that differences in interpretations offered by Pundits must have arisen from ignorance or venality.' *Ibid.*

78 Kunal Parker, 'Interpreting Oriental Cases: The Law of Alterity in the Colonial Courtroom' 107 *Harvard Law Review* 1711–1728 (1994).

79 *Id.* at 1715.

80 Letter dated Sept. 28, 1785, cited in Parker, *Id.* at 1715.

almost entirely.'[81] Unfortunately, this remains the case, and this period of colonial judges taking on themselves the task of reading, interpreting and applying the codified religious laws requires a rigorous archival study.

Janaki Nair is important voice in this context. She argues that through the colonial exercise of discovering Indian law 'the "natives" were given back their own history, of which they had been previously ignorant.'[82] However, the preference for the written over the spoken or memorised, or that of historical and factual over the mythic and legendary, only indicated that the British 'invented' themselves in inventing the Indian tradition:[83]

> One of the enduring ironies of current historical knowledge of the Indian past is that it has been derived largely from the interpretations developed over the last 200 years, and, as a result, derived from ways of studying the past which were inaugurated by the Orientalists.

The colonial interpretation of the ancient codes sketched a static view of the Indian society. The interpretive traditions aligning the *Shastras* with changing times were discarded and superseded by English common law. This fixed notion of time for the natives formed the basis of the codification. The search for the origin of pure and unadulterated Hindu and Muslim laws was a modern compulsion. Baxi summarises this phenomenon in his mapping of the sociology of Indian law:[84]

> Just as the written texts of religious laws and processes of Western-style interpretation and exegesis led to Anglicization of Hindu law, so did the neglect of custom led to the stagnation of Hindu law during the British period.

Islamic Law and the Colonial Encounter

Despite striking differences between the Hindu and the Muslim law or *Anglo-Muhammadan law*, there were similarities in the way the two were 'constructed' during colonialism. Muslim law, unlike its Hindu counterpart, did not recognise customary law as an integral part of Islamic jurisprudence.[85] But this peculiarity could not save Muslim law from stagnation. The Anglicisation of Islamic law cemented a fixed identity for the South Asian Muslims based on textual tradition

81 *Ibid.*

82 Janaki Nair, *Women and Law in Colonial India: A Social History* 20 (Kali for Women, Delhi, 1996).

83 *Ibid.*

84 Baxi, note 66 at 13.

85 Tahir Mahmood points out that 'the legal theory of Islam, on the whole does not recognize custom as an *Independent* and *formal* source of law.' It only formed a 'minor constituent' of law at the option of the jurist. See Tahir Mahmood, 'Custom as a Source of Law in Islam' 7(1/2) *Journal of Indian Law Institute* 102 (1965).

as evolved by the British courts.[86] The Hastings Plan, Michael R. Anderson argues, homogenised the interpretive traditions of Islamic law in a unidimensional manner. The Quran (the official text in the Hastings Plan) was not primarily a legal text.[87] In a remarkable similarity to classical Hindu law, it exhibited both religious/transcendental aspirations and in practice, it was a normative document for societal interactions in the community.[88] In the words of Anderson:[89]

> To apply the 'laws of Koran with respect to Mohammedans', was a project that mistook Qur'an for a code of law. The Qur'an, and even more specifically legal texts such as *al-Hidaya* had never been directly applied as sources of legal precept. Their legal relevance had always derived from a properly authoritative *quadi* whose moral probity and knowledge of local arrangements could translate precept into practice.

In the brief period when *maulvis* served as law officers, the British judges consulted the *maulvis* on the issues of personal laws in a unique manner. Without narrating the facts of the dispute to the *maulvis*, the judges asked them 'a question formulated in an abstract, hypothetical manner, often shorn of relevant details.'[90] The response to this abstract question by the Muslim law officers was applied on the facts of the dispute by the British judges. Perhaps this abstract formulation emerged from the suspicion of the *maulvis* in the mind of the colonial officers. But this process of decision-making damaged Islamic law as it removed the litigant specificity in favour of universal and mechanical rule application. The judicial reliance on the translated versions of textual sources stagnated Islamic jurisprudence. Anderson notes:[91]

> Although produced in haste, and with imperfect language skills, the unrevised eighteenth-century translations remained authoritative. A number of translating errors were discovered in *Al-Hidaya* but corrections were made *only to the Persian version* in 1807. The English version remains uncorrected.

86 The discussion in this section is limited to 'personal laws.' For a discussion on supersession of Islamic criminal law by British codification, see Radhika Singha, *A Despotism of Law: Crime and Justice in Early Colonial India* (Oxford University Press, New Delhi, 1998).

87 Michael R. Anderson, 'Islamic Law and Colonial Encounter in British India' 11 (WLUML Occasional Paper No. 7, June 1996), available at: https://cdn.atria.nl/ezines/web/WomenLivingUnderMuslimLawsOP/1996/No7June.pdf.

88 Anderson also refers to the problem of translatability. *Al-Hidaya* followed the usual route of translation: from Arabic to Persian and then translated into English from Persian by Charles Hamilton in 1791. However, due to absence of 'inheritance' as a subject, 'in 1792, *al-Sirajiyya*, a treatise on inheritance, was translated direct from the Arabic by Jones personally.' *Id.* at 13.

89 *Id.* at 11.

90 *Ibid.*

91 *Id.* at 14.

This ad-hoc treatment of the native laws resulted in a distorted picture of Muslim law in India. Contemporary Muslim law scholars have lamented this fact as this unfortunate interpretive trend continues in post-independence India. Furqan Ahmed insists that Muslim law is not a judge-made law. It is rather a jurist-made law, a fact that has not been recognised in its contemporary interpretation.[92] Ahmad argues that only a few exceptional Indian judges have recognised this distorted interpretive history aspect, Justice V.R. Krishna Iyer being one of them.[93] In the case of *Yousuf Rawther* v. *Sowramma*,[94] Justice Iyer makes the following remark which sums up the colonial inability to understand Muslim law:[95]

> Since infallibility is not an attribute of the judiciary, the view has been ventured by Muslim jurists that the Indo-Anglian judicial exposition of the Islamic law of divorce has not exactly been just to the Holy Prophet or the Holy Book. Marginal distortions are inevitable when the Judicial Committee in Downing Street has to interpret Manu and Muhammad of India and Arabia. The soul of a culture – law is largely the formalised and enforceable expression of a community's cultural norms – cannot be fully understood by alien minds.

These historical acts of interpretive violence gave birth to the rigid colonial categorisation of Hindu and Muslim identities.[96]

Fixity and Certainty: Rigor or Rigor Mortis?

Fixity, universality and certainty of law were cardinal virtues for eighteenth- and nineteenth-century legal positivists. Pierre Legrand, in his critique of the motivation of positivist lawyers, points out how in over-emphasising fixity and certainty '[w]hat we get is not rigor but *rigor mortis*.'[97] There is ample literature suggesting the deeply fraught process of codification of the Hindu

92 For a critique of some recent cases of Muslim law, see Furqan Ahmad, 'Muslim Law' L *Annual Survey of Indian Law* 901 (2014).

93 For the contribution of Krishna Iyer, J., see Furqan Ahmad, 'Understanding Islamic Law in India: An Assessment of the Contribution of Justice V.R. Krishna Iyer: A Tribute' 57(3) *Journal of the Indian Law Institute* 307–332 (2015).

94 AIR 1971 Ker 261.

95 *Id.* at 264.

96 Despite acknowledging the non-recognition of customs as integral to the Islamic jurisprudence, 'reference to 'usages' of Muslims may have been partly inspired by the position and practices of Hindu converts to Islam (Malabar, Punjab and Central Provinces) who continued to follow certain aspects of Hindu law as well as the adherence to certain regimes of customary law.' Baxi, note 66 at 18.

97 Pierre Legrand, 'Siting Foreign Law: How Derrida Can Help?' 21 *Duke Journal of Comparative & International Law* 595, 599 (2011).

personal law in India.[98] The writings of legal historians also show how despite the nineteenth-century codification of the criminal law that sought to achieve uniformity and precision,[99] the judicial interpretations consolidated and cemented differences on the basis of caste[100] as well as gender.[101] Elizabeth Kolsky, in her study of colonial rape cases, shows how the native woman came to be situated in a doubly marginalised position due to her gender, class and caste ***and*** the colonial perception of natives being 'untrustworthy':[102]

> Indian women faced a twofold challenge in colonial courtrooms. Not only were they subjected to British legal presumptions about false charges, they also had to contend with specifically colonial ideas about the unreliability of native witnesses and other prejudicial ideas about Indian culture. Indian rape victims were doubly suspect suspects.

She also demonstrates how the prejudices of caste were reiterated by the colonial judges who relied on the prejudiced precepts of medical jurisprudence.[103] The post-independence judicial discourse displays a colonial continuity in the double and triple marginalisation of legal subjects – as individuals as well as collectives – who are inscribed not merely by historical markers of caste, class and gender, but also of religion as it has played out in the post-partition, independent secular polity of India.

98 Eleanor Newbigin, *The Hindu Family and the Emergence of Modern India: Law, Citizenship and Community* (Cambridge University Press, Cambridge, 2017). Also see Madhu Kishwar, 'Codified Hindu Law: Myth and Reality' 29(33) *Economic and Political Weekly* (Aug. 13, 1994).

99 T.B. Macaulay, J.M. Macleod, G.W. Anderson and F. Millett, *A Penal Code Prepared by the Indian Law Commissioners* (published by command of The Governor General of India in Counsel) (The Lawbook Exchange Ltd., NJ, 2002). The 1837 draft of the Indian Penal Code with Macaulay's 'Introduction' and 'notes' demonstrates that the ideas of 'certainty and precision' were hallmarks of the process of codification in India.

100 See Anupama Rao, *The Caste Question: Dalits and the Politics of Modern India* (Permanent Black, Ranikhet, 2010). She traces the history of Maharashtra during the 1880s–1990s, to 'rethink India's political modernity from the perspective of the Dalits.' *Id.* at xii. For a review of this work, see Charu Gupta, 'Book Review: Anupama Rao, The Caste Question: Dalits and the Politics of Modern India' 50(1) *Indian Economic and Social History Review* 115–118 (2013).

101 For a discussion of the paternalist discourse of saving Indian women, see Lata Mani, 'Contentious Traditions: The Debate on Sati in Colonial India' in Kumkum Sangari and Suresh Vaid (eds.), *Recasting Women: Essays in Colonial History* (Zubaan, 2013). Also see Partha Chatterjee, 'The Nationalist Resolution of the Women's Question' in Kumkum Sangari and Suresh Vaid (eds.), *Recasting Women: Essays in Colonial History* (Zubaan, 2013).

102 Elizabeth Kolsky, "The Body Evidencing the Crime': Rape on Trial in Colonial India, 1860–1947' 22 (1) *Gender & History* 113 (Apr. 2010). For a recent statement on the construction of 'prostitute' as a colonial category, see Durba Mitra, *Indian Sex Life* (Princeton University Press, Princeton, NJ, 2020).

103 Kolsky, *Id.* at 113 (emphasis added).

In sum, the foundational myth of continuity, the interpretive process which supplanted the native systems of dispute resolution was superseded by the English common law. The fixity and certainty of law (and order) was attained at the cost of 'epistemicide' of native systems. In its implementation, the law became a form of universal precept to be applied to factual situations without appreciating thick narratives of the litigants before the law. This fully formed law is itself a mythic category as it obscures the necessary responsiveness of law to the emergent situations.

IV. Subaltern Engagement with the Law

The Subaltern Studies project attempted an alternative history to the frameworks of colonialist and nationalist historiography. It aimed at providing insights about the interrelationship between law and social history. The 'unreadability' of social events in their encounter with law is an important theme that surfaces in the subaltern project. Shahid Amin argues that judicial discourse de-politicised social events by stripping them of their political content.[104] Ranajit Guha shows how collective political resistance translated into the colonial legal register as the violation of codes of criminal law.[105]

One intervention which directly concerns the themes of this work is Sumit Sarkar's essay titled 'The Kalki-Avatar of Bikrampur: A Village Scandal in Early Twentieth Century Bengal.'[106] Taking the argument of unreadability forward, Sarkar raises the question of absence and erasure of mythology in the colonial legal archive. *Kalki Avatar* investigates the event of killing in a small town of *Doyhat* in Bengal. An upper-caste householder invited a Brahmin ascetic and his two lower-caste disciples. One of the disciples, Prasanna, killed his co-disciple, Ananda, molested the women of the household (asking them to strip, to kick their husband's forehead and to insert smoke-pipes inside their private parts) and finally attempted arson. The trial judge convicted the accused of

104 This is demonstrated through his reading of the 'approver' from the colonial archive. See Shahid Amin, 'Approver's Testimony, Judicial Discourse: The Case of Chauri Chaura' in Ranajit Guha (ed.), *Subaltern Studies V: Writings on South Asian History and Society* (Oxford University Press, Delhi, 1987).

105 Ranajit Guha, *Elementary Aspects of Peasant's Insurgency in Colonial India* (Duke University Press, 1999). Guha shows that the peasant insurgency on the colonial legal register could only acquire the category of a crime.

106 Sumit Sarkar, 'The Kalki-Avatar of Bikrampur: A Village Scandal in Early Twentieth Century Bengal' in Ranajit Guha (ed.), *Subaltern Studies VI: Writings on South Asian History and Society* 1–53 (Oxford University Press, New Delhi, 1989). It is quite surprising that Baxi's essay in the next volume, mapping the trajectory or presence of law in subaltern studies, fails to acknowledge this important contribution on reading the law. See Upendra Baxi, " 'The State's Emissary': The Place of Law in Subaltern Studies' in Partha Chatterjee and Gyanendra Pandey (eds.), *Subaltern Studies VII: Writings on South Asian History and Society* 247–264 (Oxford University Press, New Delhi, 1992).

homicide. The Calcutta High Court, in appeal, confirmed the conviction and issued 'stiffer sentences' against him.

As a historian, Sarkar foregrounds the surrounding mythology linked with the murderous rage, which was neglected entirely in the judicial narrative, and provides an alternative reading of the event. On this register, the accused personified himself as the mythic Lord of Death (*Yama*) and rendered sacrifice for the dawn of a fresh beginning of a new epoch (*Yuga*). Arson, for Prasanna, was equivalent to burning of the city of demons (*Lanka*), akin to the monkey-God (*Hanuman*) in the classic Hindu epic Ramayana. Sarkar reconstructs the incident[107] and shows how the erasure of the mythic social history from the judicial archive resulted in a constrained understanding of the event, and that an alternative narrative could emerge by putting together[108] the micro social history surrounding it.

Sarkar thus opens the possibility of reading Prasanna's actions, viewed from his lower-caste Dalit subjectivity, as a form of defiance of the predominant Brahmanical narrative of the mythological story of *Kalki-Avatar*. While the Kalki-myth of classical Hinduism reinstates hierarchical gender and caste-ridden social relations, Prasanna re-wrote and subverted the dominant myth (making the wives kick their husbands was one such sign). Sarkar's argument is comparable to Goodrich's narration of the erasure of the vocabulary of Haida Indians discussed earlier. Both essays narrate the violence of legal language and the impossibility of acknowledging its 'other'. Sarkar's narrative as a historian, however, explores the possibility of making legible the tribal myth in the legal landscape. Sarkar's subversive reading can be contrasted with the judicial labour invested in the reconstruction of the Hindu majoritarian myth of the birth of Lord Ram at Ayodhya in Chapter 4. This contrast also indicates that the 'mythic' version cannot be idealised as a response to the disavowal of the mythic by the secular courts. In other words, reinstating the mythic uncritically is not any guarantee of a fair and just outcome. The exercise that Sarkar undertakes focusses on the left-out, unsaid or hidden from the formal narrative. If Amin's *Approver's Testimony* reflected upon the reduction of collective political violence to narrowly constructed categories of law, *Kalki Avatar* unfolds the violence of the legal categories themselves in their potential to erase the caste and class realities. In other words, the very tools of law employed for the reconstruction of an event ended up becoming the instruments of wiping off

107 Sarkar's 'primary interest was never in reconstruction of what may have really happened' but 'in what was remembered about it, what forgotten and why.' He analyses various vernacular forms of the permeation of the myths through dramatic representations, cheap paintings of Kalighat and many other forms of renditions of the myth. This foregrounds the subtext of the mythic-historical milieu that surrounded the incident. Sarkar, note 106 at 5.

108 Sarkar explores the themes of *Kali-Yuga* and *Kalki-avatar* in Mahabharata (*vana parva*) as well as other available Sanskrit/Puranic literature around the myth. The origins of *Kalki-Puranas* are traced as early as the eighteenth century, 'possibly originating in Bengal,' which provides the myth a more concrete memory 'by giving it local habitations and names.' Sarkar, *Id.* at 5.

the social dimensions which formed the real impetus for such killing.[109] The merit of Sarkar in establishing diverse reading practices is not to idealise the 'mythic' but to remind us that an alternate or latent narrative of the text can diversify meanings and provide a richer narrative of social history.

In his essay 'Chandra's Death,' Guha illustrates how the possible multiple readings of an event can be clipped off by the law, reducing the 'range of signification to a set of narrowly defined legalities.'[110] The essay interrogates the mediation of law and its effects on the death of a woman, Chandra, in nineteenth-century Bengal. The historical re-construction of the death is based on deposition documents (*ekrars*) by Chandra's sister and mother to 'a tribunal which functioned independently of and parallel to the network of colonial courts.'[111] The depositions were about Chandra's death by consuming medicine intended for abortion. Chandra had a liaison with 'her husband's sister's husband' and had become pregnant. The two options available to her were either aborting the foetus, or accepting social banishment by going to *bhek*, a form of 'living death', for her illegitimate act. It was her choice to abort that eventually led to her death due to excessive bleeding. Guha shows that the women who stood before the law as complicit in abetting her death were indeed representing the 'strength of women's solidarity'[112] by defying the patriarchal authority of *bhek*. The legal lens entirely 'silenced' this act of 'resistance' into the codes of legality thereby, in ways similar to *Approver's Testimony* and *Kalki Avatar* reducing the act of rebellion into an act of criminality where the 'truth of an event [is] *already* classified as a crime.'[113] Such a transformation of the 'matrix of real historical experience' into 'abstract legality' and the silencing or freezing of multiple significations into a linear and singular narrative is at the heart of Guha's essay.[114]

Baxi argues that Guha's essay, despite having 'the qualities of a discourse worthy of being called a classic,'[115] confuses the conception of law with the forensic colonial law of the courts. Such colonial law of the courts is seen in opposition with the non-law of the *samaj* (community) represented by tribunals or *byabostha*. Baxi sees this slippage as induced by the colonial understanding of law as a facet of State sovereignty. How can the community mores and

109 This point is illustrated from a legal standpoint in a recent work by Latika Vashist. See Latika Vashist, *Criminal Law, Feminism and Emotions: Thinking through the Legal Unconscious* (Routledge, 2025), Ch. 2.

110 Ranajit Guha, 'Chandra's Death' in Ranajit Guha (ed.), *Subaltern Studies V: Writings on South Asian History and Society* 135, 140 (Oxford University Press, New Delhi, 1987).

111 *Id.* at 150.

112 *Id.* at 165.

113 *Id.* at 141.

114 *Id.* at 140–141. The transformations involved conversion of 'death into murder, a caring sister into a murderess, all the actants in this tragedy as defendants, and what they said in a state of grief into *ekrars*.'

115 Baxi, note 106 at 250.

practices be differentiated from the label of 'law'? In the context of Chandra's death, Baxi writes, that the 'structuration of subalternity with the ideologies of "government of sexuality" and its ultimate sanction of *bhek*, a sentence of "living death," are no different, in range and in intensity, than State law's death or life-imprisonment sentences.'[116] This again underlines that an opposition of modernity/the modern law in favour of a romantic vision of community-driven justice can be problematic. In studying the law and its 'other,' i.e. the mythic, one has to tread the path carefully without falling into romantic views of the extra/non-legal justice beyond the law. It is an important insight that any *a priori* division of 'law' and 'myth' as historically or factually separate categories can slip into an elevation of 'pre-colonial' arrangements over the modern ones.[117]

V. Colonial History of Free Exercise Clause and Religion in Public Sphere

In this section, I will sketch a brief historical impression of the free exercise of religion clauses of the Indian Constitution and the scholarship advocating for a robust engagement with religion in the public sphere. We have already noted that Warren Hastings resolved to set up a system of indigenous laws as against English common law to govern Indians. However, it was the Queen's Proclamation of 1858 which charted the map for emergence of the vocabulary of religious freedom, the shades of which can be seen in the free exercise clauses of the Indian Constitution.

After Hastings' departure to England for his impeachment trial, Charles Cornwallis, his successor, expanded and transformed the idea of religious freedom into a policy of free exercise. Regulation III of 1793 mentioned that local religious laws must be preserved to protect the natives 'in the free exercise of their religion.' During the late eighteenth and early nineteenth centuries there were rigourous debates on the possible interpretations of the free exercise clause. Did the clause encourage an active support for indigenous religion by East India Company or a complete dissociation from Indian religion?[118] This issue was settled with Queen Victoria's proclamation, which also coincided with the transfer of East India Company's authority to the British Crown.

116 *Id.* at 252.

117 For a critical review of literature on the binary of myth and modernity, see Prachi Deshpande, *Creative Pasts: Historical Memory and Identity in Western India, 1700–1960* 1–18 (Columbia University Press, New York, 2007).

118 See C.S. Adcock, *The Limits of Tolerance: Indian Secularism and the Politics of Religious Freedom* 27–30 (Oxford University Press, New York, 2014). Adcock shows that the British Evangelists were against the support or management of 'heathen' religious institutions. Co-equally they were against the idea of 'neutrality' as that would impede the pursuit of conversion to Christianity. Nonetheless, the 1858 Queen's proclamation inscribed the notion of neutrality with respect to the religious matters of the natives.

The Queen's proclamation, dated November 1, 1858, after declaring equal and impartial protection under the rule of law charged 'and enjoin[ed] all those who may be in authority under us, that they abstain from all interference with the religious belief, or worship.' Adcock describes the impact of the proclamation:[119]

> The Queen's Proclamation established the political languages that Indians would be obliged to use when addressing their colonial rulers, if they would be taken seriously. But before they could appeal to their rights as members of a religious community, Indians had first to translate their concerns in terms of the distinction between the religious and the nonreligious.

This obligation to translate into the colonial language is what she terms the politics of translation.[120] The distinction between the religious and the non-religious (or 'secular activities') finds its way into Article 25 of the Indian constitution, which I will discuss in Chapter 1. Colonial history provides the impetus for the formation of the binary of religious and non-religious which came to govern all interactions with and articulations against the Empire. This context serves as a vigorous foundation to understand this binary that will haunt the constitutional text and its interpretation in post-independence India.

Another corollary to this argument is that the vocabulary of 'religion' originated with, or more accurately in protest of, the colonial rule. There was nothing natural about a wide variety of social and cultural practices to be self-evidently religious.[121] Scholars have shown that the idea of 'religion' as doctrines, scriptures and beliefs is a European historical category.[122] However, of more relevance to this study is

> to understand the ways in which Europe, in its world-conquering project of empire, altered the conditions of the lives of non-European peoples

119 Adcock, note 118 at 38.

120 Also see Shabnum Tejani, *Indian Secularism: A Social and Intellectual History 1890–1950* (Permanent Black, New Delhi, 2007). Tejani argues that the Queen's proclamation provided a framework to articulate local grievances: 'The promise of non-interference in religious custom framed the language with which Indians sought accountability from their rulers.' *Id.* at 74.

121 Partha Chatterjee argues that 'there does not exist in any Indian language a term for "secular" or "secularism" which is standardly used in talking about the role of religion in the modern State and society and whose meaning can be immediately explicated without having recourse to the English terms.' See Partha Chatterjee, 'Secularism and Tolerance' in Rajeev Bhargava (ed.), *Secularism and Its Critics* 350 (Oxford University Press, 1998).

122 See Wilfred Cantwell Smith, *The Meaning and End of Religion: A New Approach to the Religious Traditions of Mankind* (Mentor Books, New York, 1964). Smith argues that the category of religion has specific roots in sixteenth- and seventeenth-century Europe; Peter Harrison, *"Religion" and the Religions in the English Enlightenment* (Cambridge University

> in ways that obliged them too to reconstitute themselves as members of one exclusive 'religious' community *against* others.[123]

It is in this limited sense that I will argue in Chapter 2 that the religion-economics binary which is central to the cow protection debates is insufficient to fully appreciate the validation of the anti-cow slaughter laws by the Supreme Court. I will develop the rather neglected work of C.S. Adcock on cow protection, in which she argues that religion 'in colonial India must be treated as a pragmatic category, one that described the discursive positions that were available to cow protectionists and the political ramifications of those positions.'[124] She specifically studies the Arya Samaj discourse to understand the dual idiom employed in the vernacular idioms, as against the English language literature (directed at the colonial authorities), where the language of religion fuses with that of the economy and the social sphere. I borrow this argument to study the judicial interpretation of anti-cow slaughter laws which follows a similar trajectory and cannot be fully comprehended with a priori binary of logic of economy and religion.

The engagement of the modern law with broad socio-cultural, theological and philosophically complex ideas and practices called 'religion' in India has been present since colonial times. This is not because Indian society is overtly religious by its very nature, but because religion and its interpretations were central to the encounter with the politics of the Empire. It is because of this central and often divisive role played by religion, especially religious differences understood as 'communalism,' that the Nehruvian State sought to establish a firmly secular polity in postcolonial India. But the question of religion cannot be simply erased in the espousal for a secular polity. Such an attitude would mean both the denial of this history as well as the complexity of the struggle against colonialism. A strict separation between religion and the public sphere in postcolonial India is thus rendered impossible; in the next section, I will argue that it is also not desirable in contemporary times.

Rethinking Secularism with Thick Conception of Religion

Political liberalism granted a limited role to religion as it came to be seen as a 'private' and 'individual' affair. Religion was not eradicated but privatised, and religious freedom in liberal societies became a private right.

Press, New York, 1990); Dipesh Chakrabarty, *Provincializing Europe: Postcolonial Thought and Historical Difference* (Princeton University Press, Princeton, NJ, 2000).

123 David Scott, *Refashioning Futures: Criticism After Post Coloniality* 56 (Princeton University Press, Princeton, NJ, 1999) (emphasis in the original).

124 C.S. Adcock, 'Sacred Cows and Secular History: Cow Protection Debates in Colonial North India' 30(2) *Comparative Studies of South Asia, Africa and the Middle East* 297–311, 298 (2010).

Emblematic of the United States (US) Constitution's famous wall of separation thesis,[125] Charles Taylor describes how this approach has become fundamental in imagining Western secularism. Churches 'are now separate from political structures (with a couple of exceptions, in Britain and Scandinavian countries, which are so low-key and undemanding as not really to constitute exceptions).'[126] However, even in the context of Western secularism, the sacred is only *downplayed* from the public realm without its complete *erasure*. Individual religiosity has remained untouched by the process of secularisation. Western secularisation has merely resulted in dividing the individual psyche into two halves. The private face of the subject on which a public mask is superimposed. The mask exhibits the official and formal values of secularisation in public domain. Due to the persistent tension between the personal and the political, secular values remain shallow and peripheral.[127] Sanford Levinson, a constitutional law scholar, argues that the US separation thesis had removed the theological and sacred from constitutional deliberations. But paradoxically, the constitutional text, symbols and values served as sacred supplements for the constitutional framers and the various organs of the State.[128] This has turned the US Constitution and its political institutions into a 'civil religion,'[129] as if, the repressed religiosity returned as a compulsive force obliging the framers and vanguards of the US Constitution – from James Madison to Abraham Lincoln – to turn the Constitution into a document of faith in public discourse, superseding the Bible.

From a feminist standpoint, Margaret Davies raises the question of 'uncertainties' and 'controversies' in the American separation thesis. She locates such uncertainties even in the more inclusive or 'weak constitutional principle of State impartiality towards religion' in the Australian Constitution.[130] Towards the end of the twentieth century, she argues, the 'highly visible social markers of religious difference' became an important issue for gender justice with the banning of *hijab* in France and Turkey.[131] She provocatively asks if the exclu-

125 An anti-establishment clause inserted by way of the First Amendment to the US Constitution prohibited the federal State from legislating on the affairs of the Church. Amendment I of the US Constitution reads: 'Congress shall make no law respecting an establishment of religion, or prohibiting the free exercise thereof; or abridging the freedom of speech, or of the press; or the right of the people peaceably to assemble, and to petition the government for a redress of grievances.'

126 Taylor, note 1 at 1.

127 Rodney Stark, 'Secularization, R.I.P.' 60(3) *Sociology of Religion* 249–273 (1999). The effort made to maintain the appearance only strengthened the inner religiosity, as if the outward public appearance was counterbalanced by the inner religiosity, irrational or even superstitious core.

128 See Sanford Levinson, *Constitutional Faith* (Princeton University Press, Princeton, NJ, 2011).

129 Sanford Levinson, 'The Constitution in American Civil Religion' *The Supreme Court Review* 123–151 (1979).

130 Margaret Davies, 'The Future of Secularism: A Critique' in Nadirsyah Hosen and Richard Mohr (eds.), *Law and Religion in Public Life* (Routledge, 2011).

131 *Id.* at 57.

sion of religion from public space violates the fundamental tenets of democracy and equal treatment as it marginalises the views of the religiously-minded in the structures of governance? She argues that such exclusion abdicated religion from the definition of the political. Whether by 'excluding religion from political discourse . . . we also silence those who would challenge dominant interpretations of their faith?'[132] She advocates for dissenting traditions within the religious landscape to emerge and occupy the discursive public sphere. This would avoid the essentialist view of the religion, in the hands of a few religious leaders, reinvigorating religious orthodoxy and marginalising alternative religious imaginations. Such exclusion, for Davies, is 'undemocratic' and 'unfruitful' in its potential to delegitimise the possibilities of emergence of alternative imaginations on the theological terrain.[133] Contemporary politics across the world demonstrate the increasing relevance of the sacred returning in political contestations and constitutional discourse. Thus, any attempt to salvage the legacy of constitutional secularism will have to pay heed to the presence of the sacred and the non-rational in politics and the law.

VI. Outline of Chapters

Chapter 1 focusses on the judicial doctrine of 'essential practices' (or the essential practices test, as it has come to be called). This doctrine was inaugurated by the Supreme Court of India to interpret the freedom of religion clause. After its initial appearance in 1954, this doctrine has been used to separate the 'essential' and 'integral' aspects of religion from the non-essential or secular, economic and financial ones. This separation is premised on the presupposition that only essential and integral aspects of the religion will elicit complete protection from any form of State regulations.

The doctrine has been modified over the years in the successive precedents of the Supreme Court. Initially, the Court allowed such determination by the community. In later cases, the Court gave up the 'community determination' logic, recognising that the community speaks in multiple voices and cannot be reduced to a single homogenous entity. I have discussed the evolution, use and misuse of the doctrine over the years in various cases. In recent years, we find that the Supreme Court itself has grown suspicious of the legitimacy of the doctrine. The Court has accepted the plea for a re-evaluation of the doctrine (following the decision of the Supreme Court in *Sabarimala Judgment*) and the fate of doctrine is pending, at present, before a nine-judge bench of the Supreme Court.

132 *Id.* at 63.

133 Ratna Kapur's work provides an illustration of re-imagination of alternative ways of religious traditions from a legal standpoint without falling into the trap of religious orthodoxy. See Ratna Kapur, *Gender, Alterity and Human Rights: Freedom in a Fishbowl* (Edward Elgar Publishing, 2018).

I confess that writing this chapter has been a difficult task and every draft made me question my position on the issue. Initially, I was certain and self-righteous in joining hands with the advocates of abolition of this doctrine. There are strong and convincing reasons that exist supporting this viewpoint. The primary reason is the lack of cognitive competence of the judiciary to read theological texts or traditions. The judges, after all, are trained neither in theology nor anthropology. A related, but equally weighty, reason was the eclectic (ab)use of the doctrine by the Supreme Court in at least two ways: first, in reading religion where it never existed and imposing the requirement of proof of essentiality on the petitioners who never pleaded religion in the first place;[134] and second, the misapplication of the doctrine in regressive ways by the Supreme Court.[135]

I have come to realise, while working on this issue, the limits of the position which advocates for the abolition of the doctrine. The reason behind the change in my position is linked to the central argument of the book: that there is no easy separation possible between the law and religion or the law and the mythic. Although I continue to maintain my critique of the doctrine, I have questioned the easy erasure prescription that is predominant in legal scholarship. The predominant scholarship on this issue constantly emphasises the cognitive competence argument suggesting that the judiciary should stay out of theological exegesis. However, the problematic alternative of allowing the community to decide the contents and contours of what constitutes as 'essential', without any judicial intervention, has been iterated quite uncritically. I have argued that the issues of impossibility of strict separation between law and religion/mythic on the one hand, and the dangers of community determination on the other, have remained unattended in the vast legal literature on the essential practices test.

I argue that relinquishing the essential practices test – as a rectification of the interpretational error – fails to appreciate its symbolic depth as well as historical force. This rejection hypothesis imagines neat separation of the law and judicial process from the mythic or transcendental concerns which can be cleansed entirely. These positions are informed by either a complete denial of the mythic in modern law or expulsion of this dispensable adjunct smearing the law. My argument is that such a separation of the secular law from the

134 See Amit Bindal, 'Resurrecting the Other of "Modern" Law: Investigating Niyamgiri Judgment and Legal Epistemology' 5 *NUJS The Journal of Indian Law and Society* 237–247 (Monsoon, 2015). I discuss this point in Chapter 2, on how the Supreme Court (in *Hanif Quareshi* v. *State of Bihar*, AIR 1958 SC 731) relied on this doctrine to convert the issue of livelihood into predominantly a religious issue.

135 The comments of the Supreme Court (in *Ismail Faruqui* v. *Union of India* (1994) 6 SCC 364) observing that a 'mosque is not an essential part of the practice of the religion of Islam and namaaz (prayer) by Muslims can be offered anywhere, even in open' demonstrated the partisan manner in which the doctrine can be applied. I discuss this and other related aspects of the case in Chapter 4.

transcendental or mythological is an impossibility or an unattainable *dream-work* of the secular modernity. I conclude the Chapter by arguing that a wishful withering away of the doctrine of essential practices would not eradicate but only *repress* its compelling force. I argue that the Court must encourage all available, including marginal and alternative views of reading the scriptures, customs or traditions, and validate the one(s) which comes closest to the values of the Constitution in a particular historical time and space.

Chapter 2 looks at the debate of cow protection legislations arising from the constitutional mandate for protection of the cow in Article 48. It charts out the co-existence of the sacred (myth) and secular (modernity) infused in the constitutional provision through the debates of the Constituent Assembly and the interpretive labour of the Supreme Court. It traces the trajectory of the Supreme Court's reasoning and the objectionable way in which it dealt with the issue.

I have used two central threads to unpack the cow protection debates and the judicial discourse on this issue. First, I have focused on the doctrine of presumption of constitutionality. According to this doctrine, all laws are presumed to be constitutional unless the contrary is shown by the party challenging the law in question. This doctrine has been consistently used from the very first case on anti-cow slaughter laws till the latest pronouncement on the topic. I argue that in the context of anti-slaughter laws, it has acquired a status of doctrinal myth of constitutional faith or secular mythology. This is because, despite the state[136] legislatures' repeated attempts to subvert the law laid down by the Supreme Court, the Court continues to proceed with the presumption of constitutionality of such laws. This chapter thus illustrates the complex web of modern law and mythology and suggests ways, from within the logic of modern law, of orienting the discourse of the court towards a *just* outcome.

Chapter 3 explores the interpretations given by the Court to the contentious provision in the Representation of Peoples Act, 1950 (RPA), which bars the use of religious speech or symbolism for electoral gains. I argue that the Supreme Court in its interpretation of the statutory provision has missed the social and political context. I demonstrate that this search for a *hidden meaning* of the religious symbols or speech discounts the social and political contingency of communal appeals made in election times. For example, *Om* becomes a symbol that transcends Hinduism, and in later decisions 'Hinduism' itself becomes a category transcending religion as it is a 'way of life.' The judgments in this chapter reveal the Court's attempt at finding the essence of religious motifs without any reference to the 'essential practices test,' which I elaborately discuss in Chapter 1. This establishes the fact that an abandonment of the 'essential practices test,' advocated as a panacea in contemporary legal scholarship, would do little to address the deep-seated judicial drive to

136 Throughout this book, 'State' with capital 'S' is used to refer to the overall Indian state/governmental structure, while 'state' with a small 's' is for the state law or the state governments of West Bengal, Maharashtra, etc.

engage with religion. This chapter shows the consequences of falling over by the Court towards the mythological at the expense of the historical, the social and the political. I interrogate the Court for this lapse and argue, reading attentively a few neglected decisions, that an alternate route is possible while staying within the logic of the law.

Finally, Chapter 4 attempts to explore the mythology of modern law through a careful reading of the text of the Supreme Court judgment in the Babri Masjid-Ram Janambhumi dispute at Ayodhya. Unlike other chapters, this chapter focusses on a single judgment. Through this singular, deep focus, I seek to illustrate the enveloping of the legal/rational and the mythological in one single text. Reading the 'addenda' at the end of the judgment, I argue that the 'addenda' is a perfect mythological supplement to this judgment which praises 'dispassionate objectivity' as a foundational virtue for forensic discussions. The 'addenda' exhibits the *other side* of the judgment which the Court neither denies nor fully accepts. In this sense, it is 'the juridical unconscious'[137] which illustrates the muddled relationship between rational and mythical tied together at once.

This chapter also explains a characteristic unique to Indian law – the notion of the 'Hindu idol' as a juristic or artificial legal person. I have shown how the theory of ascribing juristic personhood to 'idols' takes a perverse form in the judgment as the Court accords legal personality to idols, which it acknowledges were illegally installed. Here, the Court fails to appreciate the logic of its own precedents. It is important to put Chapter 2 in conversation with this chapter on the issue of the Hindu idol. Unlike the Hindu idol, the cow is not conferred a juristic personality in Indian law. This is despite the fact that 'cow protection' was elevated to the status of a constitutional virtue by the framers. This point is worth noticing to appreciate the novel ways in which the law and legal interpretation engage, embrace and at times distance themselves from mythological or the sacred. The conceptual boldness of the modern law about its virtues of objectivity, dispassion or autonomy hides the uncomfortable element of *faith* which constitutes its underbelly.

This study is not a nihilistic plea of doom for those who still hope for (social, economic and political) transformation through the law. Rather, it is a plea for strengthening the law by acknowledging its *other* sides, which, if repressed or disavowed, can endanger the transformative ideals of law. It is central to the argument of this book that there is as much to learn from failures and pitfalls of law[138] as from the stories of transformative constitutionalism.

137 See Shoshana Felman, *The Juridical Unconscious: Trials and Traumas in the Twentieth Century* (Harvard University Press, Cambridge, MA, 2002).

138 This point of learning from failures of law has been made in the context of LGBTQ+ politics by Ashley Tellis, 'Violence Against the Law: Reading Sexual Minority Judgements in Contemporary India' in Latika Vashist and Jyoti Dogra Sood (eds.), *Rethinking Law and Violence* 244–276 (2020). Also see Jacqueline Rose, 'Something Amiss' in Noreen Giffney and Eve Watson (eds.), *Clinical Encounters in Sexuality: Psychoanalytic Practice and Queer Theory* 391–395 (Punctum Books, 2017).

1 Interpreting the Free Exercise Clause

Reflections on the Doctrine of Essential Religious Practices

Introduction

On April 16, 1954, a seven-judge bench of the Supreme Court delivered a decision which was to become foundational for future interpretations of the religious freedom or free exercise of religion clauses of the Indian Constitution. The free exercise clauses guarantee freedom of religion as a fundamental right to both individuals (Article 25) and religious institutions (Article 26). The judgment in *The Commissioner, Hindu Religious Endowments, Madras* v. *Sri Lakshmindra Thirtha Swamiar of Sri Shirur Mutt* (*Shirur Mutt*)[1] formally[2] inaugurated the 'doctrine of essential practices' (or 'essential practices test'). This test was to become the touchstone to determine the essence of the constitutional right of religious freedom for decades thereafter. Part of the justification for the doctrine appears under Article 25 itself, which distinguishes 'secular activities' from 'religious practices' to discern which elements are amenable to State regulation and which are protected from any State intervention as constitutionally protected religious freedom.[3] The doctrine ascertains the *integral* or *essential* aspects of religion and limits the claims of religious autonomy within this compass. After the aforementioned verdict, determining these essential tenets became necessary for any religious claim to acquire the status of an enforceable fundamental right.

India's secularism, as discussed in the Introduction, consists of its own peculiarities, defined by the unique context and the fissures of colonial history

1 AIR 1954 SC 282: MANU/SC/0136/1954. B.K. Mukherjea, J. wrote the opinion of the Court. The other judges on the bench were Mehar Chand Mahajan, CJ., Sudhi Ranjan Das, Vivian Bose, Ghulam Hasan, N.H. Bhagwati, T.L. Venkatarama Aiyyar, JJ. The citations in this chapter are taken from Manupatra.

2 I write 'formally' because the idea of essential or compulsory notions as opposed to optional or non-essential exists even in the constituent assembly debates and judicial pronouncements which do not refer to the essential practices test. See the discussion on constituent assembly debates and the *Hanif Quareshi* case discussed in Chapter 2.

3 I have already outlined the historical origins of this distinction in the Free Exercise Clause (see Introduction), arguing that the vocabulary of religion in opposition with the secular affairs took shape after the Queen Victoria's Proclamation of 1858.

DOI: 10.4324/9781003398561-2

and the need for State-controlled religion in the public forum. The necessity of the doctrine appears to have sprung from the conflict between an exclusive right to religion and the interventionist compulsion for social transformation. This differentiation is clearly inscribed in Article 25 of the Indian Constitution. Religion is seen as *vis inertiae*, operating against social transformation, but at the same time as an enforceable right against the State. State intervention (for 'social welfare and reform') thus became constitutionally permissible for all non-essential facets of any religious institution.

Partha Chatterjee historically charts this tension between religious freedom and reformatory impulse against orthodox religious practices as the 'liberal paradox' of the modern Indian State.[4] One of the anomalies of the secular State in India, for Chatterjee, is the 'use of state legislation' to achieve a modernist purpose which comes directly 'in conflict with another modernist principle, of the freedom of religion.'[5] The paradox lies in the recognition of religious freedom as a fundamental right and beyond the purview of legislative action, and at the same time anticipating social reform and welfare within and from religion. The doctrine of essential practices is an outcome of this historical paradox negotiating between these two mutually contradictory impulses. It is therefore important to study the historical background and other contingencies within which the doctrine emerged. What historical and institutional necessity justified the demarcation of essential from the non-essential religious practices? Is such a demarcation possible, and that too by the judiciary? Are judges, who lack knowledge of or training in theological exegesis, competent to undertake this enterprise? These and related questions will be explored in this chapter.

I will also show how the Supreme Court of India has interpreted the doctrine in a contradictory manner. The Court, it will become clear, does not act as a cohesive institution in the application of the doctrine. The dominant strand of legal scholarship on essential practices doctrine advocates for its abandonment by the Court on account of lack of judicial competence to enter and evaluate the domain of theological discourses.[6] I will propose a critical

4 Partha Chatterjee, 'Secularism and Tolerance' in Rajeev Bhargava (ed.), *Secularism and Its Critics* (Oxford University Press, Oxford, 1998).

5 Chatterjee, *Id.* at 360. The reformist impetus for religious institutions beginning in the nineteenth century was a part of the vocabulary of the Indian ruling classes. 'Legal intervention in the cause of religious reform was not undesirable *per se*, but it was undesirable when the state was colonial.' *Ibid.* This is important to contextualise Indian secularism as historically entwined with State regulation of religious affairs. The nineteenth century reform impetus was carried over to the Indian State from colonial legislature, but it stayed as an important aspect of Indian secularism. This distinguishing feature of Indian secularism makes it at odds with the US 'wall of separation' model.

6 See Rajeev Dhavan and Fali Nariman, 'The Supreme Court and Group Life: Religious Freedom, Minority Groups, and Disadvantaged Communities' in Rajeev Dhavan, Ashok H. Desai B.N. Kirpal and Raju Ramachandran (eds.), *Supreme But Not Infallible: Essays in Honour of the Supreme Court of India* (Oxford University Press, New Delhi, 2000); Rajeev Dhavan,

evaluation of the doctrine to appreciate its failures more creatively. If the failures of the doctrine are attributed to the incapacity of the secular courts to adjudicate the theological domain, then should religious or 'unsecular' disputes be kept outside the domain of law? Who then would adjudicate the competing interpretations of the religious texts or traditions when these impinge on individual or collective rights guaranteed in the Constitution? More importantly, can the religious domain be neatly separated at all from the secular or political? I will propose that working through with these questions, largely neglected in the scholarship of religion and constitutional law, will encourage a critical engagement with the appearance of the doctrine on the landscape of Indian constitutional law.

I. Free Exercise Clause of the Indian Constitution

Article 25. Freedom of conscience and free profession, practice and propagation of religion

(1) Subject to public order, morality and health and to the other provisions of this Part, all persons are equally entitled to freedom of conscience and the right freely to profess, practise and propagate religion.
(2) Nothing in this article shall affect the operation of any existing law or prevent the State from making any law

 (a) regulating or restricting any economic, financial, political or other secular activity which may be associated with religious practice;
 (b) providing for social welfare and reform or the throwing open of Hindu religious institutions of a public character to all classes and sections of Hindus.

Explanation I The wearing and carrying of kirpans shall be deemed to be included in the profession of the Sikh religion.
Explanation II In sub clause (b) of clause reference to Hindus shall be construed as including a reference to persons professing the Sikh, Jaina or Buddhist religion, and the reference to Hindu religious institutions shall be construed accordingly.

Article 25 (1) provides religious freedom as a fundamental right to individual practitioners of religion. This must be distinguished from Article 26, which encapsulates the rights for religious institutions or denominations. Unlike any

---

'When the Judiciary Rewrites a Faith' *The Hindu* (Oct. 15, 2018). Dhavan argues that the belief of the community in tenets of religion should be accepted as the final determinant of essential aspects of religion. Also see Ronojoy Sen, *Articles of Faith: Religion, Secularism and the Indian Supreme Court* 40–72 (Oxford University Press, Oxford, 2010); Mathew John, *India's Communal Constitution: Law, Religion, and the Making of a People* (Cambridge University Press, New Delhi, 2023).

other Article guaranteeing fundamental rights in Part III of the Constitution, the clauses dealing with free exercise of religion begin with the limitations to this freedom. This can be seen in the opening words of both the Articles: 'Subject to public order, morality and health'. This is a departure from the general constitutional scheme where a right is mentioned first followed by limitations or restrictions. This indicates an apparent constitutional hierarchy between the fundamental right to religious freedom and other fundamental rights. Moreover, the Constitution further restricts only Article 25 (and not Article 26) by subjecting it 'to the other provisions of this Part.'

Article 26. Freedom to manage religious affairs

> Subject to public order, morality and health, every religious denomination or any section thereof shall have the right
>
> (a) to establish and maintain institutions for religious and charitable purposes;
> (b) to manage its own affairs in matters of religion;
> (c) to own and acquire movable and immovable property; and
> (d) to administer such property in accordance with law

The denominational right is subjected to 'public order, morality and health' but not 'to the other provisions of this Part'. Is there a constitutional hierarchy *inter se* between Article 26 and Article 25? This linguistic latitude towards the denominational right has led to various legal controversies.[7] Most notably, we will discuss this textual confusion with respect to the Supreme Court's 1957 decision in *Sri Venkataramana Devaru* v. *State of Mysore* (*Devaru*)[8] and more recently in the dispute over the entry for women into the Sabarimala temple in *Indian Young Lawyers Association* v. *State of Kerala* (*Sabarimala Judgment*).[9] The framers not only proposed a cautious religious freedom by putting limits such as public order, morality and health, but Article 25 (2) also provides a list of permissible State interventions.

Article 25 (2) distinguishes between 'existing law' (the pre-constitutional law)[10] and laws made by the State (post-independence law). Article 25 (2) (a) permits *regulation* or *restriction* by law of any 'economic, financial, political or other secular activity . . . associated with religious practice.' A positive obligation is cast upon the State under Article 25 (2) (b) to *provide for* 'social welfare and reform' or 'the throwing open of Hindu religious institutions of a public character to all classes and sections of Hindus.' Social welfare and 'reform'

7 See P.K. Tripathy, *Spotlights on Constitutional Interpretation* 100–126 (N.M. Tripathy Pvt. Ltd., Bombay, 1972).

8 MANU/SC/0026/1957: AIR 1958 SC 255.

9 (2018) SCC SC 1690.

10 The Indian Constitution specifically permits continuity with pre-constitutional laws unless they are superseded by legislative action. Article 372, Constitution of India.

are anticipated through an interventionist State for all religions. But specific mention is made of the context of caste violence in Hinduism, instructing the throwing open of the temples for all classes and sections of Hindus.[11] Chatterjee notes how historically the reformist fervour was coalesced with nation-building from the late nineteenth century onwards, resulting in the paradox where the modern Indian State rejected the strict separation between Church and State, but the 'violation of this principle of the [Euro-American] secular state was justified precisely by the desire to secularize.'[12] The strict separation was sidestepped in favour of State intervention for the reform of religious orthodoxy.

These prefatory remarks foreground a few characteristics of religious freedom in India: the Constitution aspires to an interventionist State for the purpose of 'social welfare and reform' of all religions with specific mention of the Hindu caste system. An active involvement of the State is envisaged to combat caste discrimination. This synoptic discussion is necessary to appreciate the origin of the doctrine of essential religious practices.[13]

II. Origin & Development of the Doctrine of Essential Practices

In 1952, in the case of *Nar Hari Shastri* v. *Shri Badrinath Temple Committee*,[14] a division bench of the Supreme Court approved a bylaw under the Shri Badrinath Act, 1939. It restricted the entry of priests as escorts to pilgrims at the famous Hindu temple at Badrinath. The argument of maintenance of order inside the temple premises by avoiding overcrowding had convinced the Court. The specific issue was the entry of the priests ('*pandas*') as escorts with the worshippers in the Badrinath temple.[15] The petitioners (*pandas*) claimed their right, 'by immemorial custom, to act as Pandas and "Tirtha Purohits" [pilgrimage priests] of the pilgrims at Badrinath.'[16]

The Court distinguished between *pandas* belonging to the priestly class (engaged as escorts/guides) and the worshipping priests. The petitioners (Brahmins belonging to the priestly class) contested the obstruction as unlawful restraint which denies them from 'assisting the pilgrims in the usual way at the time of

11 This provision must be read along with Article 17 of the Constitution which abolishes 'untouchability' in all its forms and compulsively mandates the State to criminalise the practice of untouchability. A detailed discussion on Article 17 and its interpretation in the context of religious freedom clause will follow later in this chapter.

12 Chatterjee, note 4 at 358.

13 The doctrine also reflects a continuation of the British colonial legacy which was interested in finding out the core of Indian religions, as discussed in the Introduction.

14 1952 SCR 849. The three judges on the bench were B.K. Mukherjea, Fazal Ali, and S.R. Das, JJ. (speaking through B.K. Mukherjea, J.) [Hereafter '*Badrinath Temple*'].

15 The temple is situated in the hills of Himalayas in the district of Gadhwal. 'The place to which the appellation of "Puri" is given, contains several temples but the principal temple is the one where the idol Badrinath along with some other subsidiary idols is installed.' *Id.* para 1.

16 *Id.* para 7.

"darshan" and worship of the deities inside the temple.'[17] The defendants (members of the temple committee and the State government) justified the restriction as necessary to avoid overcrowding. It did not restrict, they argued, any visit to the temple for the worshippers. But the plaintiffs could not be allowed to accompany their clients or receive gifts from them, which was the prevalent custom.

The Supreme Court declared that the right to entry and worship in the temple was innate and inherent as the temple was a public place. Despite acknowledging the customary right to escort the pilgrims, it validated the imposed restrictions for the purpose of decency and maintenance of order. The *pandas* were restrained from receiving gifts and presents from the clients inside the precincts of the temple. The Court noted that the restriction under the Shri Badrinath Act of 1939 was permissible for maintenance of order. This established that even an administrative requirement for the maintenance of order could supersede a long-standing customary religious practice. It also highlighted that despite rejecting the US-style Church-State separation, the Indian religious freedom is far from providing a *carte blanche* to religion. The judgment implicitly recognised the historical context of temple regulation as one of the important tasks that the independent Indian State had undertaken for itself. It is precisely this tenet of the judicial interpretation which acquired a doctrinaire form in *Shirur Mutt*.

Shirur Mutt *and the Doctrine of Essential Practices*

Shirur Mutt was the first case where provisions of a legislation were stuck down relying on the free exercise of religion clauses. It orchestrated the vocabulary of the *essential* as opposed to *non-essential* facets of religion within the Court's understanding of the religious freedoms under the Constitution. The Hindu Religious Endowments Act, 1927,[18] was enacted to take over the administration and management of the Hindu temples. This was attained by establishing 'endowment boards' which are vested with the power of such management.[19] This enactment was superseded after independence by the then-state of Madras, through the Madras Hindu Religious and Charitable Endowments Act, 1951. It abolished the Endowment Board created by the 1927 Act and vested its powers in the state government. An organised

17 *Id.* para 7.

18 The British in the initial years of rule 'took over many of the functions of patronage and administration previously carried out by Indian rulers, by middle of nineteenth century it largely renounced those responsibilities and handed them over to local trusts and committees.' Chatterjee, note 4 at 352.

19 The reform of religious institutions began by various provincial legislatures well before Indian independence from British colonial rule. The Madras Temple Entry Authorisation Act, 1947, was a noteworthy enactment as it criminalised the exclusion of any caste Hindu on the grounds of untouchability. This provincial legislation came before the enactment of Article 17 of the Constitution of India.

hierarchical structure was established under the 1951 Act, with the commissioner at the top and other government functionaries under him.[20] The scope and jurisdiction under the 1951 Act extended beyond religious endowments to include purely charitable endowments as well.

The original petition was filed in the Madras High Court by Sri Lakshmindra Theertha Swamiar, the spiritual head of the Shirur Mutt ('*muths*' are institutional spaces belonging to different religious sects where religious leaders and students live, and theological learning and rituals take place) under the 1927 enactment. He argued that the endowment board must be prohibited from interference in the affairs of the *matt*, which was founded by Sri Madhawacharya, a well-known exponent of dualist theism in Hindu religious philosophy. After the Constitution came into force in 1950, a subsequent petition was filed in 1951 by the *Mathadipati* (the head of the *Mutt*), who was the successor in authority of the previous petitioner. With the change in circumstances, this subsequent petition added an additional argument, challenging the constitutional validity of the 1951 law itself. The High Court decided the case in favour of the petitioner.

This decision was challenged by the commissioner. The Supreme Court approved the decision of the Madras High Court. Authored by Justice B.K. Mukherjea, the Supreme Court decision observed that the spiritual head could not be equated with an ordinary priest or a paid servant:[21]

> He is the head and superior of a spiritual fraternity and the purpose of Math is to encourage and foster spiritual training by maintenance of a competent line of teachers who could impart religious instructions to the disciples and followers of the Math and try to strengthen the doctrines of the particular school or order, of which they profess to be adherents. This purpose cannot be served if the restrictions are such as would bring the *Mathadhipati* down to the level of a servant under a State department.

These observations were made in the context of Sections 30 (2) and 31 of the Act, which restricted the proprietorial rights of the head priest. A secular authority was made in charge to regulate the surplus spendings for expenditure. Section 30 (2) required a previous sanction for the expenditure. This was considered too much interference as there was already a provision in the enactment (which was not challenged) that the head priest cannot use the surplus for his 'personal use.' Both these provisions were declared unconstitutional by the Supreme Court as an interference in the property rights of the head priest. It must be noted that at this point the right to property was a fundamental right under Article 19 (1) (f) of the Constitution.

20 The commissioner (the petitioner in this case) superseded the endowment board president of the 1927 Act.

21 *Shirur Mutt*, note 1, para 12.

The Court was of the view that the institutional properties cannot be neatly separated from the head priest, and it also struck down Section 56, which permitted administration of secular affairs by the commissioner as violative of Article 26 (d). A careful look at the reasoning shows that the Court was not faulting an outside authority to manage secular activities. Instead, the Court's wrath was at the overbreadth of scope of this provision, allowing an unreasonable and arbitrary power of intervention without any doubt of 'mismanagement of property or maladministration of trust funds.'[22] The Court thus declared the power of the State authorities to enter the temple at any time of the day (under Section 21) as *ultra vires* and violating the freedom of religion clause (Article 26 (b)). Distinguishing between the entry of the 'outsiders' into the 'outer portion of the temple' and into the sacred 'inner part,' it relied on what it called 'traditional custom' to declare unconstitutional the specific provision in the 1951 Act that permitted entry of the State officials into the inner part of the temple. These details are important, as most provisions in cases were stuck down not on freedom of religion clauses but for other constitutional infirmities.[23]

Following P.K. Tripathy, this minor detail opens the possibility of reading this judgment in an altogether different light. Tripathy reads this judgment not as emboldening institutional religious autonomy and diluting the secular regulations or 'sapping the vigour of secular control,'[24] which is how this judgment is generally referred to in judicial and academic writings. Tripathy finds it paradoxical that 'the judgment of Mukherjea, J., has been cited in subsequent cases with greater enthusiasm and frequency against state regulation than to uphold it.'[25] For Tripathy, the reason for this misreading lies in the 'general survey' of Articles 25 and 26 done by Justice Mukherjea in the beginning of his opinion before coming to specific provisions and validity. Much of what subsequently was attributed to *Shirur Mutt*, he argues, was *obiter dicta* and not *ratio* of the case. He notes that this general survey was not based on a meticulous analysis by the Supreme Court precisely because these were remarks offered by the way. To illustrate, Tripathy notes that while discussing the limits on Article 25,

> the important reservation couched in the words "and to the other provisions of this part," never seems to have been noticed by the Court. Not at one place does this reservation seem to have been mentioned in the entire judgment.[26]

22 *Id.* para 33.

23 For instance, in additional to right to property violation as already noted, Section 76 of the enactment was declared invalid for imposition of tax which was *ultra vires* Article 246 of the constitution (which has nothing to do with fundamental rights).

24 P.K. Tripathy, 'Secularism: Constitutional Provision and Judicial Review' 8(1) *Journal of Indian Law Institute* 1, 16 (1966).

25 *Id.* at 14.

26 *Id.* at 14–15.

Responding to the Court remarks that Article 26 (b) is 'a fundamental right which no Legislature can take away, whereas the former [Article 26 (d)] can be regulated by laws which the Legislature can validly impose', Tripathy accurately notes that this observation appears 'to ignore the opening words of article 26 which subject this right, as indeed, all others in the article, to "public order, morality and health."'[27] Nevertheless, the later Supreme Court judgments followed these observations in *Shirur Mutt* uncritically. I may add a few more ambivalent positions taken by the Supreme Court in *Shirur Mutt* as a part of the general survey. Consider this oft-quoted passage from the judgment emphasising the ***doctrinal*** tenets of a religion as the essence of the essential practices test: 'what constitutes the essential part of a religion is ***primarily*** to be ascertained with reference to the ***doctrines*** of that religion itself.'[28] This made the primary and paramount assessment as doctrinal. However, at another instance the Court dilutes this observation by suggesting the contrary:[29]

> A religion undoubtedly has its basis in a system of beliefs or doctrines . . . but it would not be correct to say that religion is nothing else, but a doctrine or belief. A religion may not only lay down a code of ethical rules for its followers to accept, it might prescribe rituals and observances, ceremonies and modes of worship which are regarded as ***integral parts of religion***, and these forms and observances might extend even to matters of food and dress.

Not only doctrines, but also ritual observances, ceremonies and modes of worship connected with belief can be integral to religion.[30] It is difficult to clearly demarcate 'food offerings' from customary practices, as these offerings have developed over time in different regions according to local conditions and preferences. Customs develop historically, adapt to changing conditions and change over time; indeed, it was this very flexibility and change in the evolution of religious customs that colonial law, as we saw in the Introduction, froze as 'timeless custom' or 'timeless tradition' when it took some current customs and turned them into fundamental tenets of Hindu or Muslim law, and discarded others as later accretions and therefore 'corruptions' of correct religious practice. The Court also insisted on the scrutiny of religious texts, practices ***and customs*** in order to find out what constitutes 'essential' to a

27 *Id.* at 15.
28 *Shirur Mutt*, note 1, para 20 (emphasis added).
29 *Id.* para 17 (emphasis added).
30 Khagesh Gautam argues that when the link between the religious action and the belief was deemed inseparable, actions too became essential and therefore worthy of constitutional protection. Khagesh Gautam, 'Protecting Free Exercise of Religion under the Indian and the United States Constitutions: The Doctrine of Essential Practices and the Centrality Test' 8(3) *Indian Constitutional Law Journal* 311 (2014). However, the language of Court appears broader as food and dress and culinary offerings are included in the passage.

particular religion. This lack of clarity between customary and doctrinal religion had existed in the colonial understanding of religion, and it continued in the Supreme Court's pronouncements. Religion, custom and tradition overlap in this formulation to a great extent. I do not want to suggest that the general survey of the Supreme Court can be seen as 'innocuous' as Tripathy seems to suggest. This is because a seven-bench opinion and its interpretation of the freedom of religion clauses would have bearings on future pronouncements. The Court cannot be excused for hasty observations even if it is a general survey. Nevertheless, one could not have selected passages from the judgment without acknowledging the fact that many of them are ambivalent. Significantly, Tripathy offers the possibility of an alternative reading of this judgment to curtail its sting of strengthening the autonomy of institutional religion.

It appears that not only subsequent pronouncements but also several Indian constitutional scholars have refused to notice this ambivalence in *Shirur Mutt*.[31] Ronojoy Sen describes the doctrine as an effort to 'cleanse Hinduism of . . . superstition, and providing it with a modernist and rationalist definition of religious error and religious truth.'[32] For Sen, the doctrine 'has served as a vehicle for legitimizing a rationalized form of high Hinduism, and delegitimizing usages of popular Hinduism as superstition.'[33] Sen subscribes to the dominant reading of the judgment, that the Court elevated the doctrinal religion over its customary practices. However, as we have seen, the Court considered both the customary practices (including food and dress) alongside the textual evidence to establish what was essential religious practice. Although over time the essential practices test may have privileged high Hinduism over popular practices, we see in these individual interpretations, as in *Shirur Mutt*, that many customary practices could find their way into the 'essential' category as well. I shall return, in the discussion of the *Sabarimala Judgment*, to Sen's division between high and popular religion, and his privileging of the latter as problematic.

Finally, we must add that *Shirur Mutt* damagingly institutes an internal point of view as determinative of the essential practices test when it observes that no outside party, but the religious community itself is the best judge to decide on what constitutes essential practice. Nevertheless, as noted previously, Tripathy's suggestion opens an alternative way to read this decision as split in its general survey as opposed to the decision on validity of the specific provisions. After all, the Court outlawed sanctions on the high priest to take personal gifts, etc., but permitted certain other regulatory mechanisms of the legislation as acceptable.

31 See Ronojoy Sen, 'The Indian Supreme Court and the Quest for a "Rational" Hinduism' 1(1) *South Asian History and Culture* 86 (2010); Gautam Bhatia, *The Transformative Constitutionalism: A Radical Biography in Nine Acts* (Harper Collins, Uttar Pradesh, 2019), Ch 5; Mohsin Alam Bhat, 'Constructing Secularism: Separating "Religion" and "State" under the Indian Constitution' 11 *Australian Journal of Asian Law* 29–55 (2009).

32 Sen, note 31 at 86.

33 Sen, note 6 at 41.

Modifications and Development of the Doctrine

The next important judgment reiterating *Shirur Mutt* and the doctrine was *Ratilal Premchand Gandhi* v. *State of Bombay* (1954).[34] The Bombay Public Trusts Act, 1950, was enacted by the Bombay state legislature 'to regulate . . . the administration of the public and religious trusts in the State of Bombay.'[35] The manager of the Jain public temple and trustees of the Parsi panchayat funds and properties challenged this Act. They challenged some of its provisions as invalid on the grounds of violation of Article 26. The Supreme Court relied upon *Shirur Mutt*, reiterating that religious freedom includes belief as well as 'the performance of outward acts' in pursuance of 'religious belief.' Further, the Court made the observation that no 'outside authority has any right to say that these are not essential parts of religion.'[36] A 'secular judge,' the Court observed, 'is bound to accept that belief it is not for him to sit in judgment on that belief.'[37] On facts, the Court declared that the provisions relating to the appointment of a charity commissioner as the trustee of the religious institutions were unconstitutional.[38] The powers vested under Sections 55 and 56 of the Act, which allowed the Court or the charity commissioner to 'divert the trust property or funds' belonging to a public trust to objects other than those intended by the donors, were declared as interfering with the free exercise of religion. However, certain other provisions requiring the institution to prepare accounts and their audit, the preparation of balance sheets of expenditure and modes of investment of the trust money were upheld as 'secular activities' associated with 'religious practice.' Therefore, we can see that the Court's judgment cemented the proposition laid down in *Shirur Mutt*, that any institutional framework set up by the state governments to regulate the religious institution's administration was in violation of the Constitution. It also put a finger on whether secular judges of the Court could at all judge religious beliefs, or whether they were simply required to accept stated religious beliefs as such. Both these cases sought to clarify the boundary not only between State and religious practice, but also between the judiciary and the very determination of religious practice, through an invocation of the idea of essential features of religion.

34 AIR 1954 SC 388. This appeal was taken up by the Court along with another appeal relating to properties of the Parsi community in *Shappoorjee Bomanjee Billimoria* v. *State of Bombay* (1954). This was a five-judge constitutional bench of the Supreme Court. B.K. Mukherjea, J. wrote the opinion for the Court. Other judges were M.C. Mahajan, CJ., S.R. Das, Vivian Bose, Ghulam Hasan, JJ.

35 *Id.* para 2.

36 *Id.* para 13.

37 *Ibid.*

38 *Shirur Mutt*, note 1, para 17 (per Mukherjea, J.) ('To allow the Charity Commissioner to function as the Shebait of a temple or the superior of a math would certainly amount to interference with the religious affairs').

Religion and Discrimination: Temple Entry Legislations

Sri Venkataramana Devaru v. *State of Mysore* (*Devaru*)[39] was a landmark decision in consolidating the doctrine of essential practices. The origin of the dispute which is central to the case can be traced to pre-independence India, when the political movements for opening of Hindu temples against caste restrictions in the early twentieth century had led to the enactment of various state legislations. One such legislation enacted by the Madras province, permitting the 'excluded classes' to enter Hindu temples, was the Madras Temple Entry Authorisation Act, 1947.[40] The trustees of the Sri Venkataramana temple located in the district of south Kanara, Mysore, who were of the Gaud Saraswat Brahmin caste, challenged the application of this law on them as an encroachment on the ancient temple.

While the case was pending, the Constitution of India came into force. In constitutional terms, a conflict appeared between the mandate of Article 25 (2) (b) to throw open Hindu temple to 'all sections of Hindus,' and the denominational right to 'manage one's own affairs' under Article 26 (b). The petitioners argued that the Venkataramana Devaru temple was denominational and a private temple that was reserved for the exclusive use of the Gaud Saraswat Brahmins, not for the Hindu community in general. Characterising the temple as 'private' was a careful stratagem to bypass the constitutionally mandated State reform in temples of a 'public character' under Article 25 (2) (b).[41] The Supreme Court rejected the 'private' temple argument on facts.[42] The genesis of the temple may have a private character but, the Supreme Court observed, it acquired a public character with the passage of time. The Court thus accepted the possibility of change over a period in custom or character of denominational property. Customary practice can undergo a change, and a private temple may acquire public character. The Court, however, accepted the denominational status of the Gaud Saraswat Brahmins for the purpose of Article 26, and the debate became centred on whether exclusion from entering a temple for worship was 'a matter of religion' according to Hindu law.

39 MANU/SC/0026/1957: AIR 1958 SC 255.

40 Section 3 (1) of the Act permitted the 'excluded classes' entry into 'any Hindu temple and offer worship therein in the same manner and to the same extent as Hindus in general.'

41 See Anupama Rao, *The Caste Question: Dalits and the Politics of Modern India* 90–117 (University of California Press, Berkeley, CA, 2010). She shows in detail how many temple trusts and institutions used this idea of the temple as private property to prevent Dalits from entering them. The colonial government wanted to control temples to tax them and manage them better because they saw them as repositories of wealth that was not properly taxed. Declaring the temples as private property was a way to get temple entry protestors arrested for unlawful entry under the criminal code.

42 Possibly, the Supreme Court saw through the ruse of the petitioners in this form of argumentation to circumvent the constitutional aspiration of throwing open temples to all sections of Hindus; the trustees never denied permission to the non-Gowda Brahmins devotees and they were allowed entry in the temple.

Approving *Shirur Matt*, the Court reiterated that both belief as well as the ritual practices were protected under the free exercise of religion clauses.[43] Despite acknowledging the denominational status to the religious sect, it validated the temple entry legislation as constitutional. The Court observed that the customary practice of untouchability in Hinduism 'denied to large sections of Hindus the right to use public roads and institutions.'[44] Such a practice based on one's birth 'could not be considered reasonable and defended on any sound democratic principle.'[45] The principle of democracy or non-discrimination became fundamental, despite the customary exclusion of Dalit*s* from Hindu temples in the classical Hindu law. In arriving at this conclusion, the Court referred to Article 17 of the Constitution and its prohibition of 'untouchability.'[46]

Two important conclusions can be gleaned from *Devaru*. First, it acknowledged that a religious institution can indeed undergo a change in character, a shift from private to public access for a temple. Second, while accepting the link between customs, usages or rituals and religious belief, the Court observed that caste stigmatisation could not secure constitutional protection. The 'affairs of religion' based on caste discrimination would be amenable to legislative and constitutional scrutiny. The denominational right under Article 26 could not trump the anti-caste discrimination principle. Article 17 became instrumental in rejecting protection to customary but violent Hindu practices. The Court observed:[47]

> The rule of construction is well settled that when there are in an enactment two provisions which cannot be reconciled with each other, they should be so interpreted that, if possible, effect could be given to both. This is what is known as the rule of harmonious construction. Applying this rule, if the contention of the appellants is to be accepted, then Article 25(2)(b) will become wholly nugatory in its application to denominational temples, though, as stated above, the language of that Article includes them . . . We must accordingly hold that Article 26(b) must be read subject to Article 25(2)(b).

The Court in harmonising the two provisions approved certain modifications made by the Madras High Court in favour of the appellant that 'during certain ceremonies and on special occasions, it was only members of Gowda Saraswath Brahmin community that had the right to take part therein, and that

43 *Devaru*, note 39, para 14 (per T.L. Venkatarama Aiyyar, J.) ('not merely its wisdom (*Gnana*) but also its devotion (*Bhakti*) and Rituals and observances (*Karma Kandas*)' are included in essential practices).

44 *Id*. para 23.

45 *Ibid*.

46 The term 'untouchability' within quotes seeks to indicate historical discrimination based on caste.

47 *Devaru*, note 39, para 29.

on those occasions, all other persons would be excluded.'[48] This, in the view of the Court, was a balancing concession to the petitioners 'without affecting the substance of the right declared by Art. 25 (2) (b).'[49] This was a surface solution which ignored the real, underlying issues involved, i.e. caste-based discrimination and practice of untouchability. By resolving the question of historical discrimination and injustice through 'harmonious construction' of conflicting rights, in effect allowing the Brahmin community to practice exclusion on 'special occasions,' the Court reveals the limits of judicial imagination in actualising the promise of Article 17. While in *Devaru* the Supreme Court said that the exclusion of certain classes was not an essential practice, it simultaneously allowed the exclusion by the back door anyway. So even though it *seems* as if it had upheld Article 17, it also diluted the importance of Article 17. The cases discussed so far have shown that no matter which side the judgment favoured, the underlying importance of determining an essential practice grew stronger with each case.

III. The Application of the Doctrine in non-Hindu Religious Disputes

The Supreme Court in *Devaru* approved the proposition of community determination of the 'matters of religion' or what is essential religious practice, citing the case of *Shirur Matt*. This consolidated the notion of complete autonomy for religious denominations to determine the contours of essential practices. It is this theory of autonomy of religious denominations which was put under a 'note of caution' in the next important Supreme Court decision, delivered in 1961.

The case, *Durgah Committee, Ajmer* v. *Syed Hussain Ali & Others* (*Durgah Committee*),[50] was related to Sufi saint Nusrat Khwaja Moin-ud-din Chisti's shrine, located at Ajmer. Khwaja Moinuddin Chishti was born in 1142 AD in an eastern province of Persia. He had arrived in India towards the end of the twelfth century and settled at Ajmer. He attracted various followers and was venerated during his lifetime. After his death, he was buried at Ajmer. During the fifteenth century, the Khilji Sultans of Malwa created a dome over his tomb which became a prominent pilgrimage site for Muslims. A five-judge bench[51] of the Supreme Court considered a dispute which arose with respect to certain provisions of the Durgah Khwaja Saheb Act, 1955, passed by the Central government. The provisions of the enactment allowed the Rajasthan government to appoint a committee which not only could advise the managing devotees (*Khadims*) but also determine their privileges

48 *Id.* para 32. This, the Court observed, 'would clearly be a denominational right.'

49 *Ibid.*

50 AIR 1961 SC 1402 [Hereafter '*Durgah Committee*'].

51 P.B. Gajendragadkar, J. wrote the opinion on behalf of four other judges. Other judges were: A.K. Sarkar, K.N. Wanchoo, K.G. Das Gupta & N.R. Ayyanagar J.J.

and regulate their presence at the tomb of the Sufi saint. Syed Hussain Ali, along with eight other *Khadims* (persons offering service to the shrine) of the tomb, approached the Rajasthan High Court at Jodhpur under Article 226 of the Constitution against the Durgah Committee formed under the statute regulating their powers and privileges.

The Rajasthan High Court declared several provisions of the legislation challenged by the *Khadims* as unconstitutional on the ground that the legislation affected the religious autonomy of the *Khadims*. It relied on *Shirur Mutt* to reiterate that no outside authority, but the community itself can decide on what practices are essential and that the statutory provisions undermining that authority were unconstitutional.

The Durgah Committee appealed against the Rajasthan High Court judgment to the Supreme Court. The Court decided the appeal considering the validity of the statutory provisions. The *Khadims* belonged to the Chisti order of the Sufis. Their claim was that they, as *Khadims*, and previously their ancestors, had managed the *Durgah* and the legislation had divested them of this right. They traced their ancestry back to Nusrat Khwaja Moin-ud-din Chisti and argued that 'the maintenance of the shrine has . . . been the sole concern of the said sect.'[52] The central issue revolved around the management and claims on the 'offerings' made by the devotees at the shrine. The appellants, from the Muslim community as well as the state of Rajasthan, challenged the claim, arguing that *Khadims* had no status or claim on the offerings, as they were merely watchguards of the shrine.[53] In effect, the argument of the appellants was that the sole maintenance of the shrine was not an essential feature of the section of the sect claiming such a right.

Tracing the Mughal and post-Mughal period of the East India Company, the Supreme Court attempted to understand the position of the sect and outlined the historic distinction between the positions of the *Sajjadanashin* (entrusted to perform religious observances) and *Muttavallis* (responsible for the administration and management of the shrine).[54] The Supreme Court observed that administration of the shrine must be distinguished from religious practices and that the administration of the shrine was purely a secular activity unconnected with anything religious. It also noted that during the reign of the Mughal emperor Akbar 'on occasions the post of the Mutawalli was held by a Hindu as well.'[55] This historical background formed the basis for the Court to establish that the sect never had the claim to the offerings or administration of the shrine. To claim it as a denominational right was thus bound to fail. Overruling the conclusions arrived at by Rajasthan High Court,

52 *Durgah Committee*, note 50, para 7.
53 *Id.* para 8.
54 *Id.* para 23.
55 *Ibid.*

the Apex Court upheld the constitutionality of the law enacted for administrative reforms of the shrine.[56]

The methodological key in arriving at the verdict was the essential practices test. It served to distinguish the essentially religious from the administrative tasks. The Supreme Court, speaking through Justice P.B. Gajendragadkar, struck a note of caution in providing complete autonomy to religious denominations to determine what is essential and constitutes matters of religion:[57]

> [I]t may not be out of place incidentally to strike a *note of caution* and observe that in order that the practices in question should be treated as a part of religion they must be regarded by the said religion as its essential and integral part; otherwise even purely secular practices which are not an essential or an integral part of religion are apt to be clothed with a religious form and may make a claim for being treated as religious practices within the meaning of Art. 26. Similarly, even practices though religious may have sprung from merely superstitious beliefs and may in that sense be extraneous and unessential accretions to religion itself. Unless such practices are found to constitute an essential and integral part of a religion their claim for the protection under Art. 26 *may have to be carefully scrutinised*; in other words, the protection must be confined to such religious practices as are an essential and an integral part of it and no other.

The emphasis on the need for judicial scrutiny of religious practices indicated the implicit apprehension of the Court in keeping judiciary entirely separate from the question of determination of essential practices, as observed in *Devaru*. For Justice Gagendragadkar, the doctrine of essential practices also served as a tool to sieve out the 'superstitious beliefs' from the ambit of religious freedom. The doctrine, in this form, followed the trajectory of the modernist reform of the religious institutions by the post-independent Indian State. Tripathy reads this judgment as prescient in its 'spotting the risk' of granting complete autonomy to the communities with respect to essential practices:

> The learned Judge [P.B. Gajendragadkar, J.], therefore, was clear in his opinion that the doctrine of autogenesis of denominational powers laid down by the Court in the *Swamiar* [*Shirur Muth*] and *Devaru* cases needed severely to be restricted if not rejected.[58]

56 *Ibid.* ('Art. 26(c) and (d) do not create rights in any denomination or its section which it never had; they merely safeguard and guarantee the continuance of rights which such denomination or its section had').

57 *Id.* para 33 (emphasis added).

58 Tripathy, note 7 at 117.

It may be noted that this welcome posture of judicial scrutiny is only acceptable if we read the remarks made in *Shirur Mutt* as obiter. Otherwise, a seven-judge bench decision would be binding on the Supreme Court. This further strengthens the suggested reading by Tripathy of *Shirur Mutt*. In Section IV, we will see how Gajendragadkar, J. articulated the role of the Court in determining the essential practices in another Supreme Court judgment. But at present I will elaborate on the 'risk' flagged by Tripathy as it turned into reality within less than a year in the excommunication case of Bohra Muslim community.

Bohra Muslims and Excommunication

An important challenge to the social reform law enacted by the Bombay state legislature, the Bombay Prevention of Excommunication Act, 1949, came up in the case of *Sardar Syedna Taher Saifuddin* v. *State of Bombay* (*Excommunication Case*).[59] Taher Saifuddin, the 51st Dai-ul-Multaq (Dai) of the Dawoodi Bohra Community, approached the Supreme Court under Article 32 challenging the constitutionality of the Bombay Act under Articles 25 and 26.[60]

The Bohra community comprises Muslims from Shia sect of *Imami Ismailis*. The head priest of the community possessed not only the powers to regulate the institutional property but also the power to excommunicate any member of the community. He challenged the Bombay Act, arguing that 'the Dawoodi Bohra community constitutes a religious denomination within the meaning of Article 26 of the Constitution.'[61] He argued that 'he, as the religious leader and Dai-ul-Mutlaq of the community, is entitled to excommunicate any member of the Dawoodi Bohra community for an offence, which according to his religious sense justifies expulsion.'[62]

The Bombay Act put a ban on the excommunication power of the head priest. The preamble denounced the practice as culminating in 'the deprivation of legitimate rights and privileges of its members.'[63] Section 4 of the Act made the practice of excommunication a criminal offence.[64] The issue before the Supreme Court was whether matters of religion which led to deprivation of civic rights could be justiciable and to what extent.

59 AIR 1962 SC 853: 1962 Supp (2) SCR 496. All the paragraphs referred to here are from SCC online edition. (Hereafter '*The Excommunication Case*').

60 A five-judge constitutional bench which decided the case was composed of B.P. Sinha, CJ, A.K. Sarkar, K.C. Das Gupta, N. R. Ayyenger and J.C. Mudholkar, J.J.

61 *The Excommunication Case*, note 59, para 3.

62 *Ibid.*

63 *Id.* paras 10, 27 & 49.

64 The relevant provisions of the Act can be found in paragraph 10 of the judgment. 'The Act has added a new offence to the penal law of the country by penalising any action which has the effect of depriving a person of his human dignity and rights appurtenant thereto.' *Id.* para 11 (per B.P. Sinha, J.).

The petitioner reiterated *Shirur Matt* to argue that customary practices and rituals are protected under Article 26.[65] He defended the excommunication power vested in him to ensure solidarity of the community which involves 'the right to enforce discipline, if necessary by taking the extreme step of communication.' As the head of a religious denomination under Article 26, he argued that such a power is constitutionally protected as a 'matter of religion' within the meaning of Article 26(b) of the Constitution. The State of Bombay (now Mumbai) contended that 'excommunication' as defined by the Act deals with rights of a civil nature 'as distinguished from religious or social rights' and thus does not violate the freedoms in Articles 25 and 26. Finally, the legislation, it was argued by the respondent, was protected by Article 25(2)(b), which permits State intervention for 'social reform.'

The Supreme Court, by majority,[66] declared the Bombay Act as violating the constitutional religious freedom clause. K.C. Das Gupta, J. remarked that the essential practices test extends to the protection of rituals and ceremonies which are integral to religion. And it is the community which will determine what constitutes as essential.[67] The judge went on to discuss more generally 'the place of excommunication in the life of a religious community.'[68] By highlighting that a member of the Bohra community takes an oath of unquestioning faith and loyalty to Dai, the Court held that excommunication served 'the purpose of maintaining the strength of the religion.'[69] Despite the important civil rights which the Act intended to protect, for the majority of the Supreme Court, the Act violated Article 26 (b) by guaranteeing freedom to religious denominations to 'manage their own affairs.'[70] N.R. Ayyangar, J. concurred with the opinion of Das Gupta and approved the disciplinary powers of the Dai as essential and beyond legislative interference. To him the denominational right had to be secured to ensure 'religious continuity' and the 'bond of religious discipline.'[71]

In contrast to these opinions, B.P. Sinha, J. wrote a dissent. Sinha acknowledged that the Bohra community constituted a religious denomination, and the Dai possessed the privilege to excommunicate. However, he tried to understand the Bombay Act considering the historical continuity where the legislature has enacted legislation to combat discrimination or uphold civil rights of the individuals. He observed that 'the Act is a culmination of the history of

65 *Id.* para 8.

66 Das Gupta, J. wrote the majority opinion for himself, A.K. Sarkar and J.C. Mudholkar, JJ. N. R. Ayyenger, J. wrote a separate opinion agreeing with the majority.

67 *The Excommunication Case*, note 59, para 33.

68 *Id.* para 34.

69 *Id.* para 39.

70 Das Gupta, J. preferred to read the religious clause of the constitution literally. 'The right given under Article 26 (b) has not however been made subject to preservation of civil rights.' *Id.* para 40.

71 *Id.* para 52.

social reform which began more than a century ago'[72] and drew comparisons between the impugned Act and the independence legislation which was called the Caste Disability Removal Act, 1850. The dissent concluded:[73]

> The impugned Act, thus, has given full effect to modern notions of individual freedom to choose one's way of life and to do away with all those undue and outmoded interferences with liberty of conscience, faith and belief. It is also aimed at ensuring human dignity and removing all those restrictions which prevent a person from living his own life so long as he did not interfere with similar rights of others.

This dissent acknowledged what Chatterjee has termed as the 'liberal paradox.' The dissent located the legislation in the historical context of social reform in colonial India. Its emphasis on social reform as a historically developed social commitment became an intrinsic part in interpretation of the religious freedom clause.[74] This historical context of social reform allowed the dissent to read the religious clause of the Constitution with emphasis on individual dignity and validating the legislation. The dissent also made an analogy with Article 17, foregrounding the social aspect of the power of excommunication:[75]

> [O]ne is inclined to think that the position of an excommunicated person becomes that of an untouchable in his community, and if that is so, the Act in declaring such practices to be void has only carried out the strict injunction of Article 17 of the Constitution, by which untouchability has been abolished and its practice in any form forbidden.

H.M. Seervai finds the analogical inspiration drawn from Article 17 problematic. In his view, 'this analogy is incorrect' as the notion of untouchability was peculiar to the 'Hindu religion and Hindu society.'[76] However, this criticism fails to appreciate the novel manner in which Sinha contained the scope of Article 26 by upholding the individual rights of the members of the community.[77] The dissent by drawing inspiration from a constitutional provision

72 *Id.* para 11.
73 *Ibid.*
74 *Id.* para 23 ('the Act is intended to do away with all that mischief of treating a human being as a pariah, and of depriving him of his human dignity and of his right to follow the dictates of his own conscience. The Act is, thus, aimed at fulfilment of the individual liberty of conscience guaranteed by Article 25(1) of the Constitution, and not in derogation of it.').
75 *Id.* para 24.
76 H.M. Seervai, ***Constitutional Law of India*** 1278 (Law and Justice Publication, New Delhi, 4th Edn., 2021).
77 Here it may be noted that Seervai in his criticism on the reliance of Article 17 does not make a distinction between using Article 17 as an analogy and against its literal application and extension to other marginal groups. In the last section of this chapter, I will explain and contrast Sinha's analogic reference to Article 17 with the literal extension of Article 17 by D.Y.

(Article 17) was able to read the removal of discrimination based on institutionalised religious practices as a mandate of the Constitution, even in the case of non-Hindu communities. Therefore, it was reading the religious freedom clause with the aid of Article 17 to combat discriminatory religious practices. The dissent had endorsed and relied on *Devaru* as a precedent in rejecting the petitioner's argument that Article 26 was hierarchically superior to Article 25: 'it is impossible to read any such limitation into the language of Art.25(2)(b).' The *Excommunication Case* demonstrated that constitutional interpretation informed by history provides a more useful tool to combat religious discrimination than one based on abstract principles of religious freedom applied in universal terms.

A Major Shift in the Doctrine: The **Nathdwara Temple Case**

In *Tilkayat Shri Govindlalji Maharaj* v. *State of Rajasthan and others* (*Nathdwara Temple Case*),[78] the constitutional validity of the Nathdwara Temple Act, 1959, was challenged before a constitutional bench.[79] The case concerns Srinathji temple, located in the town of Nathdwara in the state of Rajasthan. Constructed by Goswami priests in 1672, the temple is a pilgrimage site for the Vallabha sect of Vaishnava Hindus. In March 1959, the Rajasthan state legislature enacted the 1959 Act, describing the temple as a public temple. The provisions of the Act relegated the *Tilkayat* (the spiritual head of temple and Vallabha sect) as a mere manager of the temple property, divesting him of any substantial beneficial interest in the property of the temple. Shri Govindlalji Maharaj, who was the *Tilkayat*, filed a petition in 1959 in the Rajasthan High Court challenging the validity of the enactment.

The *Tilkayat* contended that the idol in the temple and its properties were his private properties, and the state was incompetent to pass legislation divesting him from those properties. Even if the Nathdwara temple were to be considered a public temple and he was treated as the *Mahant* (or *Shebait*), he had an interest in the office of the high priest as well as the properties of the temple.[80] As a representative of the Vallabha religious sect, he urged that the Act contravened not only his fundamental rights as an individual devotee but also of the denomination as guaranteed under Articles 26 (b) and (c)

Chandrachud J. in *Sabarimala Judgment*. Also see Amit Bindal, 'Sabarimala and the Flattening of Religious Community' 721 *Seminar* 76 (2019).

78 (1964) 1 SCR 561 (Hereafter, '*Nathdwara Temple*').

79 Bhuvaneshwar Prasad Sinha, CJ, P.B. Gajendragadkar, K.N. Wanchoo, K.C. Das Gupta and J.C. Shah JJ. The judgment was authored by P.B. Gajendragadkar J.

80 He made this latter argument relying on the constitutional provision guaranteeing the fundamental right to property (Article 19 (1) (f), now repealed). He also argued that the idols in the temple were 'private idols' and therefore there could be no public interest in the property pertaining to them. The law with respect to the legal personality of the Hindu idol and *Shebait* is elaborately discussed in Chapter 4.

of the Constitution. On the contrary, the state of Rajasthan emphasised the public character of the Nathdwara temple. It argued that *Tilkayat* 'was no more and no better than its manager' and thus had no substantial beneficial interest in the property of the temple.[81] Based on the documentary evidence, the High Court concluded that the temple was a public temple. It looked at the *firmans* [injunctions] and *sanads* [grants] (placed before the Court by the *Tilkayat*) and observed that 'the said grants supported the plea of the state that the temple was not the private temple of the *Tilkayat*.'[82] But the High Court declared the *Tilkayat* the 'spiritual head of the denomination as well as the spiritual head of the temple.' He could perform *seva* (service) at the temple, and the two minor idols of Navnit Priyaji and Madan Mohanlalji were his private idols.[83] The *Tilkayat's* rights of residence, to distribute *prasad*, to conduct or supervise the worship and the performance of *seva* [service] in the temple were recognised.[84] As to the contention of the denomination, the state argued that the law is valid as it 'did no more than regulate the administration of the property of the temple as contemplated by Art.26 (c) of the Constitution.' The High Court accepted the state's plea on this ground. The High Court thus did not hold the Act unconstitutional but struck down certain sections of the Act. This decision led to appeals and cross appeals by the state as well as the petitioners and thus the case came before the Supreme Court.

Justice Gajendragadkar (speaking for the Supreme Court) laid out the historical background of the dispute. The juridical narrative drew upon religious and cultural works viz, Haridas Bhattacharyya's *The Cultural Heritage of India* (1937), R.G. Bhandarkar's *Vaishnavism, Saivism and Minor Religious Systems* (1913) and Bhai Manilal C. Parekh's *Sri Vallabhacharya: Life, Teachings and Movement: A Religion of Grace* (1943), to construct the history of the temple and its followers. The founder of the Pushtimargiya Vaishnava Sampradaya was Vallabha who, according to legend, had acted upon a divine vision and built a small temple around 1500 AD. Vallabha was succeeded by his son, Vithalnath, who in turn was succeeded by his seven

81 *Nathdwara Temple*, note 78, para 4.

82 *Ibid.* (Relying on the *firman* issued by the Maharana of Udaipur on Dec. 31, 1934, the Court observed that 'this Firman clearly established the fact that the temple was a public temple, that the Tilkayat was no more than a Custodian, Manager and Trustee of the property belonging to the temple and that the State had the absolute right to supervise that the property dedicated to the shrine was used for legitimate purposes of the shrine.').

83 The Court thus struck down that part of the definition of temple which included the two idols within the temple of Shrinathji.

84 The High Court affirmed his beneficial interest in the properties of the temple were protected under Article 19 (1) (f). The High Court held that since the majority of the Act did not contravene fundamental rights of the *Tilkayat* under Article 19(1)(f), the Act in itself was not unconstitutional. Sections 16, 28(3), 28(3), 30(2)(a), 36 and 37, however, did contravene *Tilkayat's* fundamental rights, and so the said sections and a part of the definition of 'temple' in Section 2 (viii) were struck down by the High Court as ultra vires.

sons. The principal idol of Srinathji was entrusted to the eldest son, and other 'Swaroops' were given to the other sons who founded separate shrines at different places. The judgment recorded that the tradition of religious denominations was supported by the Mughal emperor Akbar, who issued a *firman* [injunction] in 1593 AD granting land to Vithalnathji for construction of buildings, gardens, cowsheds for the temple, and later by Shah-Jahan, who issued another *firman* in 1633 AD and granted land. The tradition continued in the reign of Emperor Aurangzeb.[85]

The rule of primogeniture had governed the succession to 'the Gaddi of the Tilkayat.' The estate faced financial difficulties during the management of *Tilkayat* Govindlalji. This led to the establishment, by the *Tilkayat* himself, of the various committees comprising 12 members in 1952 and 21 members in 1953. Whilst the 1953 committee had overseen the financial affairs of the shrine, the *Tilkayat* Govindlalji had removed some valuables from the temple, leading to excitement amongst his followers and the public. In 1957, therefore, the Rajasthan government appointed an enquiry committee. The dispute relating to the removal of valuables between the *Tilkayat* and the state government had been referred to arbitration, with the arbitrator, retired Chief Justice Mehr Chand Mahajan finding that with some exceptions, the property was the *Tilkayat's*, who had removed the items thinking them to be his personal property. It was against this background, therefore, that the state government promulgated the Nathdwara Ordinance, 1959, which was replaced by the Nathdwara Temple Act, 1959.

The first issue before the Supreme Court was whether the notion of 'public' temples was inconsistent with the tenets of the *Vallabha* denomination. The Court concluded that even though some of the temples of the sect may be private, there is nothing in the tenets or religious practices of the sect which necessarily postulate that the followers must worship in a private temple. The Court rejected *Tilkayat's* contention that the provisions of the Act contravened his property rights under Articles 19 (1) (f) and 31(2) of the Constitution. The Court noted that under Hindu law, the idol of *Srinathji* is a juridical person and therefore the temple, as well as the endowments made before the idol, were the property of the idol. While the properties of the temple would vest in the idol, the Board constituted under the Act would administer the said property as its trustee. The Court sought to maintain the sanctity of the institution of *Tilkyat*: 'the Board will act reasonably and fairly by (sic.) the Tilkayat and nothing will be done to impair his status or to affect his authority . . . concerned with the religious part of the worship in the temple.'[86]

Another contention of the appellants (Tilkayat and other petitioners) as members of the Vallabha sect was that the Act violated the autonomy granted under Article 26 (b) to every religious denomination to manage its own affairs and to administer properties in accordance with the law under Article 26 (d).

85 *Nathdwara Temple*, note 78, para 8.
86 *Id.* para 72.

In responding to this argument of denominational autonomy, Justice Gajendrajadkar, speaking for the Court in a major methodological shift, discussed the limitations of existing precedents allowing complete autonomy to the religious community to determine the meaning of 'essential.'[87] He observed:[88]

> In deciding the question as to whether a given religious practice is an integral part of the religion or not, the test always would be whether it is regarded as such by the community following the religion or not. *This formula may in some cases present difficulties in its operation.* Take the case of a practice in relation to food or dress. If in a given proceeding, one section of the community claims that while performing certain rites white dress is an integral part of the religion itself, whereas another section contends that yellow dress and not the white dress is the essential part of the religion, how is the Court going to decide the question? Similar disputes may arise in regard to food. In cases where conflicting evidence is produced in respect of rival contentions as to competing religious practices *the Court may not be able to resolve the dispute by a blind application of the formula that the community decides* which practice is an integral part of its religion, because *the community may speak with more than one voice and the formula would, therefore, break down.* This question will always have to be decided by the Court and in doing so, the Court may have to enquire whether the practice in question is religious in character and if it is, whether it can be regarded as an integral or essential part of the religion, and the finding of the Court on such an issue will always depend upon the evidence adduced before it as to the conscience of the community and the tenets of its religion.

One may recall the 'note of caution' given by the same judge in *Durgah Committee*, which took the form of an elaborate assertion here against the previous precedents for taking a monolithic view of the religious community. The Supreme Court recognised the ambivalence of the voice of the community and the difficulties of designating the religious community as a monolithic or neatly discernible entity. A religious tenet is entrenched with a multiplicity of voices, not reducible to a singular monolithic narrative. The possibility of alternative readings of the religious tradition or text can never be ruled out. The Court's notion of a 'break down' was with respect to the idea of transparent access to the community. Scholars who argue for community determination wish away this complexity in determination of the community itself, but we see the Court's recognition of this complexity in this decision.[89] The Court

87 The Court referred to the previous cases of *Shirur Mutt, Devaru* and *Durgah Committee* on the meaning of religion in Articles 25(1) and 26(b), respectively. *Id.* paras 55 and 56.

88 *Id.* para 57 (emphasis supplied).

89 Sen, note 6 at 41. Sen remarks that the 'most striking aspect of the essential practices doctrine is the attempt by the Court to fashion religion in the way a modernist state would like it to be, rather

was following the spirit of the Constitution in not allowing the community to have the last word on its own terms.

After inaugurating this conceptual shift in understanding of the doctrine, the Court went on to observe that free exercise of religion clauses accorded protection to only *religious practices* (Article 25 (1)) or the management of affairs *in matters of religion* (Article 26 (b)). A legislation engaging with purely secular practice is constitutionally permissible. The Court rejected the denomination's argument that management of the properties by the *Tilkayat* amounted to a religious practice under Article 25(1) or denomination's right to manage one's own religious affairs under Article 26(b). It concluded that it was not established that the tenets of the Vallabha denomination required that properties must be managed solely by the *Tilkayat*. In fact,

> [t]he course of conduct of the denomination and the *Tilkayat* based on that belief may have spread for many years, but . . . such course of conduct cannot be regarded as giving rise to a religious practice under Article 25(1).[90]

In other words, even if a religious denomination believed that management of properties was a religious affair, the Court did not find any merit in the argument. For the Court, the management of the property was a purely secular practice/affair and thus could not seek protection under the Constitution.

Finally, the Court took up the argument related to Article 26(d) – that the right to administer its property *in accordance with law* – has been taken away by the Act. It was argued by the appellants that the word 'law' under Article 26 (d) implies the 'law prescribed by the religious tenets' of the religious community and not a legislative enactment of a competent legislature. The Court found this argument 'wholly untenable' and ruled out the possibility of reading law as 'religious law.' It was held that 'law means a law passed by a competent legislature.'[91] The Court noted that

> [i]f the clause "affairs in matters of religion" (Article 26(b)) were to include affairs in regard to all matters, whether religious or not the provision under Article 26 (d) for legislative regulation of the administration of the denomination's property would be rendered illusory.[92]

With this decision, therefore, a major turn occurred in the determination of essential religious practices. The Supreme Court cast doubt on the

---

than accept religion as represented by its practitioners.' Sen's advocacy for the community to have a final voice inadequately responds to the concern raised by the Supreme Court that no unilateral determination of religious practice is possible because there is no monolithic community.

90 *Nathdwara Temple*, note 78, para 60.

91 *Id.* para 61.

92 *Id.* para 62.

previous precedents, which provided latitude to the religious community to have the final say in determination of what constitutes 'essential' to a particular religion. As already noted, Justice Gajendragadkar's 'note of caution' in *Durgah Committee* became an emphatic assertion in *Nathdwara Temple Case*. This variance in judicial understanding was seen by some as making 'the already narrow guarantees of freedom of religion in India [as] precarious.'[93] However, others saw this as a welcome move necessary to save the spirit of the free exercise of religion clauses from 'the dangerous theory of autogenesis of denominational authority culminating in the complete annihilation of the individual's rights enshrined in Article 25.'[94] In my view, the sacrifice of civil rights in the majority opinion of the *Excommunication Case* and the elevation of institutional authority above individual dissent within the community paved the way for this important shift in the approach of the Supreme Court. Before we discuss this point in detail, in the next section, we shall see how other kinds of practices in the public sphere associated with other sects and groups also challenged the contours of the doctrine.

IV. The Divine Dance: Peculiar Challenge to the Doctrine

One contentious practice which was challenged before the Court was that of the divine inspired dancing with skulls and tridents on the roads of Calcutta (now Kolkata) in West Bengal. The question of whether it was a part of an essential religious practice arose in two unique cases with respect to the denominational sect of the Anand Marga (literally 'a blissful path'). The issue in both these cases was unrelated to any institutional property, as we have seen in the cases thus far, but the question of belief was nevertheless at their core. The first case, *Acharya Jagdishwaranand* v. *Commissioner of Police* (*First Ananda Margi Case*),[95] arose when the Commissioner of Police issued prohibitory orders restraining the performance of divine *tandav* dance by the participants of the Ananda Marga sect on apprehension of disruption of public order because of the use of tridents and skulls by the participants. The application made to the Police Commissioner seeking permission for the dance was rejected. Previously, the Police Commissioner's repetitive orders since August 1979 had directed that

> no member of a procession or assembly of five or more persons should carry any fire arms, explosives, swords, spears, knives, tridents, lathis or any article which may be used as weapon of offence or any article likely to cause annoyance to the public, for example skulls.[96]

93 J. Duncan Derrett, 'Freedom of Religion under the Indian Constitution: Excommunication (Based on Sardar S. T. Saifuddin Saheb v. State of Bombay)' 12(2) *The International and Comparative Law Quarterly* 697 (1963).

94 Tripathy, note 24 at 18.

95 (1983) 4 SCC 522. (Hereafter '*First Ananda Margi Case*.')

96 *Id.* para 6.

Acharya Jagdishwaranand (the petitioner), the general secretary of public relations of the Ananda Marga Pracharak Sangh, filed the petition under Article 226 of the Constitution in the High Court of Calcutta against that order. The Calcutta High Court refused to entertain the petition seeking issuance of the writ prohibiting the Police Commissioner from restraining the dance performance on public roads.[97] In the Supreme Court, the petitioner raised the constitutional question against the prohibition by the instrumentality of the State (police), arguing that the chaotic dance for Ananda Marga constituted an essential practice of their religion. The Supreme Court, in its judgment, discussed the history of the religious sect.

Ananda Marga was a 'socio-spiritual organisation' founded in 1955 by Pravat Ranjan Sarkar, otherwise known as Shri Ananda Murti. The organisation was initially located in Ranchi (then in the state of Bihar, now the capital of Jharkhand), and later shifted to Calcutta. In 1966, the organisation for the first time introduced to its participants the practice of *Anand Tandav Dance*, one of the dances performed by Lord Shiva. It was one of the prescriptions that the dance should be performed every day 'with a skull, a small symbolic knife and a Trishul [trident].'[98] All these devices and instruments were held to have esoteric and symbolic significance. The contention of the sect was that such divine dance 'is an essential part of the religious rites of the Ananda Margis' and therefore such a dance can be performed both in private as well as any public place. The respondent, the Commissioner of Police of Calcutta, emphasised the violent nature of the religious organisation to challenge this contention. He argued that militancy continues to be the main feature of the organisation. The processions were taken out on the roads of Calcutta despite the order and they turned violent, leading to police intervention.

Following the argument of the High Court, this issue could have become that of conflict between 'public order' and 'morality' and the performance right of the religious denomination. Understood this way, there would be hardly any constitutional complexity. This is because both Articles 25 and 26 are subject to 'public order, health and morality.' The constitutional text categorically limits the religious freedom clause on the grounds of public order and morality. As already noted in the *Badrinath Temple* case, the Supreme Court gave way to a long-standing customary practice in order to avoid overcrowding (an issue of public order) inside the temple. However, the Court formulated the issue in terms of the essential practices test. It asked whether the Ananda Margis' procession is protected under Articles 25 and 26 and if the dance constituted an essential practice of the sect. This was because the petitioners framed the issue in the terms of proclaiming chaotic dance as an essential practice. Why the Supreme Court did not foreground the question of

97 *Ibid.*
98 *Id.* para 3.

'public order' is difficult to comprehend. Part of the answer lies in the adversarial form of the legal process where the failure of the opposing party to raise an issue in the plaint can result in an abandonment of the issue altogether.

In the judgment, Anand Marg was found to be well within the tenets of the Hindu religion and did not constitute a separate religion. But the Court agreed that it certainly possessed the traits of a religious denomination within the meaning of Article 26.[99] The next question then was regarding the centrality of the divine *Tandav* dance to the denomination. The Supreme Court decided this question by following the public-private distinction. Describing the modes and forms of dances in the tradition, it arrived at the conclusion that public performance of the dance was certainly not an essential practice of the denomination.[100]

> [T]here is no justification in any of the writings of Shri Ananda Murti that tandava dance must be performed in public. At least none could be shown to us by Mr. Tarkunde [counsel for the petitioners] despite an enquiry by us in that behalf.

An interesting turn of events triggered a second round of litigation by the Ananda Margis. Founder Anand Murti revised one of the books, titled *Carya-carya*, containing the doctrines of the denomination and included the performance of the *tandav* dance in public as an essential practice in the revised edition. Based on this revised version, the devotees pleaded for permission for the public dance from the police, which was denied. The Margis challenged this denial in the Calcutta High Court. The High Court accepted that after the revised version of the book, the chaotic dance had become an essential part of the sect. It observed that the Supreme Court in *First Ananda Margi* case had failed to appreciate this fact 'due to the non-availability of any literature or prescriptions by the founder.'[101] The High Court proceeded on the argument that it is the subjective determination of the community that discerns what is essential or integral to any religion. The Commissioner of Police of Calcutta, along with the state government, challenged this judgment in the Supreme Court. The Supreme Court, by a majority of 2:1, speaking though Justice Rajendra Babu in *Commissioner of Police & Others v. Acharya Jagdishwaranand* (*Second Ananda Margi Case*),[102] overturned the judgment of the Calcutta High Court and restored the position of the *First Ananda Margi* case.

99 Anand Marg was accepted as a religious denomination within the Hindu religion. The Court also elaborated upon the meaning of the word 'denomination' under Article 26 as requiring three considerations of 'common faith,' 'common organisation' and 'distinctive name.' All the considerations were fulfilled by the organisation of Anand Marg.

100 *First Ananda Margi Case*, note 95, paras 14–15.

101 *Commissioner of Police & Others v. Acharya Jagdishwaranand* (2004) 12 SCC 770 [Hereafter, '*Second Ananda Margi Case*'].

102 The other judge in the majority was G.P. Mathur J., while A.R. Laxmanan, J. wrote a dissenting opinion.

The issue that required thoughtful engagement was whether a practice that was declared as non-essential by the Court can be reintroduced by way of a textual amendment altering the religious doctrine. On this issue, the majority judges recognised the danger of alterations in the religious precepts after an unfavorable verdict against them. The majority opinion observed that 'it will create problematic situations if the religion is allowed to circumvent the decision of Court by making alteration in its doctrine.'[103] Anticipating this subversion of the judicial decisions, the Court declared that such an attempt

> could only be treated as a circuitous way to overcome the finding of a Court. If subsequent alterations in doctrine could be allowed to create new essentials, the judicial process will then be reduced into a useless formality and futile exercise.[104]

Although this issue merely found one short paragraph in the judgment, one can appreciate the potential danger which the Court anticipated in these remarks. Can the essence of a religion or religious sect be inserted by way of an amendment in the new edition? While religious practices and traditions undergo a change over time and no precise time can be fixed to comprehend such transformation, such editorial insertion directly after judicial verdict would truly have made a mockery of the essential practices test.

However, the central premise of the reasoning adopted by the majority in its discussion of the essential practices test took a different and unconvincing turn. It seemed to operate on an assumption that essential practices are constitutive of a fixed and unalterable character and it is 'such permanent essential parts which are protected by the Constitution.'[105] For the Supreme Court, this was the primary reason on which the Calcutta High Court verdict must be overruled.[106] The Supreme Court explained its conception of essential practice as one which was unalterable and permanent for all time.[107]

> Essential part of a religion means the core beliefs upon which a religion is founded. Essential practice means those practices that are fundamental to follow a religious belief. It is upon the cornerstone of essential parts or practices the superstructure of religion is built. Without which, a religion will be no religion . . . . If the taking away of that part or practice could result in a fundamental change in the character of that religion or in its belief, then such part could be treated as an essential or integral part.

103 *Second Ananda Margi Case*, note 101, para 11.
104 *Ibid.*
105 *Id.* para 9.
106 *Id.* para 8. According to the Supreme Court, the Calcutta High Court was 'under the wrong impression that an essential part of religion could be altered at any subsequent point of time.'
107 *Id.* para 9.

> There cannot be additions or subtractions to such part. Because it is the very essence of that religion and alterations will change its fundamental character.

Such a conception of an essential part of religion is at odds with the notion first developed and followed in *Shirur Matt* where 'forms and observances might extend even to matters of food and dress' which do not form the cardinal core of any religion, but are also necessarily subject to change and adaptation over time. The *Shirur Matt* decision did not assert that core beliefs of a religion always remained fixed and static. It seems that in describing the essential practices test as one which determines whether taking away a part or practice would result in a fundamental change in the religion, the Supreme Court was innovating a test which had little to do with the previous judicial precedents on essential practices test. This formed the basis of the conclusion that the *tandav* dance is not an essential part of the *Ananda Margi* sect: 'Had Tandava dance been the core of Ananda Margi faith, then without it Ananda Margi faith could not have existed.'[108] This logic of the Supreme Court defining 'essential' as the basic foundation on which the superstructure of religion rests obscures and complicates any coherent understanding of the essential practices test. It seems that the Court in its preoccupation with the result discounted on the process and method used in arriving at the eventual decision. As already mentioned, the judgment failed to discuss the issue of the disturbance of 'public order,' which was the basis of the restrictive orders passed by the police authorities. 'Public order' is a constitutional limitation on the exercise of freedom of religion. There is no discussion in the majority opinion that can explain how the processions carried out by Ananda Margis were posing a potential threat to public order.[109] Thus, the judgment, despite deciding an important aspect of alteration of essence of religious by textual amendment, remains inadequate in providing a convincing rationale for evoking public order exception and in its application and interpretation of the essential practices test.

Even as the *Second Ananda Margi* case sought to delimit the content as well as scope of what can be described as 'essential' to religion, the controversy about 'religious' versus 'secular' remains far from settled. This issue re-surfaces every time individual and denominational rights come into conflict. In the next section, we turn to the *Sabarimala Judgment*, where the contours of the essential practices test were tested once again in the context of sex- and gender-based exclusion from temple premises.

108 *Id.* para 10.

109 This gap in the majority opinion provided the basis for the dissent to turn the issue into one of tolerance. It pointed out that 'the Sikh community carry "kirpans" as a symbol of their religious practice and the Gurkhas the "kukris" or "dagger" . . . Persons professing Islamic Faith are allowed to take out procession during "Moharrum" Festival and persons participating in such processions beat their chest with hands and chains and inflict injuries on them and the same has been permitted as a religious practice of that community.' *Id.* para 81.

V. *Sabarimala Judgment* and the Religious Freedom Clause

The Sabarimala temple of Lord Ayyappa in Kerala excluded women in the age group of 10 to 50 from entry into the temple. This practice of exclusion emerged from an antiquated custom based on the belief that Lord Ayyappa was an ardent practitioner of celibacy (*Naishthic Brahamachari*) and therefore shunned the presence of women. The custom was legalised under Rule 3 (b) of public worship rules made under Section 3 of the Kerala Hindu Places of Public Worship (Authorisation of Entry) Act, 1965.[110] It specifically prohibited women between 10 and 50 years old from visiting Lord Ayyappa.[111]

On September 24, 1990, a petition came before the Kerala High Court on the basis of a complaint sent by K. Mahendran to a High Court judge, Justice Paripoornan. He complained that Smt. Chandrika, who held the post of commissioner of the Devasworm Board, participated in the rice feeding ceremony of her granddaughter despite the prohibition on women to enter the temple. This complaint was considered as a public interest litigation, and the Kerala High Court turned it into a writ petition filed under Article 226 of the Constitution. Notice was issued to Travancore Devasworm Board, a statutory body constituted under Travancore Cochin Hindu Religious Institutions Act, 1950, which was responsible for administration and making of rules with respect to the Sabarimala temple. The Indian Federation of Women Lawyers, Kerala Branch, filed an application to be impleaded in the case as the issue concerned the larger interest of the public and women.[112] This became the genesis of the Kerala High Court taking up the issue of restriction on entry of women as constituting gender discrimination in *K. Mahendran* v. *The Secretary, Travancore Devasworm Board* (1993).[113]

The respondent, along with one of the interveners (M.P. Gopalakrishnan), argued that 'Ayyappa devotees form a denomination by themselves, and have every right to regulate and manage its own affairs in matters of religion.'[114] The High Court accepted the denominational status of the Ayyappa devotees, stating that a 'religious denomination or organisation enjoys complete autonomy in the matter of deciding as to what rites and ceremonies are essential according to the tenets of the religion.'[115] The High Court eventually

110 Rule 3 (b) of the Kerala Hindu Places of Public Worship (Authorisation of Entry) Rules, 1965. The issues were whether Rule 3(b) violated Articles 25(1) and 15(1), and whether the rules framed under the Act were *ultra vires* the parent Act.

111 Ironically, the exclusionary rule was designed within a law meant for 'authorisation of entry' in places of public worship. Perhaps that is why the petitioners also challenged the rules as *ultra vires* the parent legislation.

112 Sri M. P. Gopalakrishnan, President of the Kerala *Kshetra Samrakshana Samithi*, also impleaded himself in the case.

113 AIR 1993 Ker 42.

114 *Id.* para 14.

115 *Id.* para 22.

upheld the prohibition as a matter of religion on account of the celibacy of Lord Ayyappa. The constitutional rationale provided by the High Court was the following:[116]

> The freedom of conscience and freedom to speak, profess and propagate religion guaranteed under Article 25 of the Constitution is subject not only to public order, morality and health, but also subject to the other provisions of Chapter III. It necessarily implies that the right to freedom of religion guaranteed under Article 25 is subject to the freedom to manage religious affairs guaranteed under Article 26(b) of the Constitution.

Although in *Devaru* the Supreme Court had clarified that Article 26 cannot be read independent of the requirements of Article 25 (2), the Kerala High Court arrived at a contrary conclusion without making any reference to *Devaru*.

In 2018, another public interest petition was filed in the Supreme Court by an association registered under the name of the Indian Young Lawyers Association. A few gender rights activists based in the state of Punjab impleaded themselves in this petition. This revived the issue and the Supreme Court took up the matter, making the state of Kerala and Devasworm Board respondents.[117] In *Indian Young Lawyers Association* v. *State of Kerala* (2018),[118] the petitioners challenged the exclusionary practice as having its origins 'upon a biological factor which [was] exclusive to women only, and which [was] based upon custom allegedly constituting an essential part of religion, can be said to be violative of their rights under Article 25.'[119] The respondents, on the other hand, pleaded the argument of complete autonomy of religious denomination of Ayyappa devotees and their right to determine what was essential for them under Article 26 (b). The respondents asserted that the practice of celibacy of Lord Ayyappa was an integral part of the sect, and the rule of exclusion was not against the tenets of the religious faith.

The Supreme Court judgment, by a majority of 4:1, invalidated rule 3 (b) of public worship rules framed by the Devasworm Board and declared it unconstitutional. It permitted the entry of women into the Sabarimala temple on the grounds that the rule violated the fundamental right of equality. All the judges who wrote the majority opinion (three separate opinions) rejected the plea that exclusion of women on the grounds exclusively of biology is an essential part of the Ayyappa sect. Chief Justice Dipak Misra (wrote the opinion for

116 *Ibid.*

117 The Court permitted various other organisations and individuals to implead as the question was of public importance.

118 (2018) SCC SC 1690 ['*Sabarimala Judgment*'].

119 *Id.* para 1 (per R.F. Nariman, J., speaking for the majority).

himself and Justice A.M. Khanvilakar) and Justice D.Y. Chandrachud evoked the notion of constitutional morality to declare the rules as unconstitutional. As both Articles 25 & 26 are subject to 'morality,' these judges interpreted this term as equivalent to constitutional morality. Justice R.F. Nariman wrote a separate opinion declaring the rules unconstitutional without taking recourse to the discourse of constitutional morality. The majority opinion found the exclusion an instance of biological determinism reinforcing the stereotypical taboo against menstruation. All three opinions of the majority judges held that such exclusion was not integral to the Ayyappa sect. Justice Chandrachud relied on the essential practices test but also raised doubts on its usefulness and implored for a reconsideration of the test in a future Supreme Court judgment. Justice Indu Malhotra wrote her dissent upholding the ban on entry of women, accepting it as an essential practice of the sect. She also raised concerns on the locus of the 'Young Lawyers Association' which was a north Indian organisation, unconnected with the devotion of Lord Ayyappa, to challenge the rule of women's exclusion: 'Courts normally do not delve into issues of religious practises, especially in the absence of an aggrieved person from that particular religious faith, or sect.'[120]

Constitutional Morality and Its Ephemeral Content

Chief Justice Dipak Misra (speaking for himself and Justice A.M Khanvilakar) and Justice Chandrachud in their separate opinions observed that the word 'morality' in Article 25 and 26 should be understood as synonymous to constitutional morality.[121] The content of the term *morality* in both the Articles must be understood in line with constitutional aspirations. Here, the liberal philosophical tenor underlying the notion of autonomous choice-making individual is at the heart of the idea of constitutional morality.[122]

The majority opinion (except for Justice Nariman) saw constitutional morality as a secular alternative to engage with religious mythology. However, despite its novel intentions, the Court's conception of constitutional morality may lead to problematic interpretations. For instance, the notion of 'unity and integrity of the nation' mentioned in the Preamble of the Constitution can,

120 *Id.* para 7.3 (per Indu Malhotra J.).

121 *Id.* para 11 (per D.Y. Chandrachud, J.) ('Individual dignity cannot be allowed to be subordinate to the morality of the mob').

122 For a general discussion on how the idea of 'constitutional morality' in Indian judicial discourse has been reduced to enforcement of fundamental rights, see Mahendra Pal Singh, 'Observing Constitutional Morality' 721 *Seminar* 14–21 (2019). Singh points out how the 'dissenting judge, Justice Indu Malhotra, also did not disagree on the interpretation of morality in terms of constitutional morality, but in her view the Constitution must be seen in the light of multiple religious groups in our country who all have to be protected in respect of their rights. In that case the religious rights of the devotees of Lord Ayyappa are to be counted for determining the content of constitutional morality.' *Id.* at 19.

in a similar manner, become a form of constitutional morality for curtailing dissent as 'morality' is also an enlisted ground of reasonable restriction under Article 19 (2).

On this register, the opinion of Nariman is discursively grounded as he arrived at his conclusion based on contradictions within the plaint to show that the practice of exclusion was based on an age-old cultural stereotype that menstruating women are 'polluted' and need to be excluded from 'sacred' spaces. Nariman used the affidavit filed by the respondent's side to demonstrate the link between the customary practice and menstruation taboo. The affidavit read:

> The problem with women is that they cannot complete the 41 days [of] vrutham [fasting] because the . . . periods will surely fall within the 41 days. It is not a mere physiological phenomenon. It is the custom among all Hindus that women during periods do not go to Temples or participate in religious activity.[123]

Nariman compared the notion of impurity of menstruation in other religious texts to conclude that the practice was an outcome of the idea of contamination based on biological essentialism. Instead of using constitutional morality, Nariman remained historically informed in asserting that Article 25 heralds a departure from these customary rules found in various religious scriptures. Further, all customs and usages are subject to fundamental rights guaranteed in the Constitution:[124]

> The fundamental right claimed by the Thanthris [Head priest] and worshippers of the institution, based on custom and usage under the selfsame Article 25(1), must necessarily yield to the fundamental right of such women, as they are equally entitled to the right to practice religion, which would be meaningless unless they were allowed to enter the temple at Sabarimala to worship the idol of Lord Ayyappa.

Janaki Nair argues that the 'absolute prohibition of women of menstruating age from worship at Sabarimala under rules 3(b)' was an *invention of tradition* as such a strict prohibition had never existed in practice in the last five decades.[125] No pure tradition of Sabarimala temple was discernible, as burgeoning *pilgrim tourism* had already threatened the local ecology and radically transformed the forms of worship that existed in ancient times.[126] We have already seen that the Supreme Court had accepted the possibility of change

123 *Sabarimala Judgment*, note 118, para 21 (per R.F. Nariman, J.).
124 *Id.* para 29.
125 Janaki Nair, 'A Pilgrim's Progress' *The Hindu* (Oct. 22, 2018).
126 *Ibid.*

of customary practice in *Devaru*. An analysis of re-formed tradition at the Sabarimala temple could have provided a way to revisit this understanding of tradition. Instead of the rhetoric of constitutional morality, I suggest, the Court could have arrived at the same verdict in a more robust manner. That might have enhanced the possibility of democratic discussion.

Expansive Meaning of "Untouchability"

D.Y. Chandrachud, J. was the only judge on the bench who accepted the argument for an expansionist reading of Article 17 of the Constitution to extend to the exclusion of women from temples. The existence of the term "untouchability" within inverted commas under Article 17 had been understood and interpreted as limited to the specific caste exclusion envisaged by the Constitution.[127] Chandrachud emphasised the phrase 'in any form' under Article 17 to encompass the exclusion of women in Sabarimala.[128] The 'use of punctuation mark cannot be construed as intent to circumscribe the constitutional width of the expression.'[129] The dissenting judge, Justice Indu Malhotra, rejected the application of Article 17 to women on the traditional lines, limiting the application of the provision to the discrimination based on caste.[130] She also relied on the Constituent Assembly debates and academic opinions in constitutional law scholarship to arrive at her conclusion.[131] Without elaborating on the conceptual problems of extending the meaning of untouchability to all women across caste and class as a whole, the dissent rejected this interpretation of Article 17 merely, and unconvincingly, on the grounds that such an interpretation did not exist in constitutional memory: 'Not a single precedent has been shown to interpret Article 17 in the manner contended by the Petitioners.'[132]

127 Article 17 reads: Abolition of "Untouchability": "Untouchability" is abolished and its practice in any form is forbidden. The enforcement of any disability arising out of Untouchability shall be an offence punishable in accordance with law.

128 *Sabarimala Judgment*, note 118, para 72 (per D.Y. Chandrachud, J.). ('The addition of the words "*in any form*" in the initial draft prepared by the Sub-Committee on Fundamental Rights is unambiguous statement to the effect that the draftspersons wanted to give the term "untouchability" a broad scope.').

129 *Id.* para 79.

130 *Id.* para 14.2 (per Indu Malhotra, J.). ('Article 17 pertains to untouchability based on caste prejudice. Literally or historically, untouchability was never understood to apply to women as a class.').

131 Reference was made to H.M. Seervai's *Constitutional Law of India: A Critical Commentary* (Universal Law Publishers, 1999) and M.P. Jain, *Indian Constitutional Law* (Lexis Nexis, New Delhi, 2010) who also take a similar viewpoint.

132 *Sabarimala Judgment*, note 118, para 14.7 (per Indu Malhotra, J.). Another strand in the reasoning of the dissenting judge, Indu Malhotra, J., focussed on the identity and geographical location of the petitioners. She argued that the petitioners do not have any claim as they are interveners and 'gender rights activists working in and around the state of Punjab . . . they learnt of the practice of restricting the entry of women . . . from three newspaper articles' (para 1). There are problems with this reasoning. First, it presupposes that only those

The opinion of Chandrachud, J., seems to be path-breaking. Gautam Bhatia in his enthusiastic evaluation of the opinion has described it as a judgment ahead of its time.[133] What was unique in the opinion of Chandrachud, J. was a literal extension of Article 17 to other forms of exclusion and not its evocation by way of an analogy. He focused on the abolition of untouchability 'in any form' but overlooked the second limb of Article 17, which required that untouchability 'shall be an offence punishable in accordance with law.' The provision has a unique historical specificity, as B.R. Ambedkar claimed that this provision in the Constitution to make caste untouchability a punishable offence required the legislature to enact legislation criminalising all forms of caste untouchability.[134] Reading other forms of discrimination under Article 17 would require the creation of fresh punishable offences, which could in turn raise the possibility of over-criminalisation. In other words, if rules of exclusion from temples are to be read as 'untouchability' as defined under Article 17, then the legislature would be bound to criminalise such exclusions. Here, it may be useful to refer to the insights of feminist scholars like Janet Halley and Prabha Kotiswaran who have argued against feminist alignment with State power, and especially the use of criminal law for feminist reforms. They have argued that such feminism, which they describe as 'governance feminism,' strengthens the repressive State apparatus in the guise of women's empowerment.[135] It is one thing to ***analogically*** refer to the constitutional basis of prohibition against ideas of human beings as agents of contamination; it is quite another to literally extend Article 17, not only in spirit but also in letter, to all forms of discriminations beyond caste. This again demonstrates the lack of attention given in the 'progressive' opinions of the courts to historical consciousness. In its zeal to broadly interpret Article 17, Chandrachud, J. disregarded the predominant voices of the contemporary feminist movement which do not align with State-based criminal law reform measures, as that would only strengthen State security discourse and reinstate paternalistic interventions as the goals of feminist politics.

---

who individually suffer injustice can challenge it in the court of law. Further, this posture of the dissent not only endorses regressive identity politics but also disavows the liberalisation of 'standing' by the Supreme Court where any public-spirited person can challenge injustice in the court of law.

133 See Gautam Bhatia, 'I Send My Soul Through Time and Space/To Greet You. You Will Understand . . .': On Sabarimala and the Civil Rights Cases' available at: https://indconlawphil.wordpress.com/2018/10/29/i-send-my-soul-through-time-and-space-to-greet-you-you-will-understand-on-sabarimala-and-the-civil-rights-cases/ (Oct. 29, 2018).

134 Untouchability (Offences) Act, 1955, was enacted in pursuance of this constitutional mandate.

135 See Janet Halley, Prabha Kotiswaran, Rachel Rebouché and Hila Shamir, *Governance Feminism: An Introduction* (University of Minnesota Press, Minneapolis, 2018). The courts need to be cautious of such interpretive leaps when feminist literature is increasingly suspicious of the use of repressive police power as transformative.

Community Determination and the Essential Practices Test

The majority judges sketched the history of the essential practices test and applied it to conclude that the rules of exclusion are not essential for the Ayyappa sect. The dissent left the issue of what constitutes 'essential' entirely on the community: 'what constitutes an essential religious practice [was] for the religious community to decide.'[136] It maintained that the judiciary should not pronounce on religious doctrines and beliefs. One exception was carved out by Indu Malhotra, J. from such judicial reticence. It is 'not for the courts to determine which of these practices of a faith are to be struck down, except if they are pernicious, oppressive, or a social evil, like *Sati*.'[137]

Some questions, however, remain unaddressed. Why would the rules of exclusion based on menstrual contamination not count as 'oppressive' or 'pernicious'? If the practice of *sati* – burning women on the funeral pyres of their husbands with religious sanction – qualifies for judicial intervention, then what is the rationale for excluding practices based on biological determinism and exclusion from judicial review? It is also worth asking why the Supreme Court did not engage with its own precedent which reflected the difficulties of community determination of essential practices (specifically, the *Nathdwara Temple* case which had rightly cautioned that 'the community may speak with more than one voice and the formula would, therefore, break down').[138]

The majority opinion of Chandrachud, J. pointed to the problems in judicial determination based on the essential practices test. This was a necessary and welcome posture, acknowledging the limits of the doctrine and its application. But, unfortunately, instead of indicating the uneven and selective way the previous precedents applied it, he suggested that except in cases of exclusionary practices ('the anti-exclusion principle'), it should be the community, and not the courts, which must decide on what is an essential or integral part of religion:[139]

> The anti-exclusion principle allows for due-deference to the ability of a religion to determine its own religious tenets and doctrines . . . The essential religious practices test should merit a close look . . . in an appropriate case in the future.

Since Chandrachud, J. relies on 'constitutional morality' framed in terms of liberal conceptions of autonomy and the 'dignity of individual,' it is submitted, his deference to the community opinion for determination of essential aspects of religion seems contradictory. While Chandrachud, J. argued that the community can decide upon the meaning of essential unless the practice was

136 *Sabarimala Judgment*, note 118, para 8.6 (per Indu Malhotra, J.).
137 *Id.* para 8.2.
138 *Nathdwara Temple Case*, note 78.
139 *Sabarimala Judgment*, note 118, para 112 (per Chandrachud, J.).

exclusionary, Indu Malhotra, J. substitutes exclusion with *oppressive or pernicious* practice. The question, then, is on what grounds do we determine what is the content of these terms? Despite the efforts in the opinion of Chandrachud, J. to identify judicial limits to community determinations of essential religious practice, he was unable to wriggle out of the problem that there is no objective formula for where such limits begin. Part of the problem lies in the lack of conversation between the judges of the Supreme Court. Chandrachud, J. did not work through the difficulty already indicated in the *Nathdwara Temple* case and Indu Malhotra, J. without engaging with the previous precedents declared that the practices and beliefs which are considered to be integral by the religious community should be regarded as 'essential' and thus given protection under Article 25.[140] This failure of the Supreme Court to speak with clarity in disagreements or in ways of employing previous precedents leads to the messiness in the Court's message, making it difficult even for legally trained minds to fully appreciate the reasoning of the Court. This is further complicated with the evocations of abstract and transhistorical categories like 'constitutional morality' which, instead of earnestly confronting the mythic, weave their own mythology. The judiciary, instead of washing off its hands, has to dirty them by entering into the quagmire of religion and perform its constitutional function by upholding that interpretation of tradition which best suits the constitutional mandate.

Conclusion

The unresolved issue of polyvocality of religious interpretations even within a specific religious community can be traced to the founding decision of the *Shirur Mutt* case, which left the question of determination of integral aspects of a religion to the religious community. Although the Court attempted a course-correction of this monolithic understanding of the community in the *Nathdwara Temple* case, the subsequent decisions and scholarly opinions remained unsure of the competence of the Court to decide on the predominant voice of the community, especially when there were divergences and disagreements within said community. The dissenting opinion in *Sabarimala Judgment* seems to have come full circle in giving up the task of determination of 'essential practices' to the community (Indu Malhotra, J.) or even surrendering the future of the doctrine itself (Chandrachud, J.).

The idea of relinquishing the doctrine finds its most recent exposition in the argument of Gautam Bhatia, who proposes 'the anti-exclusion principle as a replacement for the "essential practices test".'[141] He is careful not to apply this new principle to the category of cases dealing with 'State control over religious institutional property,' but 'where constitutional protection is sought

140 *Id.* para 13.6 (per Indu Malhotra, J.).
141 Bhatia, note 31 at 166.

for religious customs or practices, and where there is a conflict *within* religious communities.'[142] However, this idea remains fraught with conceptual difficulties. Bhatia's proposal proceeds on a rationale that the doctrine of essential practices is applied by the Court in two types of disputes: first, in dealing with religious institutional property or endowments (as in *Shirur Mutt, Devaru, Nathdwara Temple* etc.) and second, in engaging with issues about individual faith and interior belief (as in *Sabrimala Judgment* and the *Excommunication case*). His argument is that the issues of temple trusts, money and positions may be subject to judicial review while leaving the issues of personal belief and faith to community determination. But this distinction is problematic, as the question of individual faith can acquire a collective appeal and individual faiths can differ radically within a community. In that sense, even the cases which are seemingly about individual faith and interior belief are as much about the public and communitarian dimension of governing religious practice which is interlaced with power, thus warranting judicial intervention in a secular, democratic polity.

This reluctance to engage with religion cannot sufficiently tackle the liberal paradox with which I opened this chapter. The judiciary must engage with varying voices of the religion, keeping in mind the history of Constitution-making and conceptualising religion as a changing and historical phenomenon (something which colonial epistemology did not permit). The liberal paradox is foundational and constitutive of the Indian republic. Therefore, the doctrine which negotiates this paradoxical freedom requires working through. This should by no means be understood as a defense of the doctrine but a recognition that many times, its misapplication[143] is a result of its conceptualisation in universal and transcendental terms. Thus, the judicial performance of this doctrine, as explored in this chapter, cannot be understood in instrumental terms for political expediency but as a product of the contradictions *immanent* in the legal reasoning which are emblematic of the historical paradox of liberal constitutionalism.

142 *Ibid.*
143 As we will see in *Mohd. Hanif Quareshi & Others* v. *State of Bihar* (AIR 1958 SC 731) in Chapter 2 and *Dr. M. Ismail Faruqui* v. *Union of India* ((1994) 6 SCC 364) in Chapter 4.

2 Constitutionalism and the Sacred Cow

Secular Mythology of the Indian Supreme Court

Introduction

Within the dominant liberal legal tradition, religion remains the 'other' of modern law. In being heralded as 'an episteme of reason,' premised on empiricism, modern law *represses* religion and the cosmologies of faith, belief and myth. As I discussed in the introduction, this Manichean dualism separating religion from modern law has vastly impacted the literature around law and religion in India. Scholars working on the intersection of law and religion have argued against judicial attempts to 'rationalise' religion.[1] On the other hand, a few writers have defended an active and interventionist State role in regulating religious affairs. They have argued that left to itself, religion can justify cruelties such as child marriage, caste discrimination and human sacrifice. Therefore, these scholars consider that the way forward is in giving primacy to individual freedom over institutional religion when interpreting Indian constitutional provisions on religion.[2] Nevertheless, these writings still take for granted the dualism of religion and modern law which this book contests.

In contrast, a paradigmatic shift in scholarship on religion and law brings into question the very terms of this binary opposition between religion and law, or between mythology and modernity. This alternative viewpoint has exposed the fragility of this binary configuration and noted the alliances between mythology and modernity or modern law.[3] A thorough jurisprudential account of

1 Ronojoy Sen, *Articles of Faith: Religion, Secularism and the Indian Supreme Court* 40–72 (Oxford University Press, Oxford, 2010). For a critique of the Indian Supreme Court on reason-oriented interpretation of religion, see J. Duncan Derrett, 'Freedom of Religion under Indian Constitution: Excommunication (based on *Sardar ST Saifuddin Saheb* v. *State of Bombay*)' 12 *International & Comparative Law Quarterly* 697 (1963).

2 P.K. Tripathy, 'Secularism: Constitutional Provision & Judicial Review' 8(1) *Journal of Indian Law Institute* 1–29 (1966). For a different version of the same argument, see P.K. Tripathy, *Spotlights on Constitutional Interpretation* (NM Tripathy, 1972), Ch 2. Tripathy argues that 'asking the state to keep its hands off religion would amount to giving constitutional protection to social injustice.'

3 Peter Fitzpatrick, *The Mythology of Modern Law* 10 (Routledge, 1992); Peter Goodrich, 'Law and Modernity' 49 *Modern Law Review* 545 (1986).

DOI: 10.4324/9781003398561-3

modern law as Western mythology can be found in the work of Peter Fitzpatrick, who astutely remarked that 'myth is a suppressed dimension of modernity and I see its components finding a specific coherence in law as myth.'[4] This chapter aims to propel and demonstrate the significance of this insight in the context of Article 48 of the Indian Constitution. Article 48 is a unique constitutional directive to all the Indian states, providing for the protection of cows.

Article 48 has its roots in the Hindu belief that the sacred and holy nature of the cow is one of the attributes of cultural nationalism that consolidated national identity in nineteenth-century colonial India.[5] My focus on the interpretation of Article 48 is guided by the fact that this constitutional provision is one of the prominent sites at which modern law gets intertwined is shaped in line with religion. In this chapter, I seek to show how this encounter between law and religion in the courts has led to the construction of a modern doctrinaire myth within the secular reasoning of law. I will demonstrate how the use of the doctrine of constitutional interpretation constitutes a faith-based mythological approach, despite its secular pretentions. I describe this use of mythic and faith-based reasoning by courts, specifically when the constitutional validity of cow protection laws is under scrutiny, as *secular mythology*. My use of this expression is derived from Peter Fitzpatrick's argument on the mythology of law. I will show that what appears to be a secular application of a legal doctrine instead contains a trace of this mythic element, which remains unnoticed. This trace resembles a religious paradigm where presuppositions and *a priori* assumptions are applied without any necessary logical deduction. Focussing on this trace – the unresolvable contradiction between judicial reason and its repetition by way of precedent – reveals the latent or hidden mythological element within the rational, logical structure of the law. In other words, this analysis queries this element of myth which imposes itself on the secular and blurs the boundaries between the two. It is this aporia, or paradoxical blurring of the two separate categories, which I describe as secular mythology. It may be understood as referring to the interlacing of reason with faith – of myth with modernity – in the discursive logic of the Indian Supreme Court.

Another related and key aspect of secular mythology is the preferencing of abstract universal legal idioms in judicial interpretation over social and historical contexts. As is the case with the languages of mythology, judicial reasoning

4 Fitzpatrick, note 3 at 14. For Fitzpatrick, the Western enlightenment tradition defines itself in opposition to myth. However, myth has been incorporated into the foundational precepts of modernity. The 'autonomous' and 'self-sustaining' character of the law likens it to its mythic and divine counterpart, God. The omnipresence and omnipotence of the law is reflected in its claim to do anything, if not everything.

5 For the ancient historical emergence of sacredness of the cow in the Hindu tradition, see W. Norman Brown, 'The Sanctity of Cow in Hinduism' 16(5–6–7) *Economic and Political Weekly* 245 (1964) (Brown argues that the 'doctrine of cow's sanctity' only emerged in the beginning of the Christian era. It was strengthened during the Gupta period around 4 CE and largely within the Brahminical circles).

behaves as if the doctrine used for interpretation is transhistorical and universally applicable and elides the specific context in which the doctrine of constitutional interpretation is invoked. This is how I understand the mythologisation of secular law. I limit my use of the expression in this chapter to the study of constitutional validity of legislation enacted under Article 48 of Constitution of India.

My argument emerges from the analysis of Indian Supreme Court judgments between 1958 and 2005 which deal with the constitutionality of cow protection laws enacted by the legislatures of various state governments after Indian independence in 1947 and enforcement of the Constitution in 1950. As already noted in the introduction of this book, there is no dearth of critical legal constitutional scholarship problematising the taken-for-granted tension between the 'sacredness' and the 'rationality' of modern law, but little attention has been accorded to the functional dimension of law, which includes legal interpretation rooted in doctrinaire wisdom.[6] It is this vacuum which this chapter investigates for a nuanced understanding of the Supreme Court's discourse on cow protection laws and constitutionalism. The lens of secular mythology challenges the assumption of a neat distinction between religion and law. This alternative framework goes beyond the predominant approach in historical scholarship on cow protection laws and the Constitution, where economic reasoning is a veneer behind which hide the religious agenda and aspirations of those advocating for cow protection. I will show that these two forms of reasoning – economic (secular) and religious (mythological) – are deeply enmeshed in the reasoning of the constituent assembly as well as Indian constitutional courts.

This enmeshing of the religious and the secular, I argue, provides a grounded and nuanced understanding of the terms of debate and logics of constitutional interpretation. One is tempted to believe that avoiding religious scripture or theological tradition in judicial interpretation will pave a certain and clear path towards secular legal reasoning. However, this belief in clarity, in separating religion from the law, is misplaced. This is because it ignores the messy interconnection between the religious, the mythical, and the law. As I will show, the mythical permeates the otherwise rational sphere of legal interpretation. Which is why, ironically enough, we need to enter this messy terrain where law and religion interact and intersect with each other. This may provide a grounded reading because this blurring of borders between law and religion might explain how secular constitutionalism in India has bolstered the claims and demands of the cow protectionist orthodoxy which has acquired a militant and vigilante posture in recent years.[7]

6 Michael R. Anderson and Sumit Guha, *Changing Concepts of Rights and Justice in South Asia* 2 (Oxford University Press, Oxford, 1998). The authors highlight the drawback of existing legal history scholarship, in avoiding 'the questions of doctrinal development' in preference to 'statutes as definitive expressions of the law rather than looking to judicial interpretation or doctrinal exegesis.'

7 In July 2018, the Supreme Court of India issued guidelines to curb the increase in cow vigilantism in the country. See *Tehseen S Poonawalla* v. *Union of India* (2018) 9 SCC 501. For

Section I of this chapter outlines the historical foundations and textual semantics of Article 48. It briefly traces how, in nineteenth-century colonial India, the question of the cow cemented itself as an ideological symbol of cultural nationalism. Section II reviews the constituent assembly debates (CADs) on Article 48. This section shows the value and importance of returning and attending to the constituent assembly debates. The debates foreground the desires and passions of the founders which unfold implicitly, or unconsciously in the judicial discourse of the later years, and reveal the messy, contradictory strands of the Constitution, interlacing/couching the theological as economico-political. Section III focusses on the Supreme Court's decision in *Hanif Quareshi* v. *State of Bihar* (*Hanif Quareshi*),[8] the first significant decision on Article 48 interpretation, which held ground for almost 50 years. It critically assesses the Court's evaluation of anti-slaughter laws against constitutionally guaranteed fundamental rights such as freedom of trade and business and religious freedom. It will highlight the balance that the Court was trying to maintain between the utility of cow progeny[9] and the religious significance of cows for the Hindu community. Section IV analyses how the Court addressed the legislative responses of various Indian states through enactment of anti-slaughter laws, which were to circumvent the *Hanif Quareshi* decision. This section further focuses on the overlooked and forgotten constitutional bench decision in *Mohammad Faruk* v. *State of Madhya Pradesh* (*Faruk*).[10] I argue that this judgment evinces an alternative possibility of judicial interpretation informed by social and historical considerations. I will also show that *Faruk*'s judicial posture, aligning judicial reasoning to social and historical discourse, was short-lived. Finally, Section V evaluates the seven-judge bench decision in *State of Gujarat* v. *Mirzapur Moti Kassab Jamat* (*Mirzapur*),[11] which overturned the *Hanif Quareshi* decision by expanding the limits of the slaughter ban to include bulls and bullocks along with the cows. In this section, I elaborate upon the endorsement of the doctrine of presumption of constitutionality by the Indian Supreme Court in the context of Article 48. This doctrine has consistently been invoked in landmark cases

a critical analysis of lynchings of Muslims in India on account of eating beef, see Shabnum Tejani, 'Cow Protection, Hindu Identity and the Politics of Hurt in India, c.1890–2019' 3(1) *Emotions: History, Culture, Society* 136 (2019).

8 1959 SCR 629. The Supreme Court judgment uses the spelling 'Quareshi,' which I have retained throughout this Chapter while referring to this case. Rohit De uses 'Qureshi' in his book and I have used this spelling wherever I have referred to his work: Rohit De, *A People's Constitution: The Everyday Life of Law in Indian Republic* 150 (Princeton University Press, Princeton, NJ, 2018).

9 The Supreme Court uses the term 'progeny' to refer to the inclusion of 'bulls and bullocks,' as the male offspring of a cow, within cow slaughter bans. As will be discussed later, bulls and bullocks fell outside the slaughter bans until 2005. However, in 2005, the Supreme Court approved a ban on their slaughter, arguing that a total ban on the slaughter of cows also includes all the progeny thereof.

10 (1969) 1 SCC 853.

11 (2005) 8 SCC 534.

concerned with the cow protection clause in the Indian Constitution.[12] On a close reading of the majority judgment, it appears that the doctrine of presumption of constitutionality has ended up acquiring the status of secular mythology. I will show how this doctrine has acquired a mythological status within the tenets of secular law, even as the Supreme Court, by its own admission, agreed that various states' legislatures acted inappropriately – short-circuiting the law as it was laid down by the Apex Court in 1958 – in enacting cow protection laws. Nevertheless, it uncritically reiterated the doctrinal presumption to validate these very legislations.

I The Cow Protection Provision Under the Indian Constitution

Cow protection has a checkered history in India. In nineteenth-century colonial India, the cow acquired a renewed sanctity with the efforts of Swami Dayanand Saraswati, who reinvigorated it as an ancient symbol of Hindu cultural identity. Dayanand Saraswati was the founder of the Arya Samaj, a religious and cultural movement primarily in northern India that championed the return to Vedas. The protection of the cow was foregrounded as the cardinal creed of Vedic wisdom.[13] During this time, the cow – as a Hindu religious symbol – became at once an ideological category for anti-colonial resistance[14] as well as a political symbol and marker of Hindu identity in northern states.[15] Later, the Hindu Mahasabha espoused the cause of Hindu national identity by

12 The invocation of the doctrine of presumption of constitutionality has a long and complex history in Indian constitutional law. However, in this chapter, I will limit my analysis and argument with respect to its use by the Supreme Court while adjudicating on the constitutionality of the anti-slaughter laws.

13 The Arya Samaj movement emerged in the northern provinces of late nineteenth-century colonial and undivided India. Its first branch was founded at Lahore on 24 June 1877. Soon it attained a prominent presence in Punjab and the United Province (now Uttar Pradesh). Its theological idea was premised on the supremacy and infallibility of Vedic wisdom and challenged idol worship and religious symbolism. Dayanand Saraswati died in 1883, and within a decade there was an official split in the movement. In 1893, the movement was split into two main divisions in Punjab. The first was the Gurukul Party, which founded the gurukul in Kangri, Haridwar in 1901. The other wing, under the leadership of Lala Hansraj and Lala Lajpat Rai, remained in control of the major institution established in the memory of Dayanand Saraswati in 1886: the Dayanand Anglo-Vedic (DAV) school system in Lahore. See G.R. Thursby, *Hindu-Muslim Relations in British India: A Study of Controversy, Conflict & Communal Movements in Northern India* (Brill, 1975), Ch 2; C.S. Adcock, *The Limits of Tolerance: Indian Secularism and the Politics of Religious Freedom* 17–18 (Oxford University Press, 2014).

14 I use the notion of 'ideology' in the classical Marxist sense as false consciousness. The cow was a symbol of political resistance against the British on the one hand, and consolidated the Muslim as 'enemy' in the emergent idea of a Hindu nation on the other.

15 John Zavos, *The Emergence of Hindu Nationalism in India* 85–87 (Oxford University Press, 2000).

employing the cow as a political symbol of the Hindu nation.[16] This explains why the historical literature on the 'holy cow' has extensively drawn upon nineteenth-century archives to understand Hindu identity formation with the cow as a political symbol.[17] Historians of modern India, however, have challenged the ideology of a homogeneous Hindu community combating the colonial threat of cow slaughter.[18] Sandra Freitag provides a useful insight into the efforts towards the homogenisation of the Hindu identity in the late nineteenth century centred around the cow. Giving an account of how connections were forged between cities and the countryside, mobilising people around the symbol of the cow, she delineates the coercive power tactics used by Gorakshini Sabha (the Cow Protection Collective) in both formal and informal settings.[19] In his work on the Bhojpuri region in the late nineteenth century, Gyanendra Pandey demonstrates how the concern for cow protection not only distinguished Hindus from Muslims, but also led to the stigmatisation of lower-caste Hindus.[20] He shows, *inter alia*, how the lower caste adopted anti-beef eating – or pro-cow protection – attitudes in order to acquire an acceptable status and favourable attitude from the higher-caste Hindus within the stratified caste hierarchy.[21] Muslims slaughtered cows for food as well as in religious ceremonies, and lower-caste Hindus also consumed (and are still

16 The All India Hindu Mahasabha was formed in 1915 at Haridwar. It represented a coalition that formally came together to promote Hindu unity as a response to the formation of the Muslim League in 1906, as well as growing tensions between Hindus and Muslims. Previously, some Hindu sabhas (associations) existed in North India, such as the United Provinces Sabha and the Punjab Hindu Sabha, but this was eventually consolidated at an all-India level with the formation of Hindu Mahasabha. In the 1930s, under the leadership of Vinayak Damodar Savarkar, the Mahasabha acquired a prominent place in the Indian political formation. For an extensive historical analysis of its early emergence, see Richard Gordon, 'The Hindu Mahasabha and the Indian National Congress, 1915 to 1926' 9(2) *Modern Asian Studies* 145 (1975). See also, Prabhu Bapu, *Hindu Mahasabha in Colonial North India, 1915–1930* (Routledge, 2013).

17 Peter Robb, 'The Challenge of Gau Mata: British Policy and Religious Change in India, 1880–1916' 20(2) *Modern Asian Studies* 285 (1986); Anand Yang, 'Sacred Symbol and Sacred Space in Rural India: Community Mobilization in the "Anti-Cow Killing" Riot of 1893' 22(4) *Comparative Studies in Society and History* 576 (1980); Anthony Parel, 'The Political Symbolism of Cow in India' 7(3) *Journal of Commonwealth Political Studies* 179 (1969).

18 C.S. Adcock, 'Sacred Cows and Secular History: Cow Protection Debates in Colonial North India' 30(2) *Comparative Studies of South Asia, Africa and the Middle East* 297, 300 (2010) (Adcock argues that in assuming that cows are the unquestioned unifying symbol for Hindus, we 'run the risk of denying agency to non-elites' and suggesting a unity of faith in the Hindu community at large, for which there is no historical evidence).

19 Sandria B. Freitag, 'Sacred Symbol as Mobilizing Ideology: The North Indian Search for a Hindu Community' 22(4) *Comparative Studies in Society & History* 597 (1980).

20 Gyanendra Pandey, 'Rallying Round the Cow: Sectarian Strife in the Bhojpuri Region, c. 1888–1917' in Ranajit Guha (ed.), *Subaltern Studies II: Writings on South Asian History and Society* 60–129 (Oxford University Press, 1983).

21 *Id.* at 89–95. Austin

consuming) beef as a dietary staple.[22] As cultural nationalists considered cows to be religious and sacred animals, they resented both the slaughter and the consumption of cows.

Thus, the cow was transformed into a politico-cultural symbol. It at once forged a solidarity against colonial powers as well as hostility against the Muslims and lower-caste Hindus. The Arya Samaj as a movement played a key role in cementing these configurations. It placed emphasis on the Muslims' difference in their culinary preference of beef, which they shared with the British. This sectarian discourse in the rhetoric of cow protection forms the backdrop for and explains the controversial status of Article 48 since the time of independence. Granville Austin argues that Article 48 ideologically enshrines the 'Hindu sentiment' as a constitutional provision. In his words, '[a]s various provisions of the Irish Constitution show that Ireland is a Roman Catholic nation, so Article 48 shows that Hindu sentiment predominated in the Constituent Assembly.'[23]

Article 48 is in Part IV of the Indian Constitution.[24] This part provides the principles which the State must apply while making laws. Article 48 was included here despite voices in the Constituent Assembly that instead wanted to make cow protection an enforceable fundamental right. However, the drafting committee maintained that Article 48 should remain a directive or an enabling provision, rather than an enforceable claim-right, so that the goal of cow protection is attained 'without using any sort of coercion.' I will take up the discussion of the constituent assembly on Article 48 in the next section. Let us begin with a reading of Article 48 as it exists in the Constitution of India. The text of Article 48 as an artefact of its history inhabits various, and at times contradictory, textual semantic strands. It reads:

> *Organisation of agriculture and animal husbandry*: The State shall endeavour to organise agriculture and animal husbandry on modern and scientific lines and shall, in particular, take steps for preserving and improving the breeds, and prohibiting the slaughter, of cows and calves and other milch and draught cattle.

22 De, note 8 at 150.

23 Granville Austin, *Indian Constitution: A Cornerstone of a Nation* 82 (Oxford University Press, 1966). Upendra Baxi also notes that Article 48 is one of the few articles 'whose worthiness for enshrinement in the Constitution is open to question.' See Upendra Baxi, 'The Little Done, The Vast Undone: Some Reflections on Reading Granville Austin's *The Indian Constitution*' 9(3) *Journal of Indian Law Institute* 323, 346 (1967).

24 Part IV is the charter of socio-economic rights, or positive rights, of the Indian Constitution. It must be contrasted with Part III, which is the charter of civil and political rights. While rights under Part III are largely negative rights and are enforceable as claim-rights against the State, Part IV is not enforceable, yet is 'fundamental to the governance of the country' (Constitution of India, Article 37). On the importance of Part IV rights, see Rehan Abeyratne, 'Socio-economic Rights in the Indian Constitution: Toward a Broader Conception of Legitimacy' 39 *Brooklyn Journal of International Law* 1 (2014); Latika Vashist, 'Enlivening Directive Principles: An Attempt to Save Their Vanishing Present' 1(2) *ILI Law Review* 205 (2010).

This provision displays three distinct aims: the advancement of agriculture along modern and scientific lines, improvement of cattle breeds and protection of cows. There appears to be an interweaving of diverse (and perhaps conflicting) worldviews in Article 48. The aspiration of organising agriculture on 'modern and scientific lines' is combined with the 'sacred' injunction of saving the holy cow. The invocation of modernity and science with the invocation of the sacred past in one stroke is striking.[25]

II Constituent Assembly Debates (CADs): Making of the Constitutional Provision

What now appears as Article 48 was Article 38-A in the original draft of the Indian Constitution. The debates on Article 38-A are brief and terse. If we keep aside the minor comments made by way of clarifications, one finds eight voices debating the question of cow protection. These eight members include Pandit Thakur Dass Bhargava, Seth Govind Das, Sri Ram Sahai, Prof. Shibban Lal Saksena, Dr. Raghu Vira, Shri RV Dhulekar, Mr. ZH Lari and Syed Muhammad Saiadulla. Out of these eight, the last two were Muslim members who voiced their 'different views from the majority view' without any serious contestation to the text of Article 38-A. The remaining six Hindu speakers voiced their majority view generally as well as specifically with respect to the text of the Article. Only the first two can be considered as instrumental in textual design of and debates on the present Article 48. The other four speakers in their brief speeches generally supported the Bhargava's amendment and the addition proposed to it by Das. This is why one must carefully survey the reasoning, aspirations and logics of the proposals of Bhargava and Das to appreciate the formation of the cow protection clause in the Constitution of India. The amendments proposed by Bhargava and Das were put to vote in the assembly. Bhargava's motion was adopted by the assembly while an addition proposed by Das was negated by the assembly.

As we proceed to study the variance and difference (both textual and conceptual) between Bhargava and Das along with others in solidarity, I must mark certain underlying themes which surfaced in the very beginning of the debate on Article 38-A. The first is the language question, an *uncanny* return of the unresolved issues of the past. The other is the issue of the status of cow protection in the Constitutional scheme. Indeed, one of the primary reasons to evaluate the assembly debates is the striking manner in which the discursive proposals and desires manifest in the debate surreptitiously reappear in later judicial discourse. Let us note the two themes which emerge as underlying threads of the discussion on the cow.

25 Those who pushed this provision on the grounds of pushing Gandhian philosophy upon the Constitution little noticed the Gandhian anathema to modern science or Western parliamentary forms of governance as opposed to indigenous alternatives.

The question of 'language' – The issue of the tongue of the mother as opposed to colonial English diction uniquely becomes central to the discussion on Article 38-A. Bhargava, followed by Das and Sahai chose to speak in Hindi. Despite resistance, they felt that they could not speak about the cow in any other language but their mother tongue. The speeches of these members in the official text are, as it is duly noted, a translation 'of Hindustani Speech.'[26] Bhargava, from the north Indian province of East Punjab, notes that 'the subject is a very important one,' thus, he would prefer to speak in 'my own language.'[27] This turn to the mother tongue, for him, is linked with the importance of this Article:[28]

> I attach very great importance to this amendment, so much so that if on the one side of the scale you were to put this amendment and other all these 315 clauses of the draft, I would prefer the former. If this is accepted, the whole country would be, in a way, electrified.

The cow, which is incessantly described in these debates as the mother, triggers the need for the mother tongue for proper articulation. This turn to Hindi was more complex than it appears. The use of Hindi was not a simple return to 'the native tongue' as opposed to the colonial English. As Hindi or Hindustani were primarily north Indian languages, Shri S. Nagappa from the province of Madras had protested against this move. He accused the speaker of deliberately using Hindustani (which is a mixed version of the Hindi and Urdu languages) despite being well-versed in English and knowing fully well that 'a large number of South Indians cannot follow.'[29] The question of language has been one of the most contentious issues of the Indian Constitution, which goes to test the very promise of 'we, the people' as noted by constitutional law scholars who see the schism of language as the original controversy of Indian Constitution making.[30]

26 Hindustani is a term which refers to a mix of Hindi and Urdu languages. There is a complex history of how after the partition of the sub-continent, there was an attempt to make Hindi as more Sanskrit-oriented in India and Urdu more Persianised in Pakistan. Originally, there was a confluence between the two languages which was used inseparably by the natives. Nevertheless, Hindustani remained a north Indian dialect in contrast to the southern part of India which was never dominated by Hindustani dialect. I am interested in highlighting in the difficulty to find a mother tongue in the context of the constituent assembly. As even Hindustani, far less Hindi, cannot be a language which would not alienate the South Indian members of the assembly. For an excellent introduction to the historical difference forged between Hindi and Urdu and the politics of Hindi language, see Alok Rai, *Hindi Nationalism: Tracts for the Times* (Orient Blackswan, New Delhi, 2001).

27 VII *Constituent Assembly Debates* (*CADs*) 568 (Nov. 24, 1948) (Pandit Thakur Dass Bhargava).

28 *Id.* at 570.

29 *Id.* at 568.

30 See Pritam Singh, 'Hindu Bias in India's "Secular" Constitution: Probing Flaws in the Document of Governance' 26(6) *Third World Quarterly* 909–926 (2005); Sabarish Suresh, *The*

I merely note this to highlight how the issue of cow returns us to the concerns and issues which are foundational to the constitutional historicity.

The lament of Sacrifice – Bhargava in his opening speech, as well as Das in his follow-up, surfaced the theme of sacrifice. Both invoked the metaphor of sacrifice to signify the location of Article 38-A in the Directive Principles of State Policy (which cannot be en*forced* in a court of law) and not in the chapter on Fundamental Rights (which are enforceable claims). This, for them, was already a sacrifice of the cause of cow protectionists. Bhargava reluctantly accepts the fate of the provision in directive principles referring to the agreement reached in 'the Assembly that this problem should be solved in such a manner that the objective is gained without using any sort of coercion.'[31] Das dwelled on this sacrifice in a deeper sense, making a comparison between Article 17 of the Constitution and the cow protection provision.

Article 17 appears in Part III of the Constitution of India. It abolishes 'untouchability,' which was a perverted form of caste system leading of the segregation of Dalits on the basis on their caste. Article 17 not only declares the abolition of this retrograde practice but further makes its practice in any form a punishable offence. A declaration in the Constitution for the legislature to create an offence to eradicate the practice of caste untouchability is a unique fundamental right in India. Das likens the *sacrificed* cause of cow protection to Article 17 and remarks that 'just as the practice of untouchability was going to be declared an offence so also we should declare the slaughter of cows to be an offence.'[32] Das's comparison indicates the militant desire of the cow protectionist lobby in the constituent assembly. That cow protection ought to be a fundamental right, and its execution must be through criminalisation of any slaughter practice, itself shows the distance between Das and Gandhi despite the incessant invocation of the latter by Das. For our purpose, this brief detour was necessary to make sense of the future judgments where the Supreme Court tried to equate cow protection with a fundamental right throwing the constitutional logic out of the window in the judgment of *Ashutosh Lahiri* discussed in Section V. It is also noteworthy that while the sharp binary between the human and the animal might be acceptable vocabulary at the historical juncture of Constitution making, it no longer remains tenable in the contemporary moment. These marginal edges of the assembly debate require attention to understand judgments such as *Mirzapur*, where compassion for animals would lead to the expansion of ban on cow slaughter. Now let us move into the debates.

Bhargava moved the amendment and began with the economic argument drawing on detailed statistical data. He framed the issue of cow protection following a logic of utility: an economic utilitarianism of agricultural economy

Unconscious of the Indian Constitution: Traumatic Histories and Repetitions (Doctoral Dissertation, Yeshiva University, New York, 2019).

31 *CADs*, note 27 at 568.

32 *CADs*, note 27 at 571 (Seth Govind Das).

of India. To him, this Article was important as 'the whole agricultural and food problem of this country is nothing but the problem of the improvement of cow and her breed.'[33] Cow protection and improvement of cattle breeds would lessen imports and foster export possibilities for India. Following this logic of utility, Bhargava moved to the mythological importance of the cow for Hindus. The holy cow is '*Kam-Dhenu* . . . fulfiller of all our wants' in Hindu cosmology, and ancient Hindu sages had elevated it to the status of sacred animal: 'Here, Lord Krishna was born, who served cows so devotedly that to this day, in affection he is known as '*Makhan Chor*' [Butter-stealing God].'[34] Mughal rulers also abstained from cow slaughter 'not because Muslims regarded it to be bad but because, from the economic point of view, it was unprofitable.'[35] While he acknowledged that cow worship was the foundation of this constitutional provision, he maintained that this appeal was not in the name of religion, but 'in the light of economic requirements of the country.'[36]

It is precisely this focus on economic utility which Govind Das refuted, or more accurately reversed. For Das, utility was not unimportant, but it was at best second in the hierarchy of arguments advocating for the cow protection clause. Das was clear that religious concern could squarely be inscribed into the Constitution. In an extraordinary comment, Das equated religion, culture and nation-state as integral to self-determination (*Swaraj*):[37]

> Swaraj will have no meaning for our people in the absence of culture. Great important cultural issues – for instance the question of the name of the country, question of National language, question of National script, question of national anthem and the question of prohibition of cow slaughter – are before this Assembly.

Das evoked the category of *dharma* while articulating his 'religious' claims. 'It is my firm belief,' he stated, 'that Dharma had never been uprooted from the world and nor can it be uprooted.'[38] He noticed a logical possibility of dilution of the cow protection clause by focus on utility. For him, the emphasis on utility was not only limited to Bhargava's speech but also to the proposed amendment. There was a possibility that it might be read as permitting 'unfit or useless cows may be slaughtered.' Which is precisely what was to happen in the five-judge bench decision of *Hanif Quareshi* if not with respect to useless cows but with respect to useless bulls and bullocks. As a cure to this supposed

33 *Id.* at 569 (Pandit Thakur Dass Bhargava).

34 *Ibid.*

35 *Ibid.*

36 *Id.* at 570. This was followed by an imploration of the words of Gandhi suggesting that the issue of prohibition of cow slaughter 'is a great moment – in certain respects even greater moment – than that of Swaraj [self-determination].'

37 *Ibid.*

38 *Id.* at 571 (Seth Govind Das).

defect, Das proposed the definition of 'cow' to be added in the article in the following terms: 'The word "cow" includes bulls, bullocks, young stock of genus cow.' This proposed amendment was negated by the assembly. Nevertheless, as we will see later in this chapter, the seven-judge Supreme Court (without any reference to the constituent assembly) in *Mirzapur* held, overruling *Hanif Quareshi* that bulls and bullocks, despite their age or utility, should be included in the ban proposed by Article 48. One may say that Govind Das's desire finally found fruition five decades later in *Mirzapur*.

These uncanny and almost literary foreshadowings or foretellings of judicial future in the constituent assembly debates appear surprising. To take another instance, Das invoked the metaphor of 'family,' with an assimilative undertone while addressing the Muslim members of the assembly, and pleaded for 'cultural unification' despite religious diversity: 'Just as Hindu and Sikh or Hindu or a Jain can live in the same family, in the same way a Hindu and a Muslim can also live in the same family.'[39] He then remarked that 'Muslims should come forward to make it clear that their religion does not *compulsorily* enjoin on them the slaughter of the cow.'[40] Saiadulla responded to this call by clarifying that: 'In my religious book, the Holy Qoran, there is an injunction to the Muslims saying – "*La Ikraba fir Din*" or, there ought to be no compulsion in the name of religion.'[41] Nevertheless, Saiadulla was adamant on a clear distinction to be made between religious or economic arguments. We will return to this juxtaposition later. At this point, it is interesting to note that the first Supreme Court decision of *Hanif Quareshi* interpreting Article 48 will use precisely this argument of non-compulsion in Islam to dismiss the claim of Muslims under the religious freedom clause of the Constitution. Curiously, no reference was ever made to the constituent assembly debates. What followed in the assembly was affirmation of Bhargava's proposed amendment and Das's proposed additions (by Sahai, Saksena, Vira and Dhulekar), despite notes of dissent primarily exposing the untenable enmeshing of Hindu theology with economic utilitarianism by the Muslim members of the assembly (Lari and Saiadulla).

Saxena agreed with Das that 'we should not think because a thing has a religious significance, so it is bad.'[42] Reiterating the usefulness of the principles followed in the Hindu religion, he suggested the rational and statistical basis for advocating prohibition. Vira began with a Sanskrit aphorism describing violence to cows as *mahapaataki* (a paramount sin). He described the cow

39 *Id.* at 572. The innocuous familial metaphor reminds one of the metaphor of 'friendship' used by Mohandas Gandhi to argue that Muslims must voluntarily give up the cow. See Faisal Devji, 'A Practice of Prejudice: Gandhi's Politics of Friendship' in Shail Mayaram, M.S.S. Pandian and Ajay Skaria (eds.), *Subaltern Studies XII: Muslims, Dalits, and the Fabrications of History* 78–98 (Permanent Black, New Delhi, 2005).

40 *Id.* at 572 (Seth Govind Das).

41 *Id.* at 578 (Syed Mohammad Saiadulla).

42 *Id.* at 574 (Prof. Shibban Lal Saksena).

as 'the mother of the nation' and 'having precedence over the children of the family.' Dhulekar accelerated this pitch and remarked that

> I can declare from this platform that there are thousands of persons who will not run at a man to kill that man for their mother or wife or children, but they will run at a man if that man does not want to protect the cow or kill her.[43]

The dissenting Muslim members raised the concern of violent outbursts 'on the occasion of Bakrid' (against the slaughtering of cow by Muslims as a religious rite).[44] Pre-empting the clash between Hindu sentiments and Muslim practice, Lari's assertions were couched as a 'permission' by the majority to continue the minority practice:[45]

> [W]e will not stand in the way of the majority if the majority wants to proceed in a certain way, whatever may be our inclinations . . . we know that our religion does not necessarily say that you must sacrifice cow: it permits it. The question is whether, considering the sentiments that you have, considering the regard which the majority have for certain classes of animals, do they or do they not permit the minority – not a right – but a privilege or a permission which it at present has? I cannot put it higher.

The history of constitutional cases around this issue, discussed in the next part of this chapter, shows how this hope could not translate into reality. Saiadulla contested the economic argument up front. He pointed out the flaws in the methodology of arriving at figures of slaughter in both Das's and Bhargava's arguments[46] and argued that economic arguments were used as a mystifying rhetoric where Hindu religious sentiments were universalised as 'the' common good and will of the nation:[47]

> I do not also want to obstruct the framers of our Constitution, I mean the Constituent Assembly if they come out in the open and say directly: 'This is part of our religion. The cow should be protected from slaughter and therefore we want its provision either in the Fundamental Rights or in the Directive Principles.' But, those who put it on the economic front, as the honourable Member who spoke before me said, do create a

43 *Id.* at 577 (R.V. Dhulekar).

44 *Id.* at 577 (Z.H. Lari).

45 *Ibid.*

46 *Id.* at 579 (Syed Muhammad Saiadulla). For instance, he pointed out how the figures of slaughter during the war time are presented as figures of normal times and how Hindus themselves were keenly practicing the slaughter of cows. For an elaborate discussion of the rejection of economic grounds for cow slaughter, see *Id.* at 578–580.

47 *Id.* at 578.

> suspicion in the minds of many that the ingrained Hindu feeling against cow slaughter is being satisfied by the backdoor. If you put it on the economic front, I will place before you certain facts and figures which will show that the slaughter of cows is not as bad as it is sought to be made out from the economic point of view.

This was an important indictment of the self-presentation of Hindu sentiments as 'secular' (and progressive). However, the entire edifice of cow protection has historically been framed through the juxtaposition of emotive appeal with the logic of economic rationality. The use of theological vocabulary along with economics had historical continuity. The passionate desires and religious sentimentalism immanent in the CADs on the cow require careful reading as these affective moments perpetuated the violent orders of constitutionalism. Upendra Baxi's reflections on reading CADs fit the debates on Article 48: 'we ought to grasp constitutionalism as in some sense being passional rather than entirely rational. Constitutionalisms, forever, construct and reconstruct the violent orders of the desiring subjects.'[48] The narrative of mystification which cemented the symbol of the cow as worthy of constitutional protection set the stage for the way in which this clause came to be interpreted within the constitutional discourse of independent India.

III Post-independence Judicial Discourse on Cow Slaughter: The *Hanif Quareshi* Case

In this section, I will show how Article 48 of the Indian Constitution, which came into force on January 26, 1950, enabled state legislatures to enact or amend laws for cow protection. I will then critically evaluate the first significant judgment on cow protection laws by the Indian Supreme Court in *Hanif Quareshi* v. *State of Bihar*.[49] Legislatures of various states, such as Bihar, Uttar Pradesh, and Madhya Pradesh, were early pioneers of cow protection laws immediately after the commencement of the Constitution in 1950. The Bihar Preservation and Improvement of Animals Act of 1956 imposed a ban on the slaughter of all species of 'bovine cattle.'[50] The Uttar Pradesh Prevention of Cow Slaughter Act, 1955 (the UP enactment), enacted a total ban on any form of cow slaughter, irrespective of the cow's age or utility.[51] An amendment made in 1956 to the Central Provinces and Berar Act 1949 changed this definition of 'cow' to include male and female calves, bulls, bullocks, and

48 Upendra Baxi, 'Justice of Human Rights in Indian Constitutionalism: Preliminary Notes' in V.R. Mehta and Thomas Pantham (eds.), *Political Ideas in Modern India: Thematic Explorations* 268 (Sage Publications, New Delhi, 2006).

49 *Hanif Quareshi*, note 8.

50 The Supreme Court noted that 'species of bovine cattle' is expansive enough to include 'buffaloes' within the slaughter.

51 U.P. enactment, s. 3.

heifers. These laws against slaughter affected the trade and business of beef traders. Primarily, the Muslim butchers belonging to the Quareshi community were hit immensely by these new laws. Rohit De has shown that the Quareshi community which questioned the validity of these laws belonged to the poorer sect within the Muslims belonging to lower castes. They were most affected by these state laws as they were primarily butchers by occupation, and slaughtering was a significant source of their livelihood. In his study of Supreme Court records of the litigants in *Hanif Quareshi*, he notes that thousands of Muslims had signed this petition to challenge the fresh ban on the beef trade in India.[52] This led to the formation of the first constitutional bench to test the validity of the laws enacted by these states in *Hanif Quareshi*.

The Religious Freedom Argument

The constitutional grounds of challenge to this legislation included the violation of the fundamental right to equality (Article 14), the right to freedom to practice trade and business (Article 19(1)(g)) and the right to freedom of religion (Article 25). The Court began its analysis with the religious freedom argument and expressed shock at the lack of attention paid to the importance of cow sacrifice in Islam. Rohit De explains, however, why the religious freedom argument was relatively unimportant for the Quareshi community:[53]

> The Qureshis were uninterested in getting permission to sacrifice a cow once a year on Eid; they wanted to ensure the continuation of their livelihood . . . Despite Qureshi butchers' lack of interest in making a claim as Muslims, the [C]ourt tended to see their claims through this lens.

The Supreme Court referred at its own behest to *The Hedàya, or Guide: A Commentary on the Mussulman Laws*, which was originally composed in the twelfth century by Burhan al-Din al-Marghinani, a leading Muslim jurist.[54] *The Guide* notes that every mature and free Muslim is required to sacrifice one goat per person, or that seven Muslims together might sacrifice one cow or camel. The availability of an alternative option convinced the Court that the practice was not 'essential' to Islam and was therefore outside the protective zone of Article 25, the religious freedom clause of the Constitution.[55]

52 On the caste and class composition of the 3000 Muslim petitioners, see De, note 8 at 153.

53 *Id.* at 150.

54 The text was later translated by Charles Hamilton in 1791. Charles Hamilton (trans.), *The Hedàya, or Guide: A Commentary on the Mussulman Laws* (Premier Book House, 1963).

55 The discourse of an essential practices test which espouses only central or integral aspects of religion as deserving of constitutional protection acquired a doctrinal form in the Supreme Court decision of *The Commissioner, Hindu Religious Endowments, Madras* v. *Shri Lakshmindra Swamiar of Srirur Mutt*, AIR 1954 SC 282. However, the idea of compulsory religious tenets acquiring constitutional protection appears in the Constituent Assembly. To illustrate,

De points out the failure of the Supreme Court to take into consideration the caste and economic status of the Quareshi community: 'The Qureshis were *ajlafs*, or of common birth, unlike most Muslim political leaders, who belonged to the *ashraf* (aristocratic) classes and spoke Urdu.'[56] The argument of economic necessity was curtly dismissed by the Court as 'there [was] no religious compulsion.'[57] Had the Court appreciated the materiality of faith through a careful appreciation of the Qureshi caste and class, it could have considered the subtleties of the religious freedom argument instead of reducing the issue to one of monolithic religious identity. The Court failed to recognise the distinction between aristocratic non-Quareshi Muslims and non-elite Quareshi Muslims, for the economic effect of the ban was far more significant on the latter; the issue could not be reduced to just a religious identity claim.

Doctrine of Presumption of Constitutionality

After upholding the constitutionality of the ban on the grounds of religious freedom, the Court relied on the 'presumption in favour of the constitutionality of an enactment.'[58] It noted that the presumption of constitutionality of laws was based on a positive view of the legislative action in independent India, as the judiciary assumes that the legislature is best suited to understand the local conditions and that it would enact laws keeping in mind 'the needs of its own people.'[59] According to this doctrine, all laws are presumed to be constitutionally valid unless the contrary can be shown by the challenging party. The premise of the doctrine stems from the belief in democratic representation, and in the legislature as the best representative of community interests.[60] The Court therefore began with the presumption that the challenged state laws were constitutionally valid.

Seth Govind Das (a Member from then-CP and Berar, now Madhya Pradesh), during debates on Article 48, asked the Muslim members 'to come forward to make it clear that their religion does not *compulsorily* enjoin on them the slaughter of the cow.' *CADs*, note 27 at 572. Syed Muhammad Saiadulla, a Muslim Member from Assam, acknowledged in response that 'in my religious book, the Holy Qoran, there is an injunction to the Muslims saying . . . there ought to be no compulsion in the name of religion.' *Id.* at 578. Although none of the Supreme Court decisions ever referred to this exchange from the Constituent Assembly, my point in this context is that the debate on the cow slaughter as central, compulsory or essential appeared prior to the doctrine of essential practices in Indian constitutional law.

56 De, note 8 at 154. For a discussion on the status of binary and hierarchy between *ajlaf* and *ashraf* Muslims, see Imtiaz Ahmad, 'Endogamy and Status Mobility Among the Siddiqui Sheikhs of Allahabad, Uttar Pradesh' in Imtiaz Ahmad (ed.), *Caste and Social Stratification Among Muslims in India* (South Asia Books, 1978). See also Gyanendra Pandey, 'The Bigoted Julaha' 18(5) *Economic and Political Weekly* 19 (1983).

57 *Hanif Quareshi*, note 8, para 13.

58 *Id.* para 14.

59 *Id.* para 15.

60 Judicial deference to the laws made by the state legislature also emboldens the principle of separation of powers in the modern State.

Argument of Utility

Next, the Court tested the validity of the laws with a utilitarian argument. Justifying the classification of cattle based on usefulness and 'not-useful-due-to-old-age,' the Court found the laws which banned slaughter in Uttar Pradesh and Madhya Pradesh to be constitutional. By contrast, the broad phraseology of the Bihar law on the slaughter of bulls, bullocks, and buffaloes – without any reference to their utility or age – was considered unreasonable.[61] The 'age and usefulness' criterion became central to the Supreme Court's reasoning. This criterion was limited to bulls and bullocks, as the Court approved a complete ban irrespective of age and utility for cows as constitutional.[62] However, in the case of she-buffaloes, breeding bulls, and working bullocks, it compromised and permitted slaughter if they had come to the end of their usefulness.[63] This principle was upheld as an interpretation of Article 48 and thus applicable to all the states and for all laws which may be enacted in future.

Despite extolling the virtues of rationality and objectivity,[64] the Court's acceptance of Hindu religious sentiments crept into its reasoning. The Court concluded that 'Hindus in general hold cow in great reverence' and slaughter of the cow 'is repugnant to their notions and this sentiment.'[65] Although the revulsion towards cow slaughter, both pre- and post-partition, is more associated with upper-caste Hindus, not Hindus generally,[66] yet the Court's narrative collapsed any caste variances in service of its grand narrative. In the Court's construction of Hinduism, the caste question is eschewed, just as the issue of litigant specificity was made invisible by side-stepping the class and caste status of the Muslim litigants.[67] Nevertheless, the age and usefulness test for bulls and bullocks provided some latitude to various communities involved in the trade of meat and related products. However, it must be noted again that the Court distinguished cows and calves from bulls and bullocks. The test of age and usefulness was applicable only to the latter category after *Hanif Quareshi*.

61 *Hanif Quareshi*, note 8, para 15.

62 *Id.* para 45 (for a summary of conclusions by the Court: '[W]e have reached the conclusion (i) that a total ban on the slaughter of cows of all ages and calves of cows and calves of she-buffaloes, male and female, is quite reasonable and valid and is in consonance with the directive principles laid down in Art. 48.'). This point regarding the ban on cows of all ages requires emphasis, as some commentators have misread the case on this point. For instance, in an otherwise remarkable essay, De misreads the judgment when he comments with respect to *Hanif Quareshi* that the '[C]ourt did rule, however, that such a ban could not be absolute and that some categories of cattle, such as aged bulls or unproductive cows, may be slaughtered.' De, note 8 at 124. This reading is in clear contradiction with the text of Supreme Court judgment as quoted here.

63 *Ibid.*

64 *Ibid.*

65 *Ibid.*

66 Pandey, note 20.

67 De, note 8 at 166–167.

IV Legislative Responses to the Supreme Court's Judgment

In this section, I will survey and analyse various state legislatures' attempts to circumvent *Hanif Quareshi* in an assortment of ways, as well as the conflicting judicial decisions ruling on such attempts. Evaluating these conflicting decisions, this section will set the backdrop for the later judgment of *Mirzapur*,[68] which overruled all the earlier precedents – including *Hanif Quareshi* – and validated the enlarged slaughter ban on cows as well as their progeny, irrespective of their age and utility.

Circumventing the Supreme Court

The three states that were parties in *Hanif Quareshi* (Uttar Pradesh, Bihar and Madhya Pradesh) tried to bypass the age and usefulness test by setting an extremely high age threshold for slaughter in their post-*Hanif Quareshi* amended laws. This happened through legislative amendments in the state of Uttar Pradesh[69] (in 1958) and the state of Bihar (in 1959).[70] The permissible age for slaughter of she-buffaloes, bulls and bullocks was fixed at 25 years in Bihar and 20 years in Uttar Pradesh. A new piece of legislation in the state of Madhya Pradesh raised the minimum age for slaughter to 20 years.[71]

Butchers from these states challenged the excessive age thresholds, and the petitions were taken up together by the five-judge constitutional bench of the Supreme Court in *Abdul Hakim Quraishi* v. *State of Bihar* (*Abdul Hakim Quraishi*).[72] The petitioners argued that the age threshold – twenty years old or more – 'has been put so high that the practical effect is that no animals can be slaughtered.'[73] They also attributed bad faith to the legislatures for enacting these laws. This time, the Supreme Court invalidated the provisions on constitutional grounds as a violation of Article 19(1)(g), the right to practice trade and business. Accepting the petitioner's argument that the animals in question become useless after the age of 15, the Court declared Section 3 of the Bihar Act to be unreasonable.[74] In the same vein, the Court also held the 20-year age threshold in the Uttar Pradesh and Madhya Pradesh laws to be unreasonable.

The presumption of constitutionality was implicitly challenged in this case, as the petitioners alleged bad faith on the parts of the legislative bodies.

68 *Mirzapur*, note 11.

69 Uttar Pradesh Prevention of Cow Slaughter Act, 1955 (UP Act No 1 of 1956), as amended 1958.

70 Bihar Preservation and Improvement of Animals Act, 1955 (Bihar Act II of 1956), as amended 1959.

71 Madhya Pradesh Agricultural Cattle Preservation Act, 1959 (Act 18 of 1959).

72 (1961) 2 SCR 610.

73 *Id.* para 3.

74 *Id.* para 9.

However, the Court remained silent with respect to this argument. This lack of attention to the challenge to the presumption of constitutionality on account of bad faith is pertinent. The bad faith argument can be received in two ways. First, as a claim that there is bias on the part of legislature against the petitioners or the Muslim community in general. This is a difficult argument to pursue, as establishing bias against the legislature is a difficult, if not impossible, task. Second, the accusation of bad faith signifies latent discrimination where the laws in effect were meant to circumvent the *Hanif Quareshi* verdict to pursue a populist agenda. The legislative action of undoing *Hanif Quareshi* was so apparent that one wonders if the presumption that the legislature was following the constitutional spirit could remain sustainable. But for the Court it was business as usual; without acknowledging the petitioners' allegation of bad faith, the Court applied the doctrine of presumption of constitutionality and uncritically assumed that the legislative action was 'representative of the best interests of the community.'[75] This presumption prevailed, even though the legislature clearly overruled the law as laid down by the Supreme Court.

Judicial verdicts are not only about the eventual outcome, but the reasoning applied in arriving at such outcome. This is even more compelling in common law jurisdictions where the doctrine of precedent and the principle of *stare decisis* uphold legal integrity by maintaining continuity with past decisions. But material facts in this case make such continuity unnecessary. This is because the Court itself noted that the amendments made to the laws were precisely to undermine *Hanif Quareshi*. In this situation the petitioner's challenge of bad faith must have been addressed by the Court. Applying the doctrine as mere reiteration of it in *Hanif Quareshi* was inadequate to address the petitioner's challenge. Even as the *Abdul Hakim* decision produced a desirable result, it retained faith in the legislature and cemented legislative innocence into a legal principle by applying the presumption of constitutional validity.

On January 12, 1967, the Governor of the state of Madhya Pradesh issued a public notification prohibiting the slaughter of 'bulls and bullocks' at the Madar Tekdi slaughterhouse in Jabalpur.[76] Mohammad Faruk challenged this prohibition in the Supreme Court under Article 32,[77] as the notification adversely affected his occupation.[78] In *Faruk*, a constitutional bench of the Supreme Court found the notification to be violating Faruk's fundamental right to practice trade and business as espoused in Article 19(1)(g). The Court

75 *Id.* para 7.

76 Madhya Pradesh Municipal Corporation Act, 1956 (Act 23 of 1956), s 430. Prior to this notification, the state's by-laws permitted the slaughter of bulls and bullocks, along with buffaloes, sheep, goats, and pigs in premises which were fixed by the state government. The notification cancelled the by-laws to the extent that they related to bulls and bullocks.

77 Article 32 of the Indian Constitution vests the Supreme Court with original jurisdiction in cases regarding the violation of fundamental rights.

78 *Faruk*, note 10.

categorically denounced the government's attempt to subvert judicial outcomes. The Court noted that attempts were repeatedly made 'to circumvent the judgment of this court in *Mohd. Hanif Quareshi's* case.'[79] This notification was '***another attempt***, though on a restricted scale' (emphasis added).[80] This was a direct indictment by the highest court of the state government for its repeated attempts to undermine *Hanif Quareshi* in the guise of pursuing the constitutional mandate regarding cow protection.[81] The Supreme Court, contrary to its previous judgments, repudiated the presumption of constitutionality of laws. It held that the state government must prove the constitutionality of cow protection laws without the benefit of the presumption of constitutionality:[82]

> When the validity of a law placing restriction upon the exercise of fundamental rights in Article 19 (1) is challenged, the onus of proving to the satisfaction of the Court that the restriction is reasonable lies upon the State.

This statement from *Faruk* has been neglected by both legal commentators and later judicial decisions.[83] Although the judgment was delivered by a constitutional bench, Indian constitutional law scholarship entirely misses *Faruk*'s radical reversal of the presumption of constitutionality.[84] The stricter evaluation of the legislative enactments in *Faruk* which refuses to accord a mythological status to the doctrine of presumption of constitutionality emerged from judicial appreciation of socio-historical circumstances within which cow slaughter laws were enacted.

Viewed in this light, *Faruk* can be seen as a judicial effort to resist succumbing to abstract and universal doctrinaire rules, inaugurating an understanding of judicial doctrines as *contingent* rather than universal. This opened the possibility, for the future, of situating the doctrine of

79 *Id.* para 5.

80 *Id.* para 6. The reference to 'restricted scale' indicated that this was an executive order and not a piece of legislation or legislative amendment.

81 It is no coincidence that, in 1966, there was a collective demonstration of 'several hundred thousand people in favour of a national ban on cow slaughter.' D.N. Jha, *The Myth of the Holy Cow* 19 (Navayana, 2009).

82 *Faruk*, note 10, para 8.

83 The relinquishing of the presumption of validity in *Faruq* originated from the specific, contingent historical circumstances arising from the trend of state legislatures trying to subvert the ruling in *Hanif Quareshi*.

84 H.M. Seervai, for example, merely mentions this decision without any comment on the change of interpretive stance. H.M. Seervai, *Constitutional Law of India* 837–838 (vol. I, Law & Justice Publishing Co, 2021). M.P. Singh's textbook also does not accord this decision the importance it attained in the context of Article 48 interpretation. Perhaps that explains its absence from the discussion on Article 48. See M.P. Singh, *V.N. Shukla's Constitution of India* 132, 184, 368 (Eastern Book Company, 2013).

presumption of constitutionality differently – at least in the limited context of anti-cow-slaughter legislation. The Court's rejection of an uncritical reliance on the presumption of constitutional validity was not based on doctrinaire wisdom; it instead (tacitly) considered the history of the legislative–judicial struggle regarding the ambit of State power under Article 48. This is an important milestone, as anti-slaughter laws have a Hindu majoritarian sentiment which can in turn undermine the democratic law-making process.[85] The Supreme Court in *Faruk* limited the populist legislative impulse by imposing a 'heavy burden' on the State.[86] The State must establish that a 'less drastic' measure (than banning slaughter) would be insufficient to achieve its purpose. This alternative route strengthened constitutionalism by imposing limitations on State power. Unfortunately, this approach was neglected in future decisions, and the decision's potential to create an alternative constitutional interpretation of Article 48 never came to fruition. Instead, the Court gave in to the temptation of populist sentiments, as I will show now.

Reversal of Constitutional Logic

In 1982, the state of West Bengal granted an exemption to the Muslim community for a cow sacrifice for the Bakr-Eid festival. Section 12 of the West Bengal Animal Slaughter Control Act 1950 recognised 'religious purpose' as a valid ground for such an exemption. A writ petition was filed by 27 Hindu petitioners in the then-Calcutta High Court (now Kolkata). The High Court decision favoured the petitioners, reasoning that cow sacrifice was not a necessary requirement in Islam. In 1994, the state government and some members of the Muslim community appealed to the Supreme Court in *State of WB v Ashutosh Lahiri (Ashutosh Lahiri)*.[87] The appellants argued that the phrase 'religious purpose' under Section 12 could not be interpreted as 'essential' religious purpose and must be understood as 'any' religious purpose. The Court wrongly rejected this argument, relying on *Hanif Quareshi*: since cow slaughter is 'optional' and not 'mandatory' in Islam, the State has no mandate to fulfil an optional religious purpose.[88]

In this case, the state had granted permission for the sacrifice of cows on Bakr-Eid. This was not a violation of any fundamental right, but the judicial reasoning fallaciously transformed an *enabling* directive principle into an *enforceable* right. This is because, following this verdict, citizens can approach

85 Austin, note 23 at 82.
86 *Faruk*, note 10, para 8.
87 (1995) 1 SCC 189.
88 Even from a strictly legal standpoint, *Hanif Quareshi* was the wrong precedent to cite in this case, as there was no issue of the violation of specific fundamental rights.

the court if the provision, in their opinion, is insufficiently implemented. Consider the Court's observation:

> [I]t becomes obvious that if there is no fundamental right of a Muslim to insist on slaughter of healthy cow[s] on BakrI'd day, it cannot be valid ground for exemption by the State under Section 12[,] which would in turn enable slaughtering of such cows on BakrI'd.[89]

The obliviousness of what is 'obvious' to the Supreme Court leads to a constitutional anomaly. Had it been a practice essential to Islam, then no exemption would have been required in the first place. In such an event, it would have been a claim-right of the Muslim community guaranteed by the free exercise of religion clause (Article 25), barring the State from enacting any law against it.[90] Put simply, Article 48 only enables the State to take steps towards cow protection; the State cannot be forced to follow this mandate. In this case, the state of West Bengal had permitted a partial exemption to the ban on cow slaughter, but the Court declared the exemption unconstitutional. Here, it may be noted that in enforcing the ban on cow slaughter, the Court in effect enforced Article 48 – which is not a fundamental right. The discourse of the Court thus erased this federal diversity – or even antagonism – in the implementation of anti-slaughter laws by the reversal of constitutional logic. The judgment provided an impetus to any citizen to approach the judiciary for enforcing the non-enforceable constitutional provision in the future.

V The *Mirzapur* Case: An Expansion of the Slaughter Ban

In this section, I will briefly outline the background leading to the formation of a seven-judge bench of the Indian Supreme Court in *Mirzapur*, which reviewed the existing case law and interpreted Article 48 in the light of scientific developments.[91] This is by far the largest bench of the Supreme Court to have interpreted Article 48. I will critically evaluate the *Mirzapur* decision and its reasons for overturning *Hanif Quareshi* in expanding the ambit of a complete ban, irrespective of age or utility, on the slaughter of bulls and bullocks. To appreciate this constitutional approval for an extended ban on slaughter, we need to discuss another case, which serves as a backdrop to *Mirzapur*.

Another attempt to expand the slaughter ban is illustrated in the case of *Hashmatullah* v. *State of MP* (*Hashmatullah*).[92] An amendment in Madhya Pradesh, the Agricultural Cattle Preservation Act, 1959, inserted 'bulls and

89 *Ashutosh Lahiri*, note 87, para 9.

90 Article 13 of the Indian Constitution prohibits any law that purports to take away or even abridge any constitutionally guaranteed fundamental right.

91 *Mirzapur*, note 11.

92 (1996) 4 SCC 391.

bullocks' into the category of prohibited slaughter.[93] This led to an absolute ban on the slaughter of bulls and bullocks, irrespective of their age and usefulness.[94] The Supreme Court invalidated the inclusion of 'bulls and bullocks' as 'an unreasonable restriction on the fundamental rights of the appellants.'[95] The judgment indicted the state legislature for its repeated[96] attempts to bypass the law laid down in *Hanif Quareshi* on 'flimsy grounds.'[97] The Court also noted the irrelevance of the supporting material – advocating for expanding the total ban on grounds of its utility – which provided the impetus for bringing this amendment.[98] Nevertheless, it remained silent, and did not reiterate the principled position followed in *Faruk*, regarding the reversal of burden of proof. I will show in the next section how, in the *Mirzapur* case, this silence exacerbated the bypassing of this important principled position.

In *Haji Usmanbhai Hasan Bhai Qureshi & Others* v. *State of Gujarat* (*Haji Usmanbhai Qureshi*),[99] the Court dealt with the matter of the Bombay Animal Preservation Act 1964, which extended to the state of Gujarat and was amended in 1979.[100] This amendment increased the age threshold for the slaughter for bulls and bullocks to 16. This was challenged by the petitioners, who were butchers and traded in beef and beef-related items. They argued that bulls and bullocks ceased to be of any value once they reached the age of 15. The Supreme Court, however, upheld the amendment. It accepted the state of Gujarat's argument that scientific advancements had lengthened the cattle's useful lifespan.[101]

This judgment provided an impetus for yet another amendment to the Bombay Animal Preservation Act in 1994 by the Gujarat state legislature (the

93 Madhya Pradesh Agricultural Cattle Preservation (Amendment) Act, 1991 (Act No 21 of 1991). This amendment added 'bulls and bullocks' under s. 4(1) (a) of the 1959 Act. Prior to this amendment bulls and bullocks did not fall under the slaughter ban because their slaughter was permissible after obtaining due certification from the competent authority.

94 The case can be seen as part of a continuous attempt on the part of the state of Madhya Pradesh to bypass the age and usefulness formula set forth in *Hanif Quareshi*.

95 *Hashmatullah*, note 92, para 22.

96 The Court noted that it was the state's fourth attempt to entirely ban the slaughter of bulls and bullocks, even when they were of no further use.

97 *Hashmatullah*, note 92, para 19. ('We are pained to notice the successive attempts made by the state of Madhya Pradesh to nullify the effect of this Court's decisions beginning with *Mohd Hanif's* case and ending with *Mohd Faruk's* case, each time on flimsy grounds.')

98 *Ibid* ('It is obvious that successive attempts are being made in the hope that some day it will succeed as indeed it did with the High Court which got carried away by research papers published only two or three years before without realising that they . . . had nothing to do with the question of the utility of animals which have ceased to be reproductive or capable of being used as draught animals. Besides, they do not even reflect on the economical aspect of maintaining such animals for the sole purpose of dung. Prima facie it seems far fetched and yet the State Government thought it as sufficient to amend the law.').

99 (1986) 3 SCC 12.

100 Bombay Animal Preservation (Gujarat Amendment) Act, 1979.

101 *Haji Usmanbhai Qureshi*, note 99, para 17.

1994 Amendment). The 1994 Amendment extended the slaughter prohibition to 'bulls and bullocks' of all ages. Previously, such complete prohibition was limited to cows and calves, as discussed previously. The High Court of Gujarat invalidated this State action as unconstitutional.[102] The state of Gujarat, with one of the interveners, preferred a special leave petition in the Supreme Court. A five-judge bench of the Court referred this case to a larger bench, because the appellants had implored the Court to revisit *Hanif Quareshi*. This led to the formation of the seven-judge bench.

In *Mirzapur*, this seven-judge bench of the Supreme Court upheld the 1994 Amendment as 'reasonable.' In so doing, the *Mirzapur* majority expanded the category of complete prohibition on slaughter to cow offspring, irrespective of their sex, age or utility. This new interpretation of Article 48 was different to and reversed all the previous interpretations. The majority decision observed that the words 'other milch and draught cattle' in Article 48 refer to similar species of cow. Thus, like cows and calves, it argued, the entire 'cow progeny' deserved complete constitutional protection.[103] The Supreme Court also affirmed that a total ban aligned with the constitutional principle of environmental protection (Article 48-A) as well as the fundamental duty to protect living creatures (Article 51-A(g)). The Court was also persuaded by the scientific advancement and national interest arguments, and it once again resorted to the presumption of constitutionality doctrine. I will briefly comment on each of these aspects in order to demonstrate how this legal reasoning elides the socio-political context and its own principle as laid down in *Faruk*. In operating with a constricted, self-enclosed vision of law, the Court's reasoning highlights a secular mythology. The Court eschewed the socio-political context in which these laws were enacted to pursue Hindu nationalism. It even ignored its own judicial precedent in *Faruk*. In so doing, the presumption accorded to these laws was imagined as if the anti-slaughter principle were a universal and an unquestioned good. It is this abstract universalism which ignores the contingent socio-political factors which inadvertently aligned the reasoning of the Court with the vocabulary of Hindu nationalists who refuse to particularise anti-slaughter sentiment and reverence for the cow.[104]

102 *Mirzapur Moti Kureshi Kassab Jamat* v. *State of Gujarat and Others* AIR 1998 (Guj) 220.

103 *Id.* para 65.

104 See Cassie Adcock, 'Preserving and Improving the Breeds: Cow Protection's Animal-Husbandry Connection,' 42 *South Asia: Journal of South Asian Studies* 1141 (2019) (arguing that the universal plank of breed protection has historically been linked with violence in the name of cow protection); Cassie Adcock and Radhika Govindrajan, 'Bovine Politics in South Asia: Rethinking Religion, Law and Ethics' 42 *South Asia: Journal of South Asian Studies* 1095 (2019) (arguing that the Hindu cow protectionist orthodoxy pursue their cause as a universal ethical commitment eschewing the specific element of violence which appears in the political context).

The Presumption of Constitutionality as Secular Mythology

The decisions before *Mirzapur* had (correctly) attempted to strike a balance between Article 48 and Article 19(1)(g). *Mirzapur* overturned these precedents on the grounds of scientific advancements which extended cattle's useful lifespan. The Court was convinced that the argument for advancing the 'national interest' (protecting cows) should supersede the claim of 'community interest' (pursuing trade and occupation).[105]

Mirzapur found continuity with *Hanif Quareshi* in its consolidation of the doctrine of presumption of constitutionality. For the Court, the legislature necessarily represented the constituency's interests; thus, the enactment itself had to be presumed to represent the community's needs:[106]

> The Court would begin with a presumption of reasonability of the restriction, more so when the facts stated in the Statement of Objects and Reasons and the Preamble are taken to be correct and they justify the enactment of law for the purpose sought to be achieved.

How far is such a presumption constitutionally desirable without an analysis of the specifics of the affected persons? Cow protection laws in India were, and still are, interlaced with political ideology. Ironically, the *Mirzapur* decision undercut the Court's own observation that the courts must take 'into consideration . . . history of the times and matters of common knowledge and the circumstances existing at the time of the legislation.'[107] In other words, the Court overlooked the fact that various state governments on many earlier occasions had attempted to circumvent judicial verdicts based on justifications which the Supreme Court itself described as 'flimsy.'

More importantly, this proposition is in direct contradiction with the Court's own observations in *Faruk,* where the burden was imposed on the State to prove that a total ban was necessary and compelling. *Faruk* was of immediate relevance, as it dealt with the slaughter ban on bulls and bullocks.[108] But despite approvingly citing *Faruk,* the Court entirely ignored the proposition put forth in that case. This methodological approach of paying insufficient attention to precedent also raises the question of the blind spots of the judicial process. It is this universalist application of the doctrine of presumption of validity of laws, even at the risk of circumventing binding precedent, that I term the doctrinaire secular mythology of the Supreme Court.

105 *Mirzapur*, note 11, para 41.

106 *Id.* para 71.

107 *Id.* para 39.

108 The difference between the two cases is that *Faruk* was concerned with an executive order, whereas the slaughter ban of bulls and bullocks was imposed through an amendment in this case. The methodological flaw lies in the application of the doctrine without engaging with *Faruk* (which is approved and not overruled here).

I describe this posture of the Court as mythological because it applies the doctrine of presumption of constitutionality with a reverence for doctrinaire wisdom without paying attention to socio-political contexts. I propose that constitutional interpretation must be attentive to the historical and political contexts, rather than applying universal claims of truth as doctrine. This explains how the specific contexts – social, political, historical, cultural, economic – in which the laws were enacted were sacrificed to the abstract categories (or empty signifiers), such as the 'national interest,' evoked by the Court in *Mirzapur*. In the same vein, the Court discursively invoked the notions of 'gratitude' and 'compassion' for animals, reinforcing this slippage. Slaughtering animals in their 'old age' is described in the majority judgment as 'an act of reprehensible ingratitude.'[109] The Court gave its assent to and endorsed a total ban on cow progeny by evoking the fundamental duty of all citizens under Article 51-A(g) to 'protect and improve the natural environment including forests, lakes, rivers, and wildlife, and to have compassion for living creatures.'[110] Again, this plea for 'compassion' is misdirected. The temptation which must be resisted here is to read this discursive shift of the Court as 'ecological legal thinking' adapting itself beyond anthropocentrism towards an Anthropocene jurisprudence.[111] Such a reading would obfuscate the fact that such eco-law cannot be reserved only for cattle, especially when judicial discourse relies on constitutional provisions which mandate protection of the environment and all living creatures. On these terms, what would stop an extension of this logic to buffaloes or goats or sheep? Or, following the abstract logic of the judgment, why should *ingratitude* be permitted against other 'living creatures'? The Court, fallaciously, roped the anti-slaughter laws into the larger ambit of environmental protection to read them in harmony with Article 48-A.[112] However, neither the preamble nor the statement of objects of the 1994 Amendment talks about environmental protection as even a secondary aim of the legislation. But the Court continued to follow the broad interpretive logic to include even Article 48-A, which deals with preservation of the environment, in harmony with Article 48.[113]

In the same way, the majority opinion was impressed by the fact, cited twice, that '[f]armers love their bullocks'.[114] But the Court never deliberated why, if farmers deeply loved their aged cow progeny, the State would need

109 *Mirzapur*, note 11, para 67.

110 Constitution of India, Article 51(A(g)).

111 P.D. Burdon, 'Ecological Law in the Anthropocene' 11 *Transnational Legal Theory* 33 (2020); on the notion of eco-law, see generally Margaret Davies, *EcoLaw: Legality, Life, and the Normativity of Nature* (Routledge, 2022).

112 Article 48-A of the Constitution reads, 'Protection and improvement of environment and safeguarding of forests and wildlife. The State shall endeavour to protect and improve the environment and to safeguard the forests and wildlife of the country.'

113 *Mirzapur*, note 11, para 50.

114 *Id.* para 86.

legislation to ban slaughter, as the farmer would not sell it for slaughter in the first place. James Staples, in his ethnographic analysis of beef trading in South India, illustrates the role played by wilful ignorance at all levels of the beef trade in Andhra Pradesh and Telangana. He introduces the notion of 'ambivalence of love,' noting that beef eaters and cattle traders baulk at the idea of eating their own animals or even selling them in the market for consumption.[115] But he acknowledges the limits of this kinship tie, as the animals are not always treated well, and excessive labour demands made of them were commonplace.

This emphasis on the ambivalence of love is important as it destabilises the near-monolithic account of love and hatred aligned with a concern for ecology provided by the Court. In fact, the Court's reasoning sits well with vigilante cow protectionists (*gau rakshaks*) whose acts of violence are done in the name of love for the cow. Hindu nationalists do not pursue their cause as a political one, but as one which juxtaposes its religious reverence with the ethics of care, appropriating the vocabulary of animal rights activists.[116] Undoubtedly, this claim is false, as the exclusive focus on cows belies the claim of universal ethics in the Hindu nationalist imagination. Nevertheless, one must acknowledge the strategic use of the argument in order to challenge it seriously. In papering over these nuances, the *Mirzapur* majority inadvertently became entrenched with high rhetoric, feeding into the Hindu nationalist sentiment. This approach finds its zenith in the Court's wholehearted acceptance of the hyperbolic claim in the government affidavit that 'the value of dung is much more [sic] than even the famous "Kohinoor" diamond.'[117] In these polemical abstractions and empty significations, the Court aligned constitutional interpretation with mythologisation, albeit in apparently secular terms.[118]

The Court affirmed its secular credentials as the majority opinion appreciated the absence of any theological or religious argument in the pleadings of the parties:[119]

> [W]e must state, in all fairness to the learned counsel to the parties, that no one has tried to build any argument either in defence or in opposition to the judgment appealed against by placing reliance on religion

115 James Staples, 'Blurring Bovine Boundaries: Cow Politics and the Everyday in South India' 42 *South Asia: Journal of South Asian Studies* 1127 (2019).

116 Adcock and Govindrajan, note 104.

117 *Mirzapur*, note 11, para 83.

118 In his dissent, A.K. Mathur, J. struck a different chord. He questioned the bland description in the government of Gujarat's affidavits, which he asserted deserved to be taken with a 'pinch of salt' due to their internal inconsistencies. *Id.* para 170. Nevertheless, by majority, the Supreme Court posited a new law for the whole of India, when the material in the case was largely specific to the state of Gujarat.

119 *Id.* para 22.

However, viewing the 'economic' or 'ecological' argument about the cow as an instance of the Court's 'secular' approach would be a mistake. This is because the Court's position was rooted in a certain kind of faith which continued to bind the judicial discourse surrounding the cow. The majority's deferential use of the presumption of constitutionality doctrine – while the dissent stayed silent on this issue – demonstrated a profound faith in legislative wisdom. In this universalist affirmation of legislative actions, the judicial narrative placed an alternative faith in, and deference to, enacted law, even as it sought to eclipse religious or faith-based arguments. Such a heightened protection of the legislative enactments, coupled with abstract invocations of national interest, environmental protection, compassion and love served as the Court's secular mythology. It foreclosed the possibility of fathoming or foreseeing the dilution of existing constitutional protections for minorities in the secular polity by such legislative actions. Indeed, the absence of faith-based arguments in the pleadings (especially for the appellants) curiously resonated with the Arya Samaj in the nineteenth-century cow protection discourse where, as C.S. Adcock argues, the religious and the sacred were enveloped craftily within the economic argument.[120]

This is not to suggest any ulterior motive on the part of the judges, but rather to underline the affective role that abstractions can play in preventing the judicial process from adhering to its own norms, standards and rules of interpretation. This is also not to suggest that the Court could not have applied the presumption of constitutionality, but rather that the Court should have clearly distinguished the present case from *Faruk* or overruled the latter as a larger bench. The Court did neither in arriving at the eventual outcome. Instead, it ratified the state of Gujarat's hyperbolic assertion comparing cow dung with the Kohinoor diamond: stark testimony of the secular mythology of the Court.

120 Adcock, note 18 at 298. Adcock highlights a unique hurdle that legal historiography faces in ex-colonial societies because of the transplantation of an alien legal system. Adcock exposes the absence of any clear distinction between 'religion' and 'secularism' in nineteenth-century India, as they existed in the Euro-Western imagination. She outlines how the Arya Samaj relied upon the notion of 'dharma' in nineteenth-century India. 'Dharma' is a Sanskrit term which elides an easy translation in European language. This is because it simultaneously inhabits the notion of material prosperity, righteousness, and salvation. The material and the spiritual are yoked together culturally. Adcock analyses the vernacular (Hindi) pamphlets and English-language literature circulated by the Arya Samaj in the nineteenth century. She demonstrates that the dual idiom of 'dharma' was dexterously used in the speeches and writings of Dayananda Saraswati. He conveyed different meanings by using the same word. In the English literature of the Arya Samaj, written for the British colonial administration, the term strictly adheres to the material and utilitarian benefits of the cow, whereas, in vernacular Hindi, a different meaning was conveyed which infused a religious flavour as well. The purpose of this exercise is not to attribute fraudulent intent, but to emphasise the 'politics of translation' of the mythic term dharma on a secular register. See C.S. Adcock, 'Sacred Cows and Secular History: Cow Protection Debates in Colonial North India' 3 *Comparative Studies of South Asia, Africa and the Middle East* 297 (2010).

Conclusion

I opened this with Fitzpatrick's insight that the 'transcendental' dimension of the mythic worldview is only substituted, and not annulled, in modernity and modern law.[121] His formulation insists on the reversal of transcendence, or displacement of the mythic into the 'fantastic stories devised in the names of reason and history at the cost, or denigration of the non-western "other."'[122] The analysis in this chapter establishes continuity with this colonial logic in post-colonial constitutional practices in India with respect to anti-cow-slaughter laws, with the substitution of religious and caste minorities for the 'non-western other.'[123]

However, there exists an alternative possibility within the law which contests the deference of this interpretation. I have argued that *Faruk* presented such a possibility. Unfortunately, this interpretive approach flared only briefly within the judicial discourse and then vanished. Nevertheless, it continues to represent an alternative, historically informed jurisprudence: this requires a critical rereading of the law as a socio-political-affective discourse which does not shy away from pointing out and engaging with the hidden motivations that govern the process of law making. In this rereading, it is not the mask of secularity but rather the mythological supplement inherent in the secular reasoning that deserves real scrutiny for a nuanced comprehension of the uneasy coexistence of contemporary cow vigilantism and secular constitutionalism in India.

121 Fitzpatrick, note 3 at 36. ('The profane is swept up into a sacred . . . as a project and a progression towards that resolution. For the perfection of beginnings in pre-modern myth is substituted the perfection of ending.')

122 *Id.* at 46, 48.

123 On the effect of cow protection laws on caste groups and their protests, see Shivani Kapoor, '"Your Mother, You Bury Her": Caste, Carcass and Politics in Contemporary India' 3 *Pakistan Journal of Historical Studies* 5 (2018); Surinder S. Jodhka and Murli Dhar, 'Cow, Caste, and Communal Violence: Dalit Killings in Jhajjar' 38(3) *Economic & Political Weekly* 174 (2003).

3 Religion and Elections

Legal Interpretation of Hinduism as Religion

Introduction

Elections in India present a moment when the spectres of religious symbolism and religious identities incessantly surface on the political spectrum. While this fact informs commonplace knowledge of the Indian electoral scene, the Indian election law prohibits soliciting votes or any electoral gain through religious appeal. This chapter focusses on this prohibition in Indian election law and the judicial discourse around it. My inquiry is limited to a single statutory provision in Indian law which prohibits the invocation of religion ('religious appeal') during elections: Section 123 (3) of the Representation of People Act 1951 (RPA). This statutory provision forbids any religious invocation for soliciting votes leading to any electoral gain. I will show how the dominant strand of judicial interpretation in ascribing meaning to this provision ends up suffocating the very *elan vital*, the purpose of the prohibition.

Religion in the arena of electoral politics appears in its outwardly manifested form, not as an inquiry of inwardness.[1] Nevertheless, I will show that the courts have ventured into the inward, deeper meanings of religious symbols and speech. When the courts are called upon to enquire if religious appeals made during electoral campaigns are 'corrupt', the judicial scrutiny of 'religion' rests on superficial excavation of theological meanings and mythical exegesis, almost obliterating the primary objective of the law which is to outlaw appropriation of religion for material electoral gains. I will illustrate how the judicial interpretation of religion generally, and Hinduism specifically, has led to a rigid identity formation of the category of religion. The consolidation of Hindu religious identity is shaped, ironically, by highlighting the fluid, non-definable and effervescent features of Hinduism. This has contributed to strengthening Hindu identity as a militant project of the nation-state. I will

1 Jonardon Ganeri provides a useful analysis of a variety of religious traditions to expound, expand and explicate the notion of inwardness. See Jonardon Ganeri, *Inwardness: An Outsider's Guide* (Columbia University Press, 2021).

DOI: 10.4324/9781003398561-4

show this through a scrutiny of judicial interpretation in post-independence cases, culminating with the well-known decisions of the Supreme Court of India delivered in 1996, popularly called the *Hindutva Judgments.*[2]

The Supreme Court of India through the *Hindutva Judgments* has, wittingly or unwittingly, legitimised the sectarian and political appeals to Hinduism during elections. These judgments have been extensively studied by both social scientists and lawyers to understand the socio-political role of the Supreme Court in shaping the democratic polity of independent India.[3] However, predominantly in this scholarly terrain the *Hindutva Judgments* are viewed and analysed as stand-alone judicial pronouncements, unconnected with the archive of judicial precedents on election law[4] which has shaped their ultimate outcome. The *Hindutva Judgments* follow a pattern of precedents which must be examined to fully appreciate the judicial logic of these cases as well as Section 123 (3) of RPA. These decisions reveal the judicial tendency of insisting on theological/deeper meanings of religious motifs, even though the inquiry under RPA must be based on whether the invoked religious appeal (irrespective of its theological meaning and significance) sought to 'corrupt' the secular and democratic process. I will argue that the judicial interpretation obfuscates the political context in which the expression 'religious appeal' appears. Further, this mystification of the meaning of religious symbol/appeal signifies a return of the repressed polymorphous attributes of what came to be consolidated as 'Hindu' religion during the colonial encounter. As an ex-colonial society, the Indian political formation carries an anxiety around the question of religion generally and the Hindu religion in particular – the fact that Hinduism was always associated with animistic practices which could not fall within the contours of religion as understood in the Abrahamic and Euro-western contexts. This colonial anxiety, I will argue, has inspired the quest for

2 *Dr. Ramesh Yeshwant Prabhoo* v. *Prabhakar Kashinath Kunte* along with *Bal Thackeray* v. *Prabhakar Kashinath Kunte & Others* (1996) 1 SCC 130 (Hereafter, '*First Hindutva Judgment*'); *Ramachandra G. Kapse* v. *Haribansh Ramakbal Singh* (1996) 1 SCC 206 ('*Second Hindutva Judgment*') and *Murli Manohar Joshi* v. *Nitin Bhaurao Patil* (1996) 1 SCC 169 ('*Third Hindutva Judgment*').

3 See Ratna Kapur and Brenda Cossman, *Secularism's Last Sigh: Hindutva and the (Mis) Rule of Law* (Oxford University Press, New Delhi, 2001); Anil Nauriya, 'The Hindutva Judgments: A Warning Signal' 31(1) *EPW* 10–13 (1996); Arvind Narain and Mathew John, 'The Hindutva Judgments: A Comment' 9(1) *National Law School Journal* 174–177 (1997). Saumya Saxena, '*Court'ing Hindu Nationalism*: Law and the Rise of Modern *Hindutva*' 26(4) *Contemporary South Asia* 378–399 (2018).

4 Many legal scholars have shown that the ratio in the *Hindutva judgments* is traceable to a misappropriation of the 'way of life metaphor' used for Hinduism in *Shastri Yagnapurushadji* v. *Muldas Bhudardas Vaishya*, AIR 1966 SC 1119. See Ronojoy Sen, *Articles of Faith: Religion, Secularism, and the Indian Supreme Court* (Oxford University Press, New Delhi, 2010); Kapur and Cossman, note 3. However, no attention is given to the fact that the interpretive logics of election law cases in which the courts resorted to interpreting religious symbols and appeals through spiritual and mythical lens, divorced from the highly charged electoral context of material gains, paved the way for the *Hindutva judgments.*

deeper meanings, the ***hidden kernel*** of the religious categories or symbolic representations. To pursue this argument, I will track the anxious traces appearing in the court judgments dealing with the use of religious symbolism or religious speech during elections.

Gary Jeffrey Jacobsohn, while comparing the Indian conception of secularism with other jurisdictions, has devoted considerable attention to the legal provision prohibiting the invocation of religion during elections under RPA and its judicial interpretation.[5] He highlights the unique vocabulary of RPA designating the use of religion in political speech as 'corrupt speech'. Such a formulation is unthinkable in the context of the United States (US). This is because, he explains, the idea of electoral corruption in the US primarily invokes the issues of campaign funding by private corporations.[6] This makes Section 123 (3) of RPA exclusive to India, where the schism forged by religion can be traced to the blood-stained birth of the Indian republic and the partition of the subcontinent on a religious basis in 1947. The historical contingency of this provision is also noted in one of the judgments of the Indian Supreme Court, to which we will return at length later, in the following words:[7]

> Our political history made it particularly necessary that these [religious] differences, which can generate powerful emotions, depriving people of their powers of rational thought and action, should not be permitted to be exploited lest the imperative conditions for the preservation of democratic freedoms are disturbed.

The foregrounding of Indian political history explains why religious rhetoric is forbidden and is described as a 'corrupt practice' which is potentially corrosive of democratic principles. Perhaps, the prior quote from the Court is reminiscent of the caste discrimination and partition of the Indian subcontinent on religious lines as constitutive historical antecedents of the Indian Constitution itself. Significantly, the US, which cherishes its secular democratic credentials, does not, and as Jacobsohn notes *cannot*, have a similar restrictive provision in its election law. Jacobsohn argues that a similar provision cannot stand the constitutional scrutiny in the United States:[8]

> [S]tructural inequalities are in India directly and profoundly implicated in religious belief and practice, they can only be addressed through

5 See Gary Jeffery Jacobsohn, *The Wheel of Law: India's Secularism in Comparative Constitutional Context* (Princeton University Press, Princeton, NJ, 2003), Chs. 6 & 7.

6 The controversial judicial verdict in this context remains the sharply divided opinions in *Citizens United* v. *Federal Election Commission* 558 U.S. 310 (2010). For a critical discussion, see Wendy Brown, *Undoing the Demos: Neoliberalism's Stealth Revolution* (Zone Books, 2015), Ch. 5.

7 *Ziyauddin Burhanuddin Bukhari* v. *Brijmohan Ramdass Mehra & Ors.* (1976) 2 SCC 17, para 9 (Hereafter '*Bukhari*').

8 Jacobsohn, note 5 at 163.

> policies that limit religious freedom – possibly including speech – in ways that would not pass constitutional scrutiny in a polity such as the United States, where religion is much less of a factor in configuring the shape of the temporal world.

The statutory prohibition on religious speech during elections thus has a unique history.[9] Jacobsohn is accurate to remark that the legal prohibition of religious speech in elections cannot be appreciated through the abstract liberal principles of political theory[10] which presuppose a neat separation between the public and the private sphere, relegating religion to the latter.[11] A deep linkage between socio-economic inequalities and religious practices justifies the State regulation of religious freedom in India. It is precisely the

> disappearance [between the religious and the secular] that, in the case of India, renders problematic . . . the application of Rawlsian public reasoning, which, predicated on the existence of a distinct secular realm, insists on separating what may be indivisible.[12]

The same is true for caste (which is a product of religion in India and is also a prohibited category under Section 123 (3) of RPA). This makes the role of religion more complex in India than it is understood in the discourse of political liberalism. Therefore, it is not the commitment to political liberalism but the specific historical context that has shaped Indian constitutional philosophy and made the statutory regulation of incendiary religious speech in elections a desirable legislative goal.[13] This specific historical context, I will argue, requires the courts to eschew the temptation of uncovering the hidden kernel of religious symbols/appeal that lie beneath its overt form.

9 See Upendra Baxi, 'Savarkar and the Supreme Court' cited in Ronojoy Sen, *Legalizing Religion: The Indian Supreme Court & Secularism*, Policy Studies East-West Centre, Monograph Series (East West Centre, Washington, DC, 2007). Baxi describes these provisions of the Representation of Peoples Act as 'governance-oriented secularism.' He distinguishes them from the 'rights-oriented secularism' which 'entails a complex interface between rights to religion and other related rights.' Governance-oriented secularism deals with the anti-democratic features that exist alongside democratic processes of governance. Baxi insists on the distinction as the 'main focus here is with the preservation of the integrity of secular governance structures and processes.' *Id.* at 48.

10 'Indian restrictions on religious speech can be justified according to content-neutral principles that conform to contemporary conceptualizations of the liberal State; but those principles do not readily conform to the non-neutrality of the Indian State as delineated in the nation's Constitution.' *Id.* at 179.

11 See generally John Rawls, *Political Liberalism* (Columbia University Press, New York, 1996).

12 *Id.* at 171–172, fn. 36.

13 This is in continuation of my argument in Chapter 1, where we evaluated the permissible limitations on the religious freedom clause on the ground of 'social reform' generally and against caste discrimination in particular.

I. Election Law and Religious Rhetoric

RPA is a single comprehensive legislation governing election law in India at Union (or federal) as well as state levels.[14] Section 123 (3) prohibits

> the appeal by a candidate or his agent . . . to vote or refrain from voting for any person on the ground of his religion, race, caste, community or language or the use of, or appeal to, religious symbols . . . for the furtherance of the prospects of the candidate or for prejudicially affecting the election of any candidate.[15]

Another provision, Section 123 (3-A), was added by way of an amendment to RPA in 1961, which prohibits

> promotion of, or attempt to promote, feelings of enmity or hatred . . . on grounds of religion, race, caste, community, or language, by a candidate or his agent . . . for the furtherance of the prospects of the election.

This addition distinguished the two provisions in precise terms: while Section 123 (3) prohibits the invocation of any 'religious appeal' during electoral campaigns, Section 123 (3-A) prohibits promotion of animosity or enmity against a group of people on grounds of religion, race, caste, etc.[16]

Section 123 (3) was absent in the 1949 version of the British Representation of the People Act which formed the basis of RPA. There was no mention of religious invocation as a form of corrupt practice in the British statute of

14 Article 327 of the Constitution of India empowers the Parliament to 'make provision with respect to all matters relating to, or in connection with, elections to either House of Parliament or to the House or either House of the Legislature of a State.' The RPA was enacted under this provision. Article 324 of the Constitution of India vests the superintendence, direction and control of elections in the Election Commission.

15 Section 123(3) prohibits, among other things, religious speech and religious symbolism to enhance electoral prospects. Any person who is declared guilty of 'corrupt practice' under Section 123 (3) can be disqualified from casting vote in any election (Sections 8-A and 11-A of RPA) and his/her election can be declared void (Section 100 (1) of RPA) by the court for indulging in forbidden electoral practices.

16 It is noteworthy that there was a simultaneous addition of Section 153-A to the Indian Penal Code, 1860 (IPC), according to which promotion of 'disharmony or feelings of enmity, hatred or ill-will' is a punishable offence. After the introduction of new criminal laws in India in 2023, this section remains as it was as Section 196 of *Bhartiya Nyaya* Samhita, 2023 (BNS). The Supreme Court in the *First Hindutva case* pointed out the overlap between the two provisions. The 'difference in the plain language of the two provisions indicates that mere promotion of disharmony or ill-will between different groups of people is an offence under Section 153-A, IPC (or now 196 of BNS). while under sub-section (3A) of Section 123 of the RP Act, it is only the promotion of or attempt to promote feelings of enmity or hatred, which are stronger words, that is forbidden in the election campaign.' *First Hindutva case*, note 2, para 19.

1949. A brief historical sketch of the provision is apt to appreciate the original provision as it was in 1951 and the form it has acquired now. In its original form in 1951, RPA distinguished major and minor corrupt practices and required a 'systematic appeal' by the candidate to constitute corrupt practice. Section 124(5), which mentioned religious appeal, formed a part of 'minor' corrupt practices:

> Section 124 (5): The systematic appeal to vote or refrain from voting on grounds of caste, race, community or religion or the use of, or appeal to, religious and national symbols, such as, the national flag and the national emblem, for the furtherance of the prospects of a candidate's election.

The requirement of 'systematic appeal' made *repeated* appeals as an essential requirement for the application of this section. An isolated or solitary religious appeal was insufficient to fall within the prohibition in its original form. A fresh amendment was made to RPA by the 1956 amendment act which relinquished the distinction between minor and major corrupt practices. However, it retained the requirement of 'systematic appeal' to be made by the candidate, his agent or by 'any other person'.[17] In 1958, another somewhat technical amendment inserted the words 'with the consent of a candidate or his election agent' after 'any other person.' Still another important amendment was made in 1961 to 'widen the scope of corrupt practice' under Section 123(3). First, the word 'systematic' was removed from the section, which significantly enlarged the scope of the prohibition. Thus, post-1961, even a single or solitary appeal to religion became sufficient for an invalidation or reversal of electoral victory for any candidate. Second, 'language' was inserted as a prohibited category, another noteworthy addition although not the central concern of this chapter. Third, the pronoun 'his' was inserted in the provision to prohibit the candidate from soliciting votes 'on the ground of *his* religion, race, caste, community or language.'[18] The addition of the pronoun 'his' led to divergence in interpretation of the law which was eventually clarified by a seven-judge Supreme Court decision.[19] In what follows, I will evaluate the interpretation

17 Section 123(3) of the Act (as amended in 1956) read as follows: 'The systematic appeal by a candidate or his agent or *by any other person* to vote or refrain from voting on grounds of caste, race, community or religion or the use of, or appeal to, religious symbols . . . for the furtherance of the prospects of that candidate's election.' (emphasis added).

18 The amended Section 123 (3) now reads as follows: 'The appeal by a candidate or his agent or by any other person with the consent of a candidate or his election agent to vote or refrain from voting for any person on the ground of his religion, race, caste, community or language or the use of, or appeal to, religious symbols or the use of, or appeal to, national symbols, such as the national flag or the national emblem, for the furtherance of the prospects of the election of that candidate or for prejudicially affecting the election of any candidate.'

19 For the implication of the addition of the pronoun 'his' and the critical evaluation of its judicial interpretation, see Amit Bindal, 'Religion, Governance and Corruption: An Analysis of the Judicial Reasoning in the Election Judgment' 59(1) *Journal of Indian Law Institute* 57–77 (2017).

of 'religious' appeals under the RPA by the Supreme Court to discern the emergent pattern which eventually led to consolidation of aggressive *Hindutva* appeal as acceptable under the law. In doing so, I will also highlight an alternative counter pattern, an alterity to the dominant interpretation which appeared in a few marginal cases, in the formation of a judicial archive under Section 123 (3) of RPA.

Mythical Symbolism in Electoral Context

One of the earliest cases decided under Section 123 (3) of the RPA was *Shubnath Deogram* v. *Ram Narain*[20] (hereafter, *Shubnath*) dealing with general elections of 1957. The appellant (Shubnath) was an *adivasi* (tribal)[21] belonging to the 'Ho' community. He won his election for a seat in the Bihar Legislative Assembly. However, a controversy arose with respect to the use of the electoral symbol by the candidate. The electoral symbol allotted to his party was a rooster. His opponent (Ram Narain Yadab), a non-*adivasi* Hindu, challenged his election on the grounds of 'corrupt practice.' Ram Narain Yadab suspected and accused Shubnath of publishing and distributing two leaflets containing systematic appeals invoking religion. The constituency had a predominantly tribal electorate of members of the Ho, Munda and Oraon communities. The constituency also had a strong presence of non-tribals. All non-tribal communities (and a few tribal communities as well) were Hindi-speaking, while the Hos and the Oraons spoke their own respective languages.

> In one of the leaflets, written in Ho language but using Devanagari script, the rooster (the party symbol) sought votes in the following terms: "I am with you even after giving my life. You recover [from illness] even by applying a knife at my neck . . . In exchange give me *chara* [food] in the shape of a vote so I am victorious." This followed a divine threat of displeasure: "Do not forget me, otherwise I declare, ye sons of men will suffer eternal miseries . . . Yours only, Rooster."

Ram Narain Yadab (respondent) challenged this appeal as a camouflaged use of the official symbol with subtle religious undertones. The election tribunal dismissed his petition on technical grounds (failure to discharge the burden of proof with respect to the facts). On appeal, however, the Patna High Court reversed the tribunal's findings and considered the available evidence adduced as sufficient to prove the charge. The High Court invalidated the electoral victory of the candidate and noted that both the leaflets substantially qualified as

20 AIR 1960 SC 148 (Hereafter, '*Shubnath*').

21 *Adivasis* are indigenous peoples who are designated as 'scheduled tribes' in the Constitution of India.

prohibited religious appeals. Aggrieved by the High Court decision, Shubnath preferred an appeal to the Supreme Court.

The Supreme Court by 3:1 majority dismissed his appeal and upheld the verdict of the Patna High Court. The majority judges remarked:[22]

> [W]hen the leaflet stated that food should be given to the cock in the shape of votes what was meant was that the deities would be pleased if votes were cast in the box with the cock symbol. Further, the reference to the religious ceremonies involving the sacrifice of the cock and the alleviation of pain and miseries thereby, is clearly a reference to religion. If the meaning was not what we have stated earlier, it is difficult to understand why it was necessary to refer to the religious ceremonies for the happiness of the community involving the sacrifice of cocks . . . When the cock in the leaflet said 'give me *chara* (food) in the shape of vote', what it said in substance was that the giving of such votes would result in the deities being pleased.

The Court observed subtle religious symbolism in the appeal which implied that voting for the appellant would please the deities. For the Court, the reference to 'divine wrath' was a sufficient instance of religious appeal 'for the substance of it is that it would be an irreligious act not to vote for the party.'[23] Agreeing with Ram Narain Yadab, the Court highlighted the presence of subtle undertones of religion; an avowal of the fact that the appearance of the appeal may not seem religious, nevertheless, there is something on the margins of this appeal which gives the semblance of what we understand as religious. The majority verdict thus lends an ear to this tone and specifically the threat of divine displeasure which could not only be mythological analogy or lore. This important nuance of reading election symbols/speech was grimly lost in future cases. So much so that when the appeal of *Hindutva* – neither subtle nor camouflaged as an undertone – appeared before the Supreme Court, the Court saw it as legitimate.

Subba Rao, J. wrote a dissent in *Shubnath* and refused to read the leaflet as 'religious appeal.' The dissent distinguished the metaphorical use of mythology from religious speech:[24]

> This section is not obviously intended to prevent appeals in picturesque or metaphorical language drawing analogies from mythology, religion or folklore. *When most of the voters are illiterate*, the candidate or his agent can attract and enthuse the audience or drive home his points only by

22 A.K. Sarkar, J. (writing the judgment on behalf of S.K. Das and P.B. Gajendragadkar, JJ). *Shubnath*, note 20, para 16.

23 *Id.* para 18.

24 *Id.* para 27 (emphasis added).

> parables, similes or metaphors drawn particularly from religious lore *which most of the people understand and appreciate.* A distinction must, therefore, be drawn between canvassing on grounds of religion and seeking of votes in graphic or picturesque language with analogies from religious lore.

The dissent limited the statutory scope in its suggestion that all '[those] similes are drawn from religion, but they do not embody an appeal, directly or indirectly, to vote for the candidate on grounds of religion.'[25] In conclusion, Subba Rao, J. remarked:[26]

> [W]hat is the religion of the Adibasis? They are a backward community and they do not appear to have any highly evolved religion. *Presumably, they are all Hindus.* "The peculiarity of the Hindu religion is its universality. Along with its worship of gods, goddesses, and even of trees and snakes, there exists vedant philosophy which raise man himself to Godhood." These Adibasis, who are Hindus, appease different spirits alleged to govern different diseases and misfortunes, by sacrifices, which range from a cock to a buffalo, depending upon the magnitude of the calamity expected to be averted. It is well-known that not only Adibasis but also many other backward communities in India sacrifice animals to appease spirits and deities. The animal which is sacrificed is not an object of veneration, but only a convenient or conventional sacrificial medium. It cannot, therefore, be said that any reference to a sacrificing bird or animal is a reference to religion.

V.S. Rekhi, a legal commentator venturing an anthropological criticism of the dissent, argued:

> Levi Strauss has brought out the solidarity potential of mythical stories. Religious objects and mythical stories both perform the function of reinforcing solidarity of the candidate with the voter. The distinction between myth and sacrificial object is one without difference particularly in the context of elections.[27]

25 *Id.* para 27 ('to illustrate, a candidate may appeal to the electorate consisting of persons professing different religions, say Hindus, Mohammadans, Christians etc., to vote for him and say that he would sacrifice his life in the cause of his constituency just like Christ sacrificed his life to redeem the world. He may also say that like Rama, the virtuous, who killed Ravana, the rakshasa, the embodiment of evil, he would, if elected, put down corruption, nepotism and the like in Government. He may even say that he would sacrifice himself as a goat before Kali to being happiness and prosperity to his constituency.').

26 *Id.* para 29 (emphasis added).

27 V.S. Rekhi, 'Religion, Politics and Law in Contemporary India: Judicial Discourse in Critical Perspective' in Robert D. Baird (ed.), *Religion and Law in Independent India* 253 (Manohar Publishers and Distributors, New Delhi, 2005).

Rekhi at once is right, but also not quite. The legal astuteness of his criticism cannot be faulted. Nevertheless, it lacks unfolding of a nuance enwombed in the dissent which requires uncovering and a careful analysis.

Subba Rao, J. read the leaflet to argue that the category 'Hinduism' included a wide variety of animist practices that are not immediately locatable in 'scripture' and therefore difficult to define.[28] Various Indologists as well as post-colonial scholars have argued that the category of 'religion' as such has originated in Europe and is thoroughly modern.[29] The dissent therefore is not simply a misreading, or selective reading (as it disregards the bit on 'divine displeasure' in the leaflet). That it may very well be. The dissent foregrounds that the myth, folklore and religion are intertwined and are difficult to separate especially, though not only, in the context of the Hindu religion. There exists a practical difficulty in understanding Hinduism as a broader category which cannot be encompassed within the standard meaning of 'religion.' This interpretation took the form of Hinduism as a 'way of life' in the *Hindutva Judgments* and made possible the political appropriation of this complexity by aggressive Hindu nationalists. Thus, the dissent on Hinduism flagged by Subba Rao, J. must be noted.

Returning to the verdict, the specific context of elections provides a useful location where the broader meaning of Hinduism can lead to anomalous results. The dissent opens up the risk of all Hindu symbols per se being construed as non-religious and therefore outside the purview of the prohibited category.[30] While the dissent carved out myth and mythology as closely entwined with religion and having a thin distinguishing line, its stark limitation lies in its failure to appreciate that it is precisely this thin line of distinction which makes myth amenable to be appropriated as religious appeal in the context of elections.

Hindu Symbols During Elections

Another spectacular question arose in 1965 relating to Section 123 (3) of RPA, when the spectre of the symbol of 'Om' (which also signifies a hymn) appeared before the courts. Unlike the rooster in *Shubnath* which in and of

28 The question of codification of custom/myth/tradition was integral to the shaping of colonial modernity (as discussed in the introduction to this study).

29 See Talal Asad, *Genealogies of Religion: Disciplines and Reasons of Power in Christianity and Islam* 27–27 (John Hopkins University Press, Baltimore, 1993); Ratna Kapur, *Gender, Alterity and Human Rights: Freedom in a Fishbowl* 214–216 (Edward Elgar, Cheltenham, 2018).

30 The dissent observed that the appeal on the leaflet – that the candidate (like Lord Ram) would end the evil of corruption may not amount to an appeal to religion. The question is, what if the reference to Lord Ram were coupled with a divine threat (as it was in the present case)? The Indian Penal Code (IPC), Section 508, punishes any person inducing another 'to believe that he or any person in whom he is interested will become or will be rendered by some act of the offender an object of divine displeasure if he does not do the thing.' The recognition of 'divine displeasure' as a punishable category under IPC signifies the complex relationship of the secular law with the divine and mythological realm. The fact that fear of divine wrath can take the form of 'harm' sociologically is entirely eschewed in the dissenting view of the Supreme Court.

itself does not have any religious flavour, the case of *Jagdev Sidhanti* v. *Pratap Singh* (*Om Judgment*)[31] faced the question of interpretation of the 'Om' symbol, which by itself is a celebrated sacred syllable in classical Hinduism.

The elected candidate (Jagdev Sidhanti) had used flags with the inscription of 'Om' during the election campaign in the Jhajjar constituency of the (now) state of Haryana. The Punjab High Court invalidated the election of the candidate for violating Section 123 (3) of the RPA. For the High Court, 'Om' was unambiguously a religious symbol of the Hindus in general and of the Hindus belonging to *Arya Samaj* in particular. Therefore, the 'Om Dhwaj' (flag bearing the symbol of Om) flown during the election campaign constituted the use of religious symbolism prohibited by law. In appeal, the Supreme Court did not agree with the High Court's reasoning and overturned its verdict. The Supreme Court differentiated between an appeal on the ground of 'religion' with one invoking spiritual or mystical symbolism. It forcefully argued that 'Om' does not symbolise religion, or for that matter anything religious:[32]

> [I]t is difficult to regard 'Om' which is a preliminary to an incantation or to religious books as having religious significance. 'Om' it may be admitted is regarded as having *high spiritual or mystical efficacy*: it is used at the commencement of the recitations of religious prayers. But the attribute of *spiritual significance will not necessarily impart to its use on a flag the character of a religious symbol* in the context in which the expression religious symbol occurs in the section with which we are concerned . . . To 'Om' high spiritual or mystical efficacy is undoubtedly ascribed; but its use on a flag does not symbolise religion, or anything religious.

In making a distinction between an appeal which is spiritual/mystical as opposed to religious, the Court echoed the reasoning expounded by Subba Rao, J. in his dissent in *Shubnath*. While Subba Rao, J. disregarded the divine threat, in this case the Supreme Court discounted both the obvious association of 'Om' with Hinduism as well as the context of electoral platform where it was invoked. The judgment does not provide any specific theological reference in orchestrating the 'high spiritual or mystical efficacy' to the 'Om' symbol, which may be important to discern.

Om as 'preliminary to an incantation' most elaborately appears in the opening chapter of classic Hindu Upanishadic text of *Chandogya Upanishad*.[33] The syllable Om is considered venerable and chanted by sages of Vedas before issuing a call. 'They do so to honour this very syllable, because of its greatness and

31 AIR 1965 SC 183 [Hereafter, '*Om Judgment*'].

32 *Id.* para 13 (emphasis added).

33 Verse 1 of chapter 1 (*Adhyay* I) of *Chandogya Upanishad* describes Om as a venerable syllable as 'one begins the High Chant with Om.' Patrick Olivelle (trans.), *The Early Upanishads: Annotated Text and Translation* 171 (Oxford University Press, New York, 1998).

because it is the essence.'[34] However, the symbol/syllable of 'Om' was used in the context of an electoral campaign for gaining votes. Clearly, the mystical efficacy noted in the scriptures was of no relevance in the electoral context. Even otherwise, the commentaries on Upanishads consider a strong religious and even upper caste Brahmanical shade in the scriptural passage celebrating the Om symbol. R.D. Ranade in his 1926 classic work on Upanishadic philosophy describes these initial chapters from *Chandogya Upanishad* on the High Chant of Om as 'Brahamanical liturgy' or 'Brahamanism *redivivus.*'[35] He argues that the chapters containing a discussion on the Om chant have 'small cosmological argument here little philosophical disquisition there' but overall, they lack 'philosophical eminence.'[36] It appears that theologically the High Court seems to have appreciated the usage more appropriately. Indeed, Ranade admires the satirical anecdote towards the end of chapter 1 of *Chandogya Upanishad* regarding the singing of the Om chant done by one Baka Dalbhya with a material end in view.[37] He reads this satire on as 'a good invective against the Brahamanical belief in externalism.'[38] This serves as a good critique arising from within the scriptures for using Om for material benefits (such as elections). The usage of 'Om' in the *Om Judgment* could have benefitted a great deal by reading this satirical anecdote. This would have made it clear that the *mystical efficacy* is dented even theologically when it is employed for material gains and even more when it is used as a ploy for gains related to governance and sovereign power. Nevertheless, the reasoning in this case illustrates an emerging trend of the difficulty – or perhaps deliberate refusal – shown by the Courts in seeing the obvious. The Court superficially leaned towards deeper theological meaning, turning the obvious into oblivious and allowing more and more symbolism under the characterisation of its being mystical/spiritual, rather than 'religious.'

This juxtaposition of mythological and the religious appeal emerged once again before the Apex Court in 1965 in the case of *Ramanbhai Ashabhai Patel* v. *Dabhi Ajitkumar Fulsinji* (*Dhruva*),[39] another important precedent which followed the line of reasoning inaugurated by the dissent in *Shubnath* and the majority opinion in *Om Judgment.* The factual issue in the case is closer to the facts of *Shubnath.* This is because the symbol of 'star' used by one of the candidates was not, in and of itself, a religious symbol. It was the way it was associated with Hindu mythology by the candidate that made it suspect.

34 Verse 9 of chapter 1, *Chandogya Upanishad*, *Id.* at 181.

35 R.G. Ranade, *A Constructive Survey of Upanishadic Philosophy being a Systematic Introduction to Indian Metaphysics* (Oriental Book Agency, Poona, 2017).

36 *Id.* '[T]hese two chapters contain only such subjects as the significance of Om, the meaning, the kind and names of Saman, and the genesis and function of Om.'

37 *Id.*

38 *Id.* 22.

39 (1965) 1 SCR 712 [Hereafter, '*Dhruva*'].

However, the judgment of the Supreme Court unanimously decided the verdict following the reasoning of Subba Rao's, J. dissent in *Shubnath*.

Now the facts. The election dispute of this case arose in the state of Gujarat in 1962. The appellant (Ramanbhai Patel) contested and won his election as a member of *Swatantrata* party. The respondent (Dabhi Fulsinji) filed a petition before the election commission challenging the election. The official election symbol of the candidate was a star. However, the accusation against candidate Patel was that in the pamphlets he described it as the pole star, 'Dhruva,' which is associated with Hindu mythological symbolism. The election commission dismissed the accusation, but the Gujarat High Court invalidated the election on the ground of use of religious appeal. The appellant thus appeared before the Supreme Court.

One of the issues before the Supreme Court[40] was whether the mythological 'Dhruva' has any significance in the religious beliefs or practices of Hindus. The Supreme Court acknowledged that the pamphlet associated 'Dhruva' with the devotee of Hindu God Lord Vishnu and referred to its divine characteristics.[41] Nevertheless, it denied any such possible associations as constituting 'religious appeal' within Section 123 (3). It even assailed the High Court for finding out the mythological associations linked to 'Dhruva.'[42] The Supreme Court endorsed the distinction between a religious symbol and myth, and in doing so it approved the *Om Judgment* and *Shubnath* as precedents. But notice the vocabulary of the Supreme Court in its description of the election symbol:[43]

> [T]he story of Dhruva is that as a result of his steadfast devotion and complete surrender to God, Dhruva earned a boon and that was being accorded a unique place in the firmament where in relation to the rest of the sheller bodies his position is fixed. According to the Puranas he was promised this position till the destruction of the universe. This itself shows that he was not raised to the status of divinity, that is to say, he did not join the company of the 33 crore deities which are said to comprise

40 Mudholkar, J. wrote the opinion on behalf of P.B. Gajendragadkar, CJ, M. Hidayatullah, K.N. Wanchoo, and Raghubar Dayal, JJ.

41 J.R. Mudholkar, J. speaking for the Court, said: 'It is not disputed that on some pamphlets the following characteristics associated with the star Dhruva are set out: Dhruva means eternal. Dhruva means firm. Dhruva means guide. Dhruva means determined. Dhruva means one devoted to religion.' *Dhruva*, note 39, para 7.

42 *Dhruva*, note 39, para 8. ('The High Court seems to have delved deep into the Vishnu Purana, the Mahabharata and the Bhagwat for digging up the story of Dhruva and ascertaining and describing his qualities and particularly of his steadfast devotion to the creator. All that seems to us to have been wholly unnecessary because it leads us nowhere.')

43 *Id.* para 8 (emphasis added). Mudholkar, J. speaking for the Court, observed that 'the five qualities which are generally associated with Dhruva are, indeed, noble qualities but they have no significance peculiar to Hindu religion. The significance of these qualities to the Hindus would be in no way different from that to persons professing other religions or systems of beliefs.'

> the Hindu Pantheon. How then can the association of Dhruva with the star be regarded as an appeal to Hindu religious sentiments?

The Supreme Court refused that association with Hindu tradition or mythology can constitute a 'religious appeal.' Just like the precedents cited by the Court, the reasoning of this case followed the abstract universalisation and secularisation of Hinduism. 'Dhruva' of Hindu mythology was shifted from the sphere of religion to the sphere of mythology. This argument was spelled out by the Court as follows:[44]

> [I]f they are told [to] cast their vote for a particular candidate whose election symbol is associated with a particular religion just as the Cross is with Christianity that will be using a religious symbol for obtaining votes. But where, as in the case of the Hindu religion, it is not possible to associate a particular symbol with religion, the use of a symbol even when it is associated with some deity, cannot, *without something more,* be regarded as a corrupt practice.

This 'something more' is understood in terms limited to 'fear of authority' or 'hope of reward' from divinity and that too only limited to what in the Court's description are 'the illiterate, the orthodox or the fanatical electors.'[45] One can appreciate the argument of the Supreme Court in light of the fact that the symbol of star was officially allocated to the candidate. Therefore, its description as the pole star perhaps could not be a sufficient reason to overturn a democratically elected candidate. However, the reasoning of the Court is too broadly worded to exclude any mythological appeal unless it is coupled with divine fear or reward from the prohibition, or an implicit logic that the devotees of divinity, as opposed to Gods themselves, if alluded or referred to by the candidate are insufficient to fall within the prohibition of 123 (3) of RPA. Dhruva was not explicitly a deity himself, and that made the Supreme Court conclude that it was not a 'religious appeal.' This case, along with the dissent of *Shubnath*, provides a good illustration of the legal difficulties that arise in the evaluation of mythic symbolism in ex-colonial societies.

Recalling *Chandogya Upanishad*'s satirical anecdote of material benefits from the sacred chant of 'Om,' one may suggest that the electoral context constructs a distinct material meaning, a materiality of faith, other than what is ordinarily

44 *Id.* para 12 (emphasis added).

45 *Id.* para 9 ('all this only shows that Dhruva was regarded as a great devotee of Vishnu and held in reverence by Hindus. It clearly negatives the idea of Dhruva being at Godhead. Worship of mortals is so common, at least in our country, that no one can seriously attach religious significance to it. Such worship has no connection whatsoever with religion and is often motivated by fear of authority or by hope of reward.').

associated with religious symbolism. The failure to appreciate this altered meaning led to the misevaluation of symbols and their representations and eventually paved the interpretive way towards the *Hindutva Judgments* even though they were delivered in a historical moment when Hinduism had taken a more aggressive political form. Before discussing the *Hindutva Judgments*, I will discuss two more cases pertaining to religious appeals made by non-Hindu candidates where the distinction between *religious* and *political* appeal was considered and led to two diametrically opposite reasoning and outcomes.

Interpreting Sikh Religious Speech

In a 1964 case, two Sikh candidates were entangled in an electoral dispute. In *Kultar Singh* v. *Mukhtiar Singh*[46] (hereafter *Kultar Singh*), Kultar Singh (appellant) was elected on Akali Dal's ticket to the Punjab Legislative Assembly. Mukhtiar Singh (respondent) accused him of soliciting votes by making religious appeals, specifically Kultar Singh's claim that he alone was the 'proper representative of the Sikh Panth.' The appellant was also accused of deriding the respondent as a representative of a Hindu-ridden Congress party which could neither protect the Sikh religion nor the Sikh language (Punjabi). The Supreme Court referred to the disputed pamphlet issued by the diasporic Sikh community for the resident Sikhs in India:[47]

> We, who are living in Singapore, Malaya, and South East Asia, place this before you, most respectfully, that at this critical juncture it is your duty to keep high the honour of the Panth. This is not the time to criticise the weaknesses of the leaders of the Panth; the need is that in the coming General Elections you should defeat the opponents of the Panth the same way as you did in the last Gurdwara Elections. Every Sikh vote should go to the representatives of the Akali Dal, and we hope that this prayer of ours from far off will be accepted by you and you will once again preserve the honour of the Panth. Victory of the Panth will maintain the honour of the Panth. By maintaining such honour we will reach our final goal that is Punjabi Suba . . . We remain anxious to keep the honour and prestige of the Panth ever high.

The election tribunal and the Punjab High Court held that the imploration to protect the honour and prestige of the 'panth' was a direct reference to the Sikh religion. The Supreme Court however had a different view. Carving out the etymological origins of the word 'panth,' the Court described it as 'one of Sanskrit origin' which originally meant 'the path or the way.' The Court conceded that 'by itself it has come to indicate the Sikh religion because it has

46 (1964) 7 SCR 790.
47 *Id.* para 10.

been used by Sikhs to denote their religion and their denomination.'[48] Further, it clarified that the adjective 'panthic' means 'of the Panth or belonging to the Panth, and so, *prima facie*, the glory or prestige of the Panth may mean the glory or prestige of the Sikh religion.'[49] Clearly, till this juncture of the judgment, the Supreme Court shared the view taken by the Punjab High Court which invalidated the electoral victory.

However, the Supreme Court differed with the High Court in its interpretation of the pamphlet. In the initial part of the pamphlet when the word is used in honour of the Panth, 'the word "Panth" may conceivably mean the Sikh religion.'[50] But, the Court observed, 'when we go to the use of the word "Panth" in the next sentence, it becomes clear that the said word cannot possibly mean the Sikh religion.'[51] Referring to the part where the pamphlet said: 'you should defeat the opponents of the "Panth" the same way as you did in the last Gurdwara Elections,' the Court remarked that the opponents meant the opponents of the Akali Dal Party and not specifically opponents of the Sikh religion.

The Court thus differentiated religion from politics despite considerable overlaps in the religious and political identities in this context. On the one hand, the Court noted that interpreting the pamphlet in the 'cold atmosphere of a judicial chamber' was distinct from the 'surcharged' atmosphere of the campaign and that 'it would be unreasonable to ignore the question as to what the effect of the said speech or pamphlet would be on the mind of the ordinary voter who attends such meetings.'[52] On the other, the Court's own verdict was based on a fine etymological and contextual differentiation which may well have been difficult for the ordinary voter to grasp. This microscopic examination of the pamphlet to find an alternative meaning of 'Panth' ignored the spirit of the statutory provision which aims to discourage solidarity formations solely through communal identity. This further highlights the difficulty faced by the courts in separating the political from the religious. One way to read this judgment could be that it reflected the liberal attitude of the courts in allowing more latitude to the minority community.[53] Even if that were the case, such liberal posturing was misguided as it eventually became the precursor to the Court's collapsing of cultural Hinduism with the political appeal of Hindutva.[54]

48 *Ibid.*

49 *Ibid.*

50 *Id.* para 13.

51 *Ibid.*

52 *Id.* para 9.

53 It is not possible to locate any responses to the judgment of the Court in the local newspapers of the time. Therefore, I am limiting myself to the analysis of the judicial discourse.

54 For another dispute relating to two Muslim candidates, see *Abdul Hussain* v. *Shamsul Huda*, AIR 1975 SC 1612. For its analysis, see Rekhi, note 27.

"Nothing Beneath the Cloak": An Alternative Approach

A somewhat similar distinction between religious and political appeal with major overlaps within the two categories appeared before the Supreme Court out of an election dispute between two Muslim candidates. This led to a significant judicial pronouncement refusing to follow the trajectory of reasoning scrutinised thus far. The dispute arose in August 1971 elections from the Kumbharwada constituency of the Maharashtra state assembly. In *Ziyauddin Burhanuddin Bukhari* v. *Brijmohan Ramdass Mehra & Ors*,[55] the appellant, Z.B. Bukhari (a Muslim League candidate) made speeches to induce voters to believe that 'they will be objects of divine displeasure or spiritual censure if they voted for Shaukat Currimbhoy Chagla [as] he alone stood for all that was Muslim whereas Chagla represented all that was against Muslim religion and belief.'[56] The appellant accused his opponent of not being a true Muslim. This was due to his opponent's affiliation with the party (Congress Party) that was committed to bringing about legislative changes in the Muslim Personal Law. The appellant (Bukhari) told the audience that Muslim personal law was a matter of religious faith and if the Congress government brought in 'amendments in our religious law,' the 'battle would be fought in every street' as 'the question of religion has arisen.' The appellant was charged under Sections 123 (3) & (3-A) for six separate speeches delivered at different places. He advocated for staunch religiosity and adherence to Islam without any dilution in the faith.[57] The trial court and the Bombay High Court declared various speeches as violating Section 123 (3) and others as inflammatory enough to come within Section 123 (3-A). Bukhari appealed to the Supreme Court against the judgment of the High Court.

In the Supreme Court, the appellant argued that the essence of speeches made by him amount to opposing any changes in Muslim personal law. In other words, essentially the appeal was on differences which were about political and not religious matters. The implicit argument was that the religious issue was at best an incidental one. '[C]hange of personal law is, it is suggested, only a secular matter, opposition to its change could not become an appeal on grounds of religion.'[58] Dismissing the argument, the Supreme Court noted:[59]

> To accept this argument would be to view the appeal to the voters after turning it upside down, or, perhaps, inside out. We are not concerned so much with the real nature of what is opposed or supported as with

55 *Bukhari*, note 7.
56 *Id.* para 2.
57 *Id.* para 32 ('It contained allegations against Chagla's faithfulness to Muslim religion on the ground that he advocated inter-communal and inter-caste marriages and that he wanted a Hindu to be a member of the Haj Committee . . . Bukhari claimed that he could die for Islam.').
58 *Id.* para 41.
59 *Ibid.*

> the grounds on which a candidate claims support over a rival. *We have to primarily examine the cloak which the appeal wears to parade in and not only what lies beneath it.*

The Supreme Court discerned that the primary examination ought to be of 'the cloak which the appeal wears to parade in and not only what lies beneath it.' This is in contrast with the Court's approach in *Dhruva*, *Om Judgment* and *Kultar Singh* where, as we have seen, the Court went into the latent content of the religious speech/symbolism and ignored the *form* which encompassed the religious appeal. In this case M.H. Beg, J. argued that the 'religious cannot be understood in binary opposition with temporal affairs which ought to be secular.' Commenting on the distinction between secular and religious matters, he observed:[60]

> If all human activity in this world could be labelled 'secular', on the ground that it appertains to 'this world' as against 'the other world', all religious thought and activity could be described as 'secular', as it takes place in this world. But the term is not used so broadly.

The point made by the Supreme Court of taking the *form* of religious speech seriously[61] is crucial in unmasking the secular garb placed on the essentially religious nature of the appeal.[62] The judgment emphasises the need for a scrutiny of the *form* or appearance of the speech challenged under Section 123 (3) of RPA. Unfortunately, this line of reasoning did not receive sufficient attention as it deserves in the later cases.

II. Way of Life: The Hermeneutics of Hinduism in Law

Before an evaluation of the *Hindutva Judgments*, it is useful to understand another Supreme Court decision (unrelated to electoral law) which heavily influenced the operative logic of the *Hindutva Judgments*. This was a judgment which had immense historical implications for Indian political rhetoric and juridical interpretation. In 1966, 30 years before the *Hindutva Judgments* were to be pronounced, the Supreme Court of India in *Shastri Yagnapurushadji*

60 *Id.* para 42. (Beg, J. also added: 'It is a convenient label to distinguish all that is done in this world without seeking the intervention or favour of or propitiating a Superhuman or Divine Power or Being from that which is done professedly to please or to carry out the will of the Divinity.')

61 Beg, J. reiterates this point as follows: 'To return to the precise question before us now, we may repeat that what is relevant in such a case is what is professed or put forward by a candidate as a ground for preferring him over another and not the motive or reality behind the profession or ostensible ground that very secular or mundane. It is the professed or ostensible ground that matters.' *Id.* para 46.

62 Beg, J. unfortunately drew some rather sharp contrasts between 'primitive' and 'modern' man's understanding of religion. *Id.* para 44 (per Beg, J.).

v. *Muldas Bhudardas Vaishya* found an opportunity to discuss the meaning and category of 'Hinduism.'[63] The judgment famously announced that Hinduism 'may broadly be described as a way of life and nothing more.' It is a simple sentence. But it carries spectres of the ex-colonial past and implications for the future, way beyond the context of the legal dispute within which it was situated. Hinduism was declared by the Supreme Court a way of life and nothing more. The *nothing more* refers to the traditional notion of religion. Hinduism is not a religion having any well-established or 'official' canonical scriptures as compared to its Abrahamic counterparts. It is a way to live. A way is also a path or even a style, but without the attributes of traditional religion in its European genealogy. In its own terms, and before we attend to its proper context, this statement can be read as a voice of the Court against colonial history of hasty codification of the native laws (led by Warren Hastings) despite the resistance of Hinduism for any such enterprise as we noted in the Introduction. More importantly, this sentence became an impetus to cement the future trajectory of a militant form acquired by Hinduism in the *Hindutva Judgments* by placing reliance on the way of life metaphor.

'It may broadly be described as a way of life and nothing more.' The sublime – 'may broadly be' – must be underscored. It may be interpreted 'broadly' as a way of life which is different from saying that Hinduism is only or merely a way of life. The *Hindutva Judgments* endorsed this statement without much attention to 'may broadly be' or attending to the entirely different circumstances where it appeared. The circumstances of the dispute in the *Satsangi Judgment* indicate an entirely different context in which this sentence appeared. This judgment, as noted earlier, was unrelated to RPA. It pertained to a temple entry legislation enacted by the (then) state of Bombay – Bombay Hindu Places of Public Worship (Entry Authorisation) Act, 1956 (Bombay 1956 Act). The state legislature was following the constitutional aspiration, to throw open 'Hindu religious institutions of a public character to all classes and sections of Hindus.'

The Swami Narayan sect (*Satsangis*) wanted to bypass the provisions of the Bombay 1956 Act. This statutory mandate was specifically against the exclusion of Dalits from the Hindu temples. The *Satsangis* employed an interesting strategy to dilute the reformatory power of the enactment. They argued that despite the Hindu flavour to the legacy of their denomination they indeed are not Hindus nor within the Hindu fold. Therefore, the mandate of the Constitution and this legislation was inapplicable to them. This was the context within which the Court broached a broader definition of Hinduism and rejected this contention to ensure the application of temple entry law to the *Satsangi* sect.

The origin of this controversy dates to the pre-constitutional epoch. Few provincial legislatures had begun to enact laws for the reform of religious practices. One such reform legislation was the Madras Temple Entry Authorization

63 AIR 1966 SC 1119 (Hereafter '*Satsangi Judgment*').

Act, 1947. It made it a punishable offence to prevent any person from entering or worshipping in a Hindu temple on the ground of untouchability. The Act was immediately followed by similar legislations in the Central provinces, Bihar, Bombay etc and finally the temple entry provisions of the Constitution of India. The Bombay 1956 Act was initially challenged by the *Satsangis* in the Bombay High Court. The High Court had decided against them, holding that they followed Hindu religion and the legislation applied to them.

Against this decision of the Bombay High Court, in January 1966, the *Satsangis* preferred an appeal before the Supreme Court. They argued that the Swaminarayan sect was a 'distinct and separate religious sect *unconnected with the Hindus* and Hindu religion.'[64] They are not strictly Hindus despite the Hindu flavour in the doctrines and legacy of the founder of the sect, *Swami Sahjananda*. The appellants supported their claim by highlighting the absence of traditional Hindu idols in their temples and their belief that 'the sect propagated the ideal that worship of any God other than Swaminarayan would be a betrayal of his faith.' The Supreme Court rejected their arguments and discussed the theological category of 'Hinduism'. Citing extensively from *Encyclopedia of Religion and Ethics,* Monier William's *Hinduism* (1882) and then President Radhakrishnan's *The Hindu View of Life* (1927), the Supreme Court remarked that 'unlike other religions and religious creeds, Hindu religion [was] not tied to any definite set of philosophic concepts as such.'[65] This broader conception of Hinduism enabled the Court to hold that the *Satsangis* cannot be outside the scope of Hindu religion.

In this context, the Court remarked that Hinduism 'does not appear to satisfy the narrow traditional features of any religion or creed. It may broadly be described as a *way of life* and nothing more.'[66] Jacobsohn praised the decision as an instance of 'ameliorative secularism.'[67] Jacobsohn's treatment of this judgment focuses on the Supreme Court's interpretive labour which in effect reinstated the spirit of social reform. The author of the four-judge bench judgment, PB Gajendragadkar, J. has been credited by another legal commentator as a 'predominantly reformist' judge in the sphere of freedom of religion.[68] The judgment deserves a careful reading, for it uses scriptural logic against the scriptural orthodoxy of Hinduism. This was the first time that a Supreme Court decision referred specifically to verses from *Bhagwadgita* and it was done to subvert the traditional core of rotten caste hierarchies, as the outcome of the judgment demonstrates. In what follows, we must proceed to investigate how this *opening* in the margins of the judgment ended up as terrifying future in 1996.

64 *Id.* para 1 (emphasis supplied).

65 *Id.* para 36.

66 *Id.* para 29 (emphasis supplied).

67 Jacobsohn, note 5.

68 P.K. Tripathy, 'Mr. Justice Gajendragadkar and Constitutional Interpretation' 8(4) *JILI* 488 (1966).

The Hindutva Judgments

The Supreme Court in 1996 delivered three important decisions which shaped the electoral future of India. These decisions, commonly described as the *Hindutva Judgments*, confronted various important issues.[69] One of them was whether the invocation of 'Hindutva' constituted a 'religious appeal' and therefore fell afoul of Section 123 (3). Another was the constitutional validity of the provision itself, whether it violated the free speech clause of the Indian Constitution. Finally, there were vitriolic individual speeches by the candidates or their agents which were alleged as foul play under Section 123 (3) of the RPA if it withstood the constitutional challenge.

The *First Hindutva judgment* was allegedly based on three speeches which were delivered by Bal Thackeray on behalf of Shiv Sena candidate, Ramesh Prabhoo. The contents of the provocative speech were undisputed, as the 'candidate himself admitted the content of the public speeches' in one of the pleadings in the Court. The High Court of Bombay declared all three speeches as offending both Sections 123 (3) and (3-A) of the RPA. This led to the appeal before the Supreme Court by Ramesh Prabhoo. The arguments on both sides followed a predictable trope. Ram Jethmalani, the lawyer for the appellant, argued that 'Hindutva' only 'mean[t] Indian culture and not merely Hindu Religion.' On the contrary, Ashok Desai, the lawyer for the respondent, argued that 'the term "Hindutva" used in election speeches is an emphasis on Hindu religion bearing no relation to . . . Indian culture.'

The Supreme Court acknowledged that an indirect appeal would suffice to elicit the prohibition of the section. However, the Court added that for

> understanding the meaning and effect of the speech, the context has to be found *in the speech itself and not outside it with reference to any other background* unless the speech itself imports any earlier fact in the context of that speech.[70]

This strange observation by the Supreme Court indicating the judicial scrutiny in isolation of the text was never explained. The only justification provided by the Court was that 'the public speeches during election campaign ordinarily are addressed to audience comprised of common men' and they must be distinguished from 'academic debate.' It appears that the meaning of academic in the Court's lexicon was historicity, for historically the word *Hindutva* was associated with reclaiming of the Hindu identity as a nation-state as opposed

69 The High Court of (then) Bombay invalidated the electoral victories of all three concerned candidates for use of corrupt practices: Ramesh Yeshwant Prabhoo, Murli Manohar Joshi and Ramachandra Kapse. All of them filed appeals against the High Court decisions to the Supreme Court.

70 *Id.* para 12 (emphasis mine).

to the fluid notion of Hinduism which, we already noted, finds difficulty in identity or identification as a religious category.

The Court also made an important clarification: that the use of religion 'as such' was not prohibited by the provision. If a candidate evoked religion for the protection of secular polity or unfavourable treatment to a particular religion by any political party, then such an invocation was well within the permissible limits of election law:[71]

> It cannot be doubted that a speech with a secular stance alleging discrimination against any particular religion and ***promising removal of the imbalance*** cannot be treated as an appeal on the ground of religion as ***its thrust is for promoting secularism.*** Instances given in the speech of discrimination against any religion causing the imbalance in the professed goal of secularism . . . In other words, ***mention of religion as such in an election speech is not forbidden*** by sub-section.
>
> (3)

This clarification from the Supreme Court could also be extended to the other prohibited categories in the section. For example, an appeal on the ground of 'caste' is permissible if it is meant to remove caste imbalance or discrimination which was a constitutional aspiration. Similarly, an appeal on the ground of 'language' would not be barred by this section if it was meant to preserve it from danger of extinction. Thus, this interpretation was in line with the constitutional mandate which guarantees the fundamental right to 'any section of the citizens' to preserve and conserve one's language and culture.[72]

Constitutional Validity of RPA Provisions

The three judge bench of the Supreme Court, writing through J.S. Verma, J. upheld the constitutional validity of Sections 123 and 123 (3-A) of the RPA.[73] It found the provisions within the 'reasonable restrictions' clause under Article 19 (2) of the Constitution. The Court concluded that 'seeking votes at an

71 *Id.* para 16 (emphasis added).

72 Article 29 of the Constitution of India. The Court made its point referring to the legislative debates where the Law Minister pointed out that 'If you say Bengali language in this area is being suppressed or schools closed because they bore a particular name, then, you are speaking not to fight in an election but you are also really seeking to protect your fundamental rights, to preserve your own language and culture. That is a different matter. But "I am a Bengali, you are all Bengalis, vote for me," or "I am an Assamese and so vote for me because you are Assamese speaking men," I think, the entire House will deplore that as a hopeless form of election propaganda.' *Id.* para 14.

73 The vires of Section 123(3-A) was challenged previously in *Dr. Dasrao Deshmukh* v. *Kamal Kishore Kadam* (1995) 5 SCC 139. Here, a Shiv Sena candidate had provocatively espoused teaching a lesson to the Muslim community. The Court had upheld the section as a 'reasonable restriction' on the fundamental right to freedom of speech and expression.

election on the ground of the candidate's religion in a secular State, is against the norms of decency and propriety of the society.'[74]

Next, the Court discussed the issue of appeal of Hindutva under a separate section in the judgment titled 'Meaning of "Hindutva" and "Hinduism."' The Court equated the speech against religious discrimination with a speech for 'preservation of Indian culture.' In the same breadth it concluded that

> mere use of the word "Hindutva" or "Hinduism" or mention of any other religion in an election speech does not bring it within the net of sub-section (3) and/or sub-section (3A) of Section 123, unless the further elements indicated are also present in that speech.[75]

The interchangeable use of 'Hindutva' and 'Hinduism' and their awkward alliance with 'preservation of Indian culture' make this passage both abrupt and unconvincing.

The Court heavily relied on and extensively cited the *Satsangi Judgment.* Unmindful of the context of *Satsangi Judgment,* which was about temple entry legislation (and not electoral appeal), the Court concluded:[76]

> [N]o precise meaning can be ascribed to the terms 'Hindu', 'Hindutva' and 'Hinduism'; and no meaning in the abstract can confine it to the narrow limits of religion alone, excluding the content of Indian culture and heritage. It is also indicated that *the term 'Hindutva' is related more to the way of life* of the people in the sub-continent.

This context obfuscation or abuse of precedent is not only erroneous but a blow to fundamental norms of judicial process. As already noted, the expansive interpretation of Hinduism in *Satsangi Judgment* was premised upon expanding the scope of temple entry laws to all sects of Hindus. But selective citations of passages from different judgments is quite a significant feature of the case. The *First Hindutva Judgment* demonstrates the malaise of judicial discourse which permits extraction of passages from precedents without referring to the larger argument or contexts. Approvingly citing the cases of *Kultar Singh* and *Om Judgment,* the Court concluded:[77]

> [T]he words 'Hinduism' or 'Hindutva' are not necessarily to be understood and construed narrowly, confined only to the strict Hindu religious practices unrelated to the culture and ethos of the people of India,

74 *First Hindutva Judgment,* note 2, para 29. For a criticism of using the 'decency and morality' clause by the Apex Court, see S.P. Sathe, *Judicial Activism in India* 190 (Oxford University Press, New Delhi, 2003).

75 *First Hindutva Judgment,* note 2, para 33.

76 *Id.* para 37 (emphasis mine).

77 *Id.* para 42.

> depicting the way of life of the Indian people . . . these terms are indicative more of a *way of life* of the Indian people.

The approach of the Court can be summed up in its insistence to interpret the section of the statute narrowly while expounding Hindutva very broadly. Paradoxically, this broadening of Hindutva by the Court's interpretation politically meant a narrowing down of its canvas as a cohesive religious identity which can be militantly collapsed with the confines of nation-state. The ironies are far from over. The Court referred to *Bukhari's* case as an 'assurance to the correctness of the construction made by us of these provisions.'[78] *Bukhari,* if anything, goes entirely against the trajectory of the reasoning adhered to in the case. The Supreme Court stayed with the search of 'true meaning' of Hinduism and Hindutva, despite *Bukhari*'s insistence on 'the cloak which the appeal wears . . . and not only what lies beneath it.'[79]

One legal commentator concludes that 'Verma's additional move of equating Hindutva with "Indianization" gave the Court's seal of approval, in a sense, to the Hindu nationalists' conception of the nation.'[80] In short, even as the Court declared Bal Thackeray's speech to be corrupt and worthy of prohibition, it opened a space for the legitimation of the ideology underlying his speech.

On facts, the Court declared that the speech by Bal Thackeray fell within the prohibitions of both Sections 123 (3) and (3-A). In his first speech, Thackeray had remarked that '[w]e are fighting this election for the protection of Hinduism. Therefore, we do not care for the votes of the Muslims. This country belongs to Hindus and will remain so.'[81] In his second speech, the assertions exacerbated: 'Anybody who stands against the Hindus should be showed or worshipped with shoes. A candidate by name Prabhoo should be led to victory in the name of religion.'[82] The Court concluded that 'all the three speeches of Bal Thackeray

78 *Ibid.*

79 *Bukhari*, note 7, para 41.

80 Ronojoy Sen, note 6 at 38. Sen argues that in equating Hinduism with Hindutva, Verma, J. 'also gave a highly political twist to the judicial discourse on Hinduism.' *Ibid.* The Court cited from Maulana Wahiduddin Khan's book *Indian Muslims – The Need for a Positive Outlook* (Al-Risala Books, India, 1994) to argue that 'Hindutva' is equivalent to 'Indianisation'. The Supreme Court said that 'considering the terms *Hinduism* or *Hindutva* per se as depicting . . . intolerance towards other religious faiths or professing communalism, proceeds form an improper appreciation and perception of *the true meaning* of these expressions.' A.G. Noorani has shown that the judgment has wrongly cited Wahiduddin Khan's book as the author was critical and not in support of Hindutva as Indianisation. See A.G. Noorani, 'A Shocking Judgment with Selectivity in Quotation' *The Statesman* (Dec. 26–27, 1995).

81 *First Hindutva Judgment*, note 2, para 54.

82 *Id.* para 59 ('The first speech also makes derogatory reference to Muslims by calling them "snake" and referring to them as "lande" (derogatory term used for those practising circumcision). The language used in the context, amounted to an attempt to promote feelings of enmity or hatred between the Hindus and the Muslims on the ground of religion. The first speech, therefore, also constitutes and corrupt practice under sub-section (3A).').

amount to corrupt practice under sub-section (3), while the first speech is a corrupt practice also under sub-section (3A) of Section 123 of the R.P. Act.'[83] This case laid the principled position which was followed in the other two cases as well.

In the *Second Hindutva judgment*, Ram Kapse was elected as the BJP (Bhartiya Janta Party) candidate for Lok Sabha defeating the respondent (who belonged to the Congress (I)). The High Court of Bombay declared him guilty under both Sections 123 (3) and 123 (3-A). Two of the three speeches were held as 'corrupt' by the High Court. These speeches were delivered by Sadhvi Reethambara and Pramod Mahajan on behalf of the appellant. The Supreme Court reversed the findings of the High Court on the technical grounds of insufficient evidence.[84] The High Court found the evidence sufficient as it relied on the manifesto of the political party (Bhartiya Janta Party) which contained religiously motivated appeals to invalidate the election of the appellant. The Supreme Court, however, reversed this decision. It observed: 'Ex facie contents of a manifesto, by itself, cannot be a corrupt practice committed by a candidate of that party.'[85] The Court thus refused to rely on the manifesto to declare the campaign corrupt.

It is difficult to comprehend the Court's reasoning on two grounds. First, while the Court referred to the provision under the RPA where every party must file an affidavit showing its allegiance to constitutional principles (including secularism), the controversial manifesto posed no issue as far as its status as a registered political party was concerned. The Court, remarkably, found no inconsistency between the allegiance to the constitutional principle of secularism and its explicit rejection in the party manifesto. How could a party manifesto be immune from judicial scrutiny under Section 123 (3) or (3-A) when the party was registered under the RPA? Why did the Court not address this apparent contradiction in the affidavit and the party manifesto? A nine-judge bench of the Supreme Court in *S.R. Bommai* v. *Union of India* (1994)[86] had previously castigated the manifesto of political parties going against the ethos of secularism. The non-appearance of *Bommai* as a precedent in any of these cases foregrounds the pervasive problem of judicial cherry-picking of the precedents and the failure of the Apex Court to work as one institution that speaks in one voice. Second, the Court's reasoning proceeded on the grounds that the candidate could not be held accountable for making religious appeals

83 *Id.* para 61.

84 The Court cited lack of witnesses to depose about the speech and its contents as well as Kapse's unawareness about Sadhvi's utterances as the reasons. In a nutshell, the Supreme Court reversed the findings of the High Court on the grounds of insufficient evidence provided by the respondent.

85 *Second Hindutva Judgment*, note 2.

86 (1994) 3 SCC 1 [Hereafter, '*Bommai*']. The majority of nine-judge bench confirmed the imposition of president rule in BJP ruled states immediately after Babri demolition as the BJP manifestoes contained communal overtones. I will discuss the *Bommai* case in Chapter 4 more elaborately.

that resonated with the claims in the manifesto, if he had neither drafted nor specifically used the controversial part of the manifesto in his campaign. S.P. Sathe remarks that this 'means that a candidate who stood for election under a party ticket was presumed not to share the party's programme and ideology. This strikes at the very root of the party system in parliamentary democracy.'[87]

The *Third Hindutva judgment* was decided on the same day by the same bench. It concerned the speech of Murli Manohar Joshi where 'in the meeting held on 24.2.1990 at Shivaji Park, Dadar, he had stated that 'the first Hindu State will be established in Maharashtra.'[88] The issue was whether this is a 'religious appeal.' In a brief response to this question, the Supreme Court observed:[89]

> In our opinion, a mere statement that the first Hindu State will be established in Maharashtra is by itself not an appeal for votes on the ground of his religion but *the expression, at best, of such a hope.*

The Supreme Court conceded that such a statement was despicable but he dismissed it as merely 'a hope.' This was a new interpretive ruse. Thus far, we have seen the differentiation of mystical, mythic, mythological, cultural as failing to fulfil the requirement of '*religious* appeal.' This time the emphasis shifted from religious to the word 'appeal' itself. The Court seems to be saying that what the law requires is an appeal which is religious. However, this is not an *appeal* but only a *hope*, although this hope is pressed on and expressed in electoral campaigns. To Jacobsohn, this posture of the Court made little or no sense. He noted that this hope, if realised, would be contrary to the basic structure and features of the Constitution as described by the nine-judge bench in *Bommai*. For Jacobson, this statement presented a juridical anomaly 'that if Chief Minister Joshi, rather than Candidate Joshi, had publicly expressed the aspiration for a Hindu state of Maharashtra, a dismissal of his government under President's Rule could, following *Bommai*, plausibly be upheld by the Supreme Court.'[90] This 'hope,' remarkably, remained permissible in the electoral context.

A review petition was filed before the Supreme Court[91] on the incorrectness of the three *Hindutva judgments* which had completely bypassed *Bommai*, a prominent precedent on the issue. J.S. Verma, J. dismissed the review petition:[92]

> We may observe that the decision of this Court in [*Bommai*] did not relate to the construction of, and determination of the scope of subsections (3) and (3A) of Section 123 of the Representation of the People

87 Sathe, note 74 at 189.
88 *Third Hindutva Judgment*, note 2, para 30.
89 *Id.* para 62 (emphasis mine).
90 Jacobsohn, note 5 at 195.
91 *Mohd. Aslam* v. *Union of India & Others*, AIR 1996 SC 1611.
92 *Id.* para 3.

> Act, 1951 and, therefore, nothing in the decision in *S.R. Bommai* is of assistance for construing the meaning and scope of sub-sections (3) and (3-A) of Section 123 of the Representation of the People Act. Reference to the decision in S.R. Bommai is, therefore, inapposite in this context.

All this presupposes that apposite and appropriate contextualising is well in place in the reasoning of the judgment. And therefore, there is no need to orient oneself out of context. The contrary is the script which we find encrypted in the *Hindutva judgments.* As mentioned earlier, the *Satsangi judgment*, which was central to the Court's reasoning, did not relate to the RPA in any manner and was thus quite 'inapposite' in itself. The *Hindutva judgments* illustrate every *faux pas* that can possibly appear in writing a legal judgment by the novice law student. Nevertheless, what these cracks make visible is a nostalgia and longing for a lost past: a theological memory of *another* theology that existed in some ex-colonial past. These judgments and the host of other precedents display a hysterical desire to conjure up that past. The irony is that these attempts only bury such a fluid, open and non-identitarian idea of theology and turn Hinduism into an instrument of electoral politics, thereby destroying any real potentiality of the idea of 'religion without religion' to emerge.[93] This is the irony that in the anxious rush to excavate the past, the Indian courts present a Hinduism which has a solidified identity, of nation-state, of vote politics in hasty speed to acquire sovereignty. This sovereign Hinduism, or theology in the service of sovereignty is what we find as ultimately cemented. All this mimics, repeats, retraces the steps of the colonial past which in the eighteenth century precisely did the same to native theologies as we have discussed in the Introduction. The word 'Hindutva' in Sanskrit origins is a coupling of 'Hindu' and 'Tva.' The suffix '*tva*' denotes the essence or quality of the prefix to which it is attached. This would make the translation as the state of being Hindu, the quality or more acutely the essence of being Hindu. What if Hinduism foregrounds its non-identitarian amorphousness which constitutes the essence of Hinduism, which in a way is essentialised as a rigid identity by the Court in pretending to take it seriously?

One can notice a similar compulsive denial to see something amiss in Upendra Baxi's defensive brief for JS Verma, J. in response to Jacobson's diagnosis of the rotten core of these pronouncements. Baxi's laments, written after a decade of these decisions, are the following:[94]

> I continue to think that too much is made of Brother Verma's reference to Hindutva as 'way of life.' It was neither a kiss of life to Hindutva forces nor a kiss of death for Indian constitutional secularism; rather, the

93 See John Caputo, *On Religion* (Routledge, New York, 2019), Ch 4. Caputo argues that his idea of religion is to 'stake out a third way, neither traditional confessional religion nor a modernist anti-religious-secularity, to take up the cause of religion understood *otherwise.*' *Id.* at 93.

94 Upendra Baxi, 'Understanding Constitutional Secularism in "Faraway Places": Some Remarks on Gary Jacobsohn's *The Wheel of Law*' 1 *Indian Journal of Constitutional Law* 231, 242 (2007).

> issue concerned the invocation of differently constituted Utopias during the campaign speech-making; how may Justices and legislators prohibit freedom of speech and expression as forms of constitutionally dreaded Dystopia? . . . Put another way, where as a matter of principle may Justices draw bright lines between the Utopic and the Dystopic?

Neither *eros* for the force of *Hindutva* which are legitimately enforced, nor *thanatos* to the Enlightenment ideal of constitutional secularism. But if legislators and justices cannot draw the lines between constitutionally dreaded dystopia and its reverse, if the value of freedom for speech and expression even during campaign speech-making is so high, then what grants the kiss of love to the constitutional validity of Section 123 (3)? The sexual metaphor of kiss used by Baxi is interesting. It is the kiss of love (for a memory, an imagined revenant resurrected) which is the kiss of death for the present Utopia. Perhaps the blindness of fraternal brotherhood makes it difficult to ask, was it only a coincidence that Brother Verma remained reticent and silent on constitutional secularism as he penned his dissent in the *Bommai* case?

Conclusion

The provisions of the RPA discussed in this chapter demonstrate the prominence as well as the slipperiness of the category of religion in the political history of India. The centrality of religion in India goes beyond the proverbial presence of religion in the everyday lives of Indian people. This chapter has sought to demonstrate how Sections 123 (3) and (3-A) of the RPA are an extension of the State's attempt to regulate the political and electoral rhetoric when it is entwined with religious rhetoric. Despite the absence and impossibility of similar provisions restricting speech in other jurisdictions, they are needed in our context to ensure that religion does not become an instrument to corrupt the principles and ideals of the Indian republic.

This chapter showed how the judicial reasoning in the *Hindutva judgments* stands in line within a trajectory of long-standing precedents. The methodology of the Supreme Court in this line of cases discounted the apparent *prima facie* literal meaning and spirit of Section 123 (3) in preference for some deeper, hidden or true meaning of 'religion.' While approving the constitutional basis of the RPA provisions, the Apex Court eroded their very spirit through its interpretations of the term 'religious.' It incessantly differentiated between the 'religious' and the cultural, mythological, mythic, mystical or spiritual, and termed electoral appeals as permissible if they fell within the realm of the latter. Such differentiations ultimately left little in the sphere of the 'properly religious' that the RPA provisions sought to prohibit. But an alternative line of reasoning does exist in the judicial corpus, most notably in the majority of *Shubnath* and in *Bukhari*.

On the one hand, this chapter underscores the need for more contextual and historically informed adjudicative practices to emerge. On the other, it proposes to take seriously the judicial *faux pas* as an anxiety that lies hidden, latent, as a crypt within the judicial script about excavation of the deeper, true and hidden meaning of the religious speech. How far is this anxiety peculiar to ex-colonial societies? To what extent can they be seen as a desire of a future which is already the past, already yesterday, due to colonialism? We can allow these questions to wait as quick answers have never helped. But we cannot miss these judicial moments as undoing precisely what they set out to do. This much is certain: that no wall of separation between religion and law can ever even get a glimpse, much less assuage the anxious nostalgia for the memory which is lost or yet to arrive.

4 Mythology as/and History in Indian Courtrooms

The Ayodhya Dispute

Introduction

The Indian Constituent Assembly deliberated for almost three years (two years, 11 months and 18 days) to give shape to the Indian Constitution after the end of British colonialism. The enthusiasm of the birth of the new republic was tied with the traumatic event of the partition of the subcontinent primarily based on religion. The partition created the Islamic republic of East Pakistan and West Pakistan (now Bangladesh). Sandwiched between them was India, which constitutionally decided not to be a theocratic State. Curiously, in between the few months of the adoption of Indian Constitution (November 24, 1949) and its commencement (January 26, 1950), on January 16, 1950, we find the institution of the first civil suit which brought the Babri Masjid-Ram Janambhumi dispute to courts of independent India.

The civil suit, filed in Faizabad district court, Ayodhya, in the state of Uttar Pradesh (U.P.) in India, was only a new fold in the long-standing historical combat spanning way back to the sixteenth-century Mughal era on the ownership of land of 1500 square yards of land on which stood the Babri Mosque and some adjoining Hindu sites of worship. The Babri Mosque was built during the reign of Emperor Zahīr ud-Dīn Muhammad, or Babur in 1528. The Hindus had contested that this mosque was built on the remains of a Hindu temple dedicated to Lord Ram, the protagonist of the epic poem Ramayana which describes the city of Ayodhya as his birthplace (*janambhumi*). This cultural memory acquired the shape of a civil suit in 1950 as modern law was called upon to traverse this dispute and adjudicate this entwined collapse of myth and history.

In 2019, the Supreme Court of India finally settled the civil dispute of ownership of the land. The Court was mindful of this historicity spanning the Mughal empire, British colonial rule and the present constitutional regime. Perhaps, that is why we find the description of the origins of the dispute, in the opening page of the judgment, as coterminous with 'the idea of India itself.' This judgment, titled *M. Siddiq (D) Thr Lrs* v. *Mahant Suresh Das &*

DOI: 10.4324/9781003398561-5

Others (*Ayodhya Judgment*),[1] will be the focal point in this chapter. The Court decided that the entire land belonged rightfully, as a matter of right, to the 'Hindu side' as they have proved their title and are thus entitled to it.[2] Unusual for a judicial verdict, the judgment ended with the proposal of the new temple of Lord Ram which may be constructed on the site – which now stands on the site, and was inaugurated with a national celebration on January 22, 2024 – and even mentioned who should be a part of the management of the temple. The Court's verdict was a political euphoria for the Bhartiya Janta Party (BJP), which was the ruling party in the state of Uttar Pradesh in 2019 (under the leadership of Chief Minister Yogi Adityanath) and in power at the central or federal level (under the leadership of Prime Minister Narendra Modi). The enthusiasm was fitting as BJP labouriously forged a movement for reclaiming the Hindu temple as the forefront of its agenda in the late twentieth century. There could not have been a better vindication than a legal stamp given by the Apex Court.

This judgment overturned the 2010 Allahabad High Court pronouncement in the same dispute. The High Court by a majority of 2:1 had preferred a tripartite division of the land between the Muslim side (represented by Sunni Waqf Board) and other two parties (Nirmohi Akhada and the Deity). We will turn to these parties and their standing in the following.

An important milestone to be underscored in the legal battle is the immediate aftermath of the conquest of British East India company over the Mughals in 1856 in the then-province of Oudh where the immovable property of the dispute is located. As if foreshadowing the partition of the subcontinent on a religious basis, in 1856–57, following a communal riot between the Hindus and the Muslims, the colonial British government had partitioned the land of the disputed site into two halves. A grill-brick wall of separation had divided the disputed land into what came to be known in the legal vocabulary as the 'inner' and 'outer' courtyards.[3] The inner portion of the courtyard, where the mosque was situated, was demarcated for exclusive worship by the Muslims. The outer portion, which had structures of religious significance for the

1 (2020) 1 SCC 1 ('*Ayodhya Judgment*'). All references from the judgment are from the official Supreme Court website, ***available at***: www.sci.gov.in/pdf/JUD_2.pdf. ***Id.*** at 6 (para 2). The following five judges constituted the five-judge bench which delivered the verdict: Ranjan Gogoi, C.J., S.A. Bobde, J., D. Y. Chandrachud, J., Ashok Bhushan, J. and Abdul Nazeer, J. In an unprecedented move, the unanimous Supreme Court judgment kept the authorship of the judgment anonymous. This authorial anonymity continued with an addendum written by one of the five judges.

2 The terms Hindu and Muslim used in this chapter follow the usage by the Supreme Court in *Ayodhya Judgment*. It will become clear during the discussion that the reference to the communities does not represent the views of these communities in totality. Indeed, there was a conflict between the Hindu parties, discussed later, representing the deity (Suit no. 5) and the managing of the affairs of the temple (Suit no. 3). The usage is more a matter of clarity than representative of claims made by the communities at large.

3 *Ayodhya Judgment*, note 1 at 63 (para 46).

Hindus (*Sita ki rasoi* (Sita's kitchen) and a platform called the Ram *chabutra*), was given exclusively to the Hindus. Till December 1949, this position remained intact. Of course, not without combats, transgressions leading to tensions between the Hindus and the Muslims. On December 22–23, 1949, idols of Lord Ram (described as *Ram lalla*; the suffix 'lalla' is a north Indian dialect for infants or toddlers as the idol installed was of Lord Ram as a toddler) were installed inside the central dome of Babri Masjid situated in the inner courtyard. This led to major altercations and disturbances of the public order. This led to the filing of the first civil suit (Suit no. 1) in the district court of Faizabad, seeking permission to worship the idols placed inside the mosque. Suit no. 2, instituted by Paramhans Ram Chandra Das on December 5, 1950, was like the first suit, but was withdrawn on December 18, 1990. Suit no. 3 was instituted on December 17, 1959, by the Nirmohi Akhara, a branch of the Ramanandi sect. The Nirmohis impleaded themselves as managers (*shebaits*) of the temple. Their fundamental grievance was that with the attachment of the property they were 'wrongfully deprived of the management and charge of the temple.'[4] Suit no. 4 was filed by Sunni Central Waqf Board and nine Muslim residents as a representative suit for the Muslim community on December 18, 1961 seeking for the declaration, and pursuant relief, that the disputed property was a sixteenth-century public mosque.[5] Lastly, suit no. 5 was filed on July 1, 1989, by the Hindi idol of Lord Ram, through plaintiff Sri Deoki Nanadan Agarawala, a former judge of the Allahabad High Court, for the ownership and title of the disputed land.[6] He acted in the capacity of the 'next friend' of the deity, the idol, *Sri Ram Lalla Virajman* (first plaintiff) and the land, *Asthan Sri Ram Janambhumi*, Ayodhya (second plaintiff).

All these suits were taken together by the Allahabad High Court, which delivered its verdict on September 30, 2010.[7] As noted previously, the High Court, by a majority of 2:1, decided on a three-way partition of the disputed land.[8] Justice Sudhir Agarwal and Justice Sibghat Ullah Khan, speaking for the majority, awarded a one-third portion to the Hindu idol (Suit no. 5). One-third of the open area of the outer courtyard was given to Nirmohi Akhara (Suit no. 3), who were claiming the property as managers of the temple. Finally, the leftover share in the inner courtyard was awarded to the Sunni

4 *Id.* at 36 (para 36). Nirmohi Akhada repeatedly asserted that no mosque ever existed on the site. It was always a temple of Lord Ram, from which the Nirmohis managed and received offerings.

5 *Id.* at 38–39 (para 38).

6 *Id.* at 45 (para 40).

7 *Gopal Singh Visharad* v. *Zahoor Ahmad*, 2010 SCC OnLine All 1935 [Hereafter, '*Allahabad High Court judgment*']. The entire text of the judgment with annexures is available on the official website of the Allahabad High Court, available at: http://elegalix.allahabadhighcourt.in/elegalix/DisplayAyodhyaBenchLandingPage.do.

8 The majority judges clarified that partition of the land must be done in such a way that the portion of the inner courtyard, where idols were installed in 1949, must be given to the Hindu community.

Central Waqf Board (Suit no. 4) that represented the Muslim side. Justice Sharma dismissed the entire case of the Muslim side and awarded the entire disputed land to the Hindus.

In the High Court judgment, a question arose regarding Suit no. 5 being barred by limitation since it was filed in 1989. Justices Dharam Veer Sharma and S. Aggarwal decided that limitation could not bar a claim for the idols because they must be considered as perpetual minors. This is a point on which, we will see later in this chapter, the Supreme Court will disagree with the High Court despite allowing the suit of the idol for different reasons.[9] Striking an alternative chord, S.U. Khan, J., despite his agreement with the outcome of tripartite partition, dismissed the arguments accepted by his co-judges about the non-application of limitation law on the deities due to their claim of perpetual minority. He also rejected the claim that the site where the idols were placed constituted a legal person. In this sense, despite his agreement with the eventual outcome, Khan J. had major disagreements from the reasoning adopted by the other two judges.[10] This judgment of the Allahabad High Court was appealed in 2010 by all the parties challenging the tripartite partition in the Supreme Court of India.

The central aim of this chapter is to uncover the hidden aspects in the narrative of the Supreme Court judgment, focusing on what it tries to suppress, exclude, elide and erase. As in our reading of *Hindutva Judgments* in Chapter 3, we noted the ruse of judicial misinterpretation, misreading or selective use of the previous precedents, in this chapter I will follow a similar approach with respect to other related cases which are linked with the Ayodhya dispute. I will also show how the Supreme Court judgment eclectically engages with those aspects of the Allahabad High Court judgment which suit its narrative construction but conveniently bypasses those parts which highlight the complicity of the executive and the judicial wing in their partisan logic. In mapping this trajectory, I hope to excavate the political theology that guides the jurisprudence of the Supreme Court despite all its attempts to veil it in the language of law.

Section I deals with the event of the demolition of the Babri mosque in 1992, the varied legal and political questions raised by the demolition and how the Supreme Court of India opened two pathways to engage with the event. The

9 One may find a deeper indictment, a divine dictum, about the Ayodhya dispute. Have we not reduced the Gods to a position of minority *perpetually* and acquired a position of majority by making them fight the battles of property, the very material eros of modernity against which the idol of salvation (moksha) in Hinduism is situated? How would one theologically understand the talionic pursuit of saving Gods or saving Gods' property? For a synoptic overview of the *Ayodhya Judgment* from this perspective, see Amit Bindal, 'Saving the Gods, Not Listening to Them' 755 *Seminar* 29–37 (2022).

10 I will devote Section III of this chapter to his judgment and demonstrate that he was the only judge who foregrounded the question of violent dispossession of the mosque and the role played by the administration and the judiciary in perpetuating criminal actions by the Hindu side.

1994 nine-judge bench verdict of *S.R. Bommai* v. *Union of India* (*Bommai*)[11] shows the first path, where the Apex Court took the political context of the demolition head-on to uphold the secular fabric of the Constitution. The second way to approach the event was illustrated in *Ismail Faruqui* v. *Union of India*,[12] decided in the same year but after *Bommai*, which underplayed the violence of demolition of the mosque and alienated the Muslim community.

Section II explains and analyses the historical events of 1949 when the idol of Lord Ram was installed inside Babri Masjid. Careful attention to this episode provides a clear perspective to understand the *Ayodhya Judgment* as well as other precedents related to it. Section III will continue probing the installation of idols by focussing on that part of S.U. Khan's J. judgment which maps an alt-history of the Ayodhya dispute by highlighting executive and judicial complicity. Section IV outlines the central tenets and legal principles of civil law applied in arriving at the final decision of the ownership of disputed land. It shows the awkward, messy and at times colossal misreading of the factual situation to arrive at the eventual denouement in the *Ayodhya Judgment*. Section V explains the unique tenet of Indian law which grants juristic personality to the Hindu idol. It will also discuss how the *Ayodhya Judgment* rejected the claim of holy land to be granted the status of juristic person in and of itself. Finally, Section VI evaluates the anonymous ***addendum*** which is affixed as a supplement to the *Ayodhya Judgment*. At once a part and not a part of the judgment, I argue that this appendix serves as an illustration of law as mythology inasmuch as it collapses all distinctions between faith/fact, mythology/history and belief/evidence. Let us begin by recalling the most shocking event in the history of post-independence India, the demolition of the Babri Masjid orchestrated by a mob of Hindu worshippers which was and is a blow to both political promise and judicial imagination of equality, liberty and justice.

I. The Demolition of the Babri Mosque and Its Aftermath

On December 6, 1992, the Babri mosque was destroyed. A mob of Hindu worshippers dismantled the Masjid in violation of law and judicial orders. This event was bemoaned even in the Supreme Court's *Ayodhya Judgment* as 'an egregious violation of the rule of law.'[13] Many high functionaries of various state governments had applauded this event as a retaliation against the past injustice. The demolition subsequently led to the dismissal of the state

11 *S.R. Bommai* v. *Union of India* (1994) 3 SCC 1 [Hereafter, '*Bommai*']. The reader might recall that we have referred to *Bommai* and its absence in the *Hindutva judgments* in Chapter 3. I will discuss the context and outcome of this case in this chapter more elaborately.

12 *Dr. M. Ismail Faruqui* v. *Union of India* (1994) 6 SCC 364 [Hereafter, '*Faruqui*'].

13 *Ayodhya Judgment*, note 1 at 914 (para 788). All the suits pending in the local courts were transferred to the Allahabad High Court for final decision in July 1989. On Aug. 14, 1989, an interim order was passed by the High Court to maintain the *status quo* on the disputed land till the final adjudication by the Court. The 1992 demolition took place despite these orders.

legislature by the central/federal government. This was done by invoking a unique constitutional provision (Article 356) which allows the federal government to take over the state government ('President's Rule') on proven disregard and failure of constitutional machinery in any state resulting in the failure of constitutional governance. President's Rule was imposed in three Indian states: Rajasthan, Madhya Pradesh and Himachal Pradesh. The official grounds of imposition of President's Rule were tacit or express collusion of some of the highest public officials in the demolition.[14]

This broached the context for the nine-judge bench of the Supreme Court verdict in *Bommai*. The Court adjudicated on the validity of President's Rule imposed on the states. A majority of 7–2 judges in *Bommai* approved the President's Rule in all three states. The Court declared that actions of the state governments tended to jeopardise the constitutional principle of secularism which, the Court declared, are a part of the basic structure of the Indian Constitution. What came before the Court in *Bommai* was a spectre of eruption of mob violence in the name of religion and an audacious disregard of the law and the orders of the Court. More importantly, how the heads of the states endorsed this illegality as festivity was a testament to how structural violence can acquire a macabre form. By approving the dismissal of state legislative assemblies, the majority judges in *Bommai* reinforced the relative autonomy of the judiciary in annulling democratically elected governments when principles of secular constitutionalism are thwarted openly.

The relevance of *Bommai* lies in not shying away from the political context and engaging in a direct confrontation with political [in]action if it infringes upon the essential aspects of the Constitution. *Bommai* described the process, resulting in eventual demolition, as 'serious blow' to the peace and harmony of the nation and an event having adverse international reverberations. The *Ayodhya Judgment* in its discourse on secularism devotes nine full pages to a legislation (The Places of Worship (Special Provisions) Act, 1991) that in explicit terms excluded the present controversy while giving only half a page, bereft of any context, to *Bommai*, where the discussion of secularism appeared in the context of the demolition of the Babri Mosque.[15] This fugitive approach to and non-engagement with *Bommai* is a symptom in the judgment representative of its larger attempt to bury the past and silence the political dynamics, making it complicit in maintaining an insular approach in comprehending the Ayodhya dispute.

In the *Ayodhya Judgment*, the Court does not want to confront the atrocious event of the mosque demolition despite its relevance to the dispute. This is conspicuous in the Court's eliding *Bommai* and reducing it to a decorative

14 The legislative assembly in the state of Uttar Pradesh, the state in which the town of Ayodhya is situated, was dissolved as Chief Minister Kalyan Singh himself resigned after the demolition.

15 S.5 of the Places of Worship (Special Provisions) Act, 1991 in specific terms excludes its application to Ram Janma Bhumi-Babri Masjid.

precedent. Let alone foregrounding the context, the Court did not find it worthy to even mention what led to *Bommai*. After a solitary quote from *Bommai*, the discussion in the judgment safely returns to the Places of Worship Act and its relevance to secularism, something on which the Court had already spent substantial judicial ink. The case of *Bommai* is never returned to judgment thereafter. Perhaps it was necessary for the Supreme Court to underplay the context and elaboration of secularism in *Bommai*. The spectre of demolition of Babri Masjid in contumacious disregard of the law shows how the Ayodhya dispute in the nineties became a militant aggression rather than a question of faith or religion. To settle the dispute, could any court ever arrive at the verdict that closed the controversy by declaring the Hindus as the rightful owners of the disputed land, if the mosque were not demolished in 1992? That would have required the demolition of the existing mosque to execute the order of the Court! These and many other questions remain muted in the uncomfortable silence on *Bommai* and the Court's lack of engagement with the Babri Masjid demolition. Now I must turn to the case of *Faruqui*, which presents an alternative route in approaching the demolition.

Exactly a month after the demolition on January 7, 1993, an ordinance was issued by the President of India (which here meant the federal/central government). This ordinance was later superseded by the Acquisition of Certain Areas at Ayodhya Act, 1993. Section 4 (2) of the Act allowed the central/federal government to acquire the disputed land of Ayodhya and the land adjacent to the disputed site. Section 4 (3) provided for abatement of 'all the suits and legal proceedings,' extinguishing the judicial remedy available to the parties. The enactment and consequent acquisition of land by the central government were challenged before a five-judge bench of the Supreme Court in *Faruqui*. The Supreme Court by a thin majority of 3:2 upheld and approved the acquisition of the land. However, the Court was unanimous in invalidating the clause of the enactment where judicial review of the dispute was declared as impermissible. This revived the claims of the title to the disputed land which were pending in the Allahabad High Court.

For the majority of judges in *Faruqui*, the acquisition of the mosque as a place of worship was permissible in law, as the mosque is on par with other places of worship which too can be acquired by the State.[16] Section 7(2) of the Act ensured the *status quo* and non-alteration of 'the position existing before the commencement of this Act.' The position, which existed before the midnight or night of January 6, 1993 (date of the Presidential ordinance), was thus maintained. The challenge to the legislation was made on the ground that it gave preferential treatment to the Hindu community and thus was a

16 '[a] temple, church or mosque etc. are essentially immovable properties . . . [e]very immovable property is liable to be acquired . . . a mosque does not enjoy any additional protection which is not available to religious places of worship of other religions.' *Faruqui*, note 12, para 81 (per JS Verma, J.).

violation of the principle of secularism. The majority judges, rejecting this argument, stated:[17]

> While offer of prayer or worship is a religious practice, its offering at every location . . . would not be an essential or integral part of such religious practice unless the place has a particular significance for that religion . . . Places of worship of any religion having particular significance for that religion, to make it an essential or integral part of the religion, stand on a different footing and have to be treated differently and more reverentially.

This abstract statement discounted the fact that the inner portion of the site had belonged to Muslims since colonial times. A *status quo* meant that worship by the Hindu community continued despite demolition. The sting of injustice became more poignant as idols (whose worship was legitimised by this decision) were placed at the disputed site on December 6, 1992, after the demolition (these idols, it may be noted, were installed in addition to the ones placed inside the mosque during the events of 1949).

While the majority of *Faruqui* allowed the worship of these idols without any hesitation, it did not permit the Muslims to offer prayers. To this end, J.S. Verma, J. made a curious remark: '[a] mosque is not an essential part of the practice of the religion of Islam and *namaz* (prayer) by Muslims can be offered anywhere, even in open.'[18] The issue whether offering of *namaz* (prayer) inside a mosque is essential to Islam or not was never raised by either of the parties in the first place. The embarrassment of such slips of the court becomes obvious in 2018, when a three-judge bench of the Supreme Court had to clarify that these remarks were made by way of *obiter dicta* and cannot be considered binding law.[19] Further, the majority noted that the maintenance of *status quo* by the Act was indeed detrimental to the Hindu community. This is because the Hindus had to pay the price of the mob violence in the form of a curtailed right to worship, as the mob also caused some damage to the outer courtyard which was now no more available to Hindu worship. The Hindu community, the majority of judges of the Supreme Court observed, had to 'bear the cross' on its chest.[20]

17 *Id.* para 78.
18 *Id.* para 82.
19 In 2018, the question with respect to these observations was raised before a three-judge bench of the Supreme Court. The bench had to clarify that the observations on 'mosque' and 'namaz' must be read as limited to the facts of the case. The 'observation need not be read broadly to hold that a mosque can never be an essential part of the practice of the religion of Islam.' *M. Siddiq (D) Thr. Lrs.* v. *Mahant Suresh Das & Others* (2018) SCC online SC 1677 (per Ashok Bhushan, J., for himself and Deepak Misra, J., decided on Sep. 27, 2018). *Id.* para 59.
20 *Faruqui*, note 12 at 14, para 53.

The two dissenting judges (A.M. Ahmadi and P. Barucha, JJ.) took a contrary view and arrived at the conclusion that the entire legislation was unconstitutional. To them, permitting worship of the trafficked idols betrayed the spirit of the constitution:[21]

> [N]o account is taken of the fact that the structure thereon has been destroyed in a most reprehensible act (sic) . . . No account is taken of the fact that there is a dispute in respect of the site on which puja is to be performed . . . the disputed structure was being used as a mosque; and that the Muslim community has a claim to offer namaz thereon.

The reasoning and logic of majority opinions in *Bommai* and *Faruqui* represent two distinct approaches to the episode of demolition. The obiter remark of Justice Verma which invited a clarification from the Court itself, and his silence on secularism in *Bommai* (as he was one of the two dissenting judges) became an issue of academic scrutiny.[22] However, for our purpose, this section sufficiently provided a preliminary narrativisation of the Ayodhya dispute from within the judicial archive. So far, we have referred to its context through tangential precedents, or by circling around the issue, though not exactly on the issue of the title of land or property rights. In what follows, we must enter the thicket of events which led to the filing of the title suit.

II. Idols Inside Babri Masjid: The Events of December 22/23, 1949

Krishna Jha and Dhirendra K. Jha in their laborious ethnographic account have constructed the events of placement of idols.[23] The following prefatory context is useful to appreciate and fully knit the threads spilled over in the judgment. On the night of December 22, 1949, Abhiram Singh, a militant Vaishnavite ascetic belonging to the Ramanandi sect, entered the Babri Masjid in the inner courtyard. Accompanied by a few others, they planned on installing the idols of Lord Ram inside the central dome of Babri Masjid. The trespass required precise and calculated timing just before the midnight hour, '[f]or a Muslim guard, Abul Barkat, was to take charge after that.'[24] By the time the new guard took his duty, the idol with the silver throne was

21 *Ibid.*

22 Gary Jacobsohn has noted the avoidance of Verma, J. to discuss secularism in *Bommai* with his avoidance of *Bommai* in the *Hindutva Judgments.* He develops this by knotting together *Bommai*, its absence in in *Hindutva* and the tie-breaking verdict written by Verma, J. in *Faruqui.* See, Gary J. Jacobsohn, *The Wheel of Law: India's Secularism in Comparative Context* (Princeton University Press, Princeton, 2005), Ch 7.

23 Krishna Jha and Dhirendra K. Jha, *Ayodhya the Dark Night – The Secret History of Rama's Appearance in Babri Masjid* 74 (Harper Collins, Delhi, 2016).

24 *Ibid.*

taken inside with other materials required to perform worship. Gopal Singh Visharad, a prominent member of the Hindu Mahasabha, who instituted the first civil suit in the Faizabad district court on January 16, printed pamphlets and posters 'which announced the "miracle" of reclaiming Babri Masjid.'[25] He also exhorted the Hindus to gather at the spot in large numbers to witness the 'miracle.' A gathering of Hindu worshippers arrived around the site the next morning. As planned, Abhiram Singh, along with his conspirators, began the worship of idols and lit the lamp inside the mosque in the early hours of the morning celebrating the appearance of Lord Ram. 'The compassionate god has miraculously appeared' (*Bhaye prakat kripala deen dayala*), chanted the gathering of Hindu worshippers. The ascetics in huge numbers started performing elaborate ceremonies and religious hymns (*kirtan*).

The encouragement for the *kirtan* was provided by Shakuntala Nair. She was the wife of the district magistrate of Faizabad district, K.K.K. Nair. Nair's active participation in legitimising the worship of the illegally trespassed gods inside the mosque, archived in the Allahabad High Court judgment will be discuss in the next section. His complicity in consolidating the installed idols enabled him to retire early from public life. He and his wife were duly rewarded politically for their efforts.[26] The installation of the idols was just one of the many phases in the long-standing Ayodhya dispute. However, this event became the cornerstone for the dispute to enter the judicial process in independent India.

The strain between the Hindus and the Muslims was high due to the partition of India resulting in the death of millions. The backdrop of the partition aided the Hindu nationalist forces in appropriating the Ayodhya dispute to link the Hindu identity as a nationalist demand for the formation of the Hindu temple at Ayodhya.[27]

The event of idol installation was not an isolated event. It was preceded by a month of confrontations between the two communities. A few ascetics (*bairagis*) 'infiltrated a Muslim cemetery near the masjid, squatted on the graves and ignited sacred fires there to emphasize their claim that the area was originally Hindu religious space.'[28] Harold A. Gould argues that the idol-installing incident was 'carefully orchestrated . . . by . . . civil servants with

25 *Id.* at 77.

26 Shakuntala Nair was offered a ticket from the Gonda constituency by All India Hindu Mahasabha. She became a Member of Parliament (M.P.) in 1952. K.K.K. Nair became an M.P. in 1967 'on a ticket from Jana Sangh, an off shoot of Hindu Mahasabha.' *Jha and Jha*, note 23 at 92.

27 Decades later, two prominent leaders of Bhartiya Janata Party (BJP) echoed this sentiment, linking Ayodhya to the nationalist cause. Atal Bihari Vajpayee remarked that 'the campaign for a *mandir* in Ayodhya has proved to be a unifying factor . . . not only for the Hindu society but for the whole nation' *Hindustan Times* (Sep. 24, 1990). Lal Krishna Advani described the issue as 'the basis of nationalism in India.' *The Telegraph* (Sep. 13, 1990). Cited in A.G. Noorani, *The Babri Masjid Question*, 1528–2003, vol. I, xxxiii (Tulika, New Delhi, 2014).

28 Harold A. Gould, *Grass Roots Politics in India: A Century of Political Evolution in Faizabad District* (1994), cited in A.G. Noorani, note 27 at 209.

a very definite political agenda.'[29] One of them, the aforementioned district magistrate K.K.K. Nair, 'was notoriously pro-Hindu, a member of the Rashtriya Swayamsevak Sangh (RSS).'[30] Nair vehemently resisted the attempts of the government to restore the state of things by the removal of idols transported illegally inside the mosque. He pleaded that violence would ensue if any attempt was made to remove the idols. This led to the disputed property legally being taken into custody by an official receiver by the order of the judicial magistrate.

Nair played an important role in ensuring that worship of the idols continued despite the attachment of the property.

> Under the Magistrate's order, only two or three *pujaris* were permitted to go inside the place where the idols were kept, to perform religious ceremonies like *bhog* and *puja*. Members of the public were restricted from entering and were only allowed *darshan* from beyond the grill-brick wall.[31]

The Hindus in general offered worship from outside the locked door. The Muslims were entirely debarred from offering *namaz* at the place which was a mosque before the incident.

As already noted, Suit no. 1 was filed by Gopal Singh Visharad before the civil judge of Faizabad, a plea of an ardent Hindu devotee denied his right to worship the idols inside the mosque by the local administration. He alleged that government officials, including Nair, one of the defendants, prevented him from offering worship to the deities. His role in publishing pamphlets to mobilise Hindu worshippers to arrive at the site on the morning of November 23, 1949, was peacefully erased in the legal discourse.

After almost seven decades, on November 9, 2019, the Supreme Court of India, in its final verdict, declared that the 'right of the plaintiff in Suit 1 to worship at the disputed property is affirmed subject to any restrictions imposed by the relevant authorities.'[32] Merely a few pages earlier, the Court noted, in the context of surreptitious installation of idols in 1949, that the 'ouster of the Muslims on that occasion was not through any lawful authority but through an act which was calculated to deprive them of their place of worship.'[33] How can an unlawful act manoeuvred to dispossess Muslims from the site of the mosque find affirmation by the Supreme Court? If the deities were put inside the mosque in violation of law, then by what logic could the worship of illegitimately placed deities be pleaded in the first place in Suit no. 1? The suit for

29 *Ibid.*
30 *Id.* at 208.
31 *Ayodhya Judgment*, note 1 at 11 (para 12).
32 *Id.* at 927–928 (para 805).
33 *Id.* at 922 (para 798).

worship was instituted by the plaintiff who was complicit in the act of installation. Neither his complicity nor the organised conspiracy of the local administration was adequately addressed or adversely commented upon by the Apex Court. What should one make of the condemnation by the Apex Court of the events of 1949? This and many such compelling elisions and erasures haunt the judicial reasoning in its final resolution, or dissolution, of the Ayodhya dispute.

III. Complicity in Securing the Idol of Lord Ram

Peter Goodrich has remarked that the 'language of law carries with it all that is unsaid, that has been driven within, hidden from view: it carries its failures within as an indelible past, as the memory of battle, as litigation.'[34] Drawing from the Allahabad High Court judgment of S.U. Khan, J., I will foreground the *unsaid* of the *Ayodhya Judgment* in this section. Anupam Gupta in his comment on the Allahabad High Court judgment remarks the following about Khan's J. opinion: 'The great merit of Justice Khan's judgment is his unravelling of the criminality of 1949 and the illegality of 1986, the two landmarks in the modern history of Babri masjid before its demolition.'[35] However, no other legal commentators nor the Supreme Court took into account the malaise of illegalities and judicial mala fides which were highlighted in his judgment. In this section, I take this remark to carefully read Khan's J. opinion to show how it constructs an alternative history of the Ayodhya dispute from within the available judicial archive.

Justice Khan, almost in an act of conjuring buried ghosts of the archive, presents a manic schema orchestrated by the administration in 1949 and judiciary in 1986. He takes note of the partisan attitude of the district magistrate, as described previously, both prior to and after the fatal night when the idols were secreted into the mosque. He notes that the possibility that idols might be installed was suspected by the Muslim community almost a month before its occurrence.[36] Summoning the original file notes regarding the incidents on the night of November 22, 1949, he made some startling revelations. A letter written by the superintendent of police, Kripal Singh, addressed to K.K.K. Nair, anticipated in clear terms the apprehensions of mosque capture by Hindu ascetics. It mentions the dismantling and digging of several Muslim graves during the grand event organised by the Hindu community:

> Several thousand Hindus, Bairagis and Sadhus . . . intend to continue the present Kirtan [worship accompanied with music] till the full moon

34 Peter Goodrich, *Languages of Law: From Logics of Memory to Nomadic Masks* 16 (Weidenfeild & Nicholson, London, 1990).

35 Anupam Gupta, 'Dissecting the Ayodhya Judgment' 45(50) *Economic and Political Weekly* 35 (2010).

36 *Allahabad High Court Judgment*, note 7 at 25 (per S.U. Khan, J.).

> night. The plan appears to be to surround the mosque in such a way that entry for the Muslims will be very difficult and ultimately they might be forced to abandon the mosque.[37]

The police superintendent noted, a month before idol placement, a 'strong rumour, that . . . the Hindus [would] try to force entry into the mosque with the object of installing a deity.'[38]

Khan, J. cites at length from the report/diary prepared by Magistrate Nair immediately after the incident. In the report he feigned ignorance of any such apprehension. The news, Nair mentioned in the report, came to him as a 'great surprise,' as something like this had neither been suspected nor reported. Khan, J. notes that Nair's 'surprise d[id] not appear to be genuine as there was a clear mention of such a plan in the above letter of S.P.'[39] He further highlights the contradiction in Nair's previous letter, written to the state government on December 16, reassuring that things were under control, and his later surprise over the incident in his report/diary.[40] This narration illustrates how the support of high-level administrative functionaries formed the backdrop of the installation of the idols.

Khan, J. also notes the refusal of magistrate Nair to remove the idols. His report/diary on December 27 notes, 'if the Government still insisted that removal should be carried out in the face of these facts, I would request to replace me with another officer.'[41] Magistrate Nair's letter to the chief secretary of the Uttar Pradesh government pleaded for continuation of the Hindu worship of the deities. His 'solution to offer for government's consideration' involved the attachment of the premises of the mosque excluding both Hindus as well as Muslims, 'with the exception of the minimum number of pujaris . . . who would offer pooja and *bhog* before the idol.'[42]

On December 29, 1949, the property was attached, under Section 145 of the Criminal Procedure Code of 1898, in the order passed by the judicial magistrate attaching the inner courtyard and appointing a receiver to

37 Letter by Kripal Singh, S.P. to K.K.K. Nair, DM, dated Nov. 29, 1949, quoted in the *Allahabad High Court Judgment*, note 7 at 27.

38 *Ibid.*

39 *Allahabad High Court Judgment*, note 7 at 28 (per S.U. Khan, J.).

40 In K.K.K. Nair's letter to the state government, dated Dec. 16, 1949, demonstrating the manner in which instead of taking action, Nair blamed the Muslims for 'exaggerating these happenings' due to heightened Muslim anxiety 'by the recent Navanh (sic.) Ramayan Path, a devotional reading of Ramayan by thousands of Hindus.' Dismissing the complaints from the Muslim community as 'grossly exaggerated,' Nair assured the government that 'the situation was entirely in control and police picket was functioning efficiently.' *Id.* at 29–31.

41 *Id.* at 34–35.

42 'Letter from Deputy Commissioner, Faizabad, dated Dec. 27 1949, to Chief Secretary, Government of UP' in Noorani, note 27 at 215– 216.

manage it.[43] After taking charge, he submitted a 'scheme' of arrangements stating that '*the most important* item of management is the maintenance of bhog and puja in the condition in which it was carried on when I took over charge.'[44] Therefore, Hindu worship conducted for less than two weeks superseded the *status quo* that had existed over several hundred years. Almost in accordance with Nair's proposition, two or three pujaris were permitted inside to the exclusion of all others who were not permitted to cross the grilled brick wall.

An additional development took place in 1986. Umesh Chandra Pandey, a practicing lawyer in Ayodhya, filed an application in the court of the deputy *munsif* on January 25, 1986, to open the locks and allow access to the Hindu community in general to perform worship and offer prayers which was limited to the pujaris till 1986. Umesh Pandey was neither a party member, nor was he representing any party. The court did not pass any orders because the matter was pending in the Allahabad High Court. Nevertheless, Umesh Pandey approached the court of the district judge in Faizabad on January 31, 1986. On the very next day, the district judge, KM Pandey, without possession of the case file, allowed the appeal and passed an order for the opening of the locks on the gate of the mosque: 'If the Hindus are offering prayers and worshipping the idols, though in a restricted way, for the last 35 years, the heavens are not going to fall . . . if the locks are removed.'[45]

Mohammed Hashim, a plaintiff in Suit no. 4, filed an application to be impleaded in the case on the very next day, February 1, 1986. But the district judge rejected the application on the grounds that it was 'unnecessary and improper.' The multiple fault-lines in the court order are bemoaned by Khan, J. Other than the technical glitches in the order,[46] he found it appalling that

> a person who was a party in the connected suit which was leading case (sic) was considered to be neither necessary nor proper party by the District Judge, however, Mr. Umesh Chand Pandey who was not a party in the suit was held entitled to file appeal which was also allowed.[47]

43 The *Allahabad High Court judgment* mentions another act of judicial impropriety in this order by the judicial magistrate. 'At the end of the order . . . there was a line which was admittedly scored off by the Magistrate himself . . . The Magistrate stated that he scored off the sentence before signing the orders as it was redundant . . . [But] the cutting does not bear initials.' Nevertheless, the High Court with 'great difficulty' made sense of the scored off sentence. 'It is to the effect that *puja darshan* shall continue as was being done at that time (presently).' *Allahabad High Court Judgment*, note 7 at 39–40 (per S.U. Khan, J.) (emphasis in the original).

44 *Id.* at 40 (emphasis added).

45 *Umesh Chandra Pandey* v. *State of U.P. & Others*, Civil Appeal No. 66/198, in Noorani, note 27 at 267–269.

46 The order of the *munsif* never decided anything and therefore appeal could not lie against it. The order was passed without the judge even having the file of the case (which was in the High Court where the case was pending) that made it all the more suspect.

47 *Allahabad High Court Judgment*, note 7 at 90 (per S.U. Khan, J.).

Undoubtedly, this partisan judicial interruption of the 35 years of ***status quo***, in an extraordinarily erroneous fashion, provided the necessary stimulus to the eventual demolition of the mosque, as this was the time when politically the Ram janambhumi movement was gaining momentum.[48]

Khan's J. eight-page analysis of the incident of the unlocking of doors exposes how the judiciary became implicated in the failure to find a just resolution for this age-old conflict. He asserted that the proverbial wisdom that justice must not only be done but must also seem or appear to have been done was mutilated in the ***modus operandi*** of the district judge.[49] His opinion rendered great service by inaugurating the tradition of critical analysis in judicial reasoning which unfortunately found no echo in the judgment of the Supreme Court. He described this farcical order by the district judge, K.M. Pandey, as a 'real tragedy' because this 'shook the faith' of the affected parties, who were largely unaware of these proceedings, in the judicial system itself. The Supreme Court, which invested much of its intellectual labour on 'faith and belief,' did not find this landmark event that shook the faith of people in the judiciary as worthy of any elaboration. No critical comment on this sordid episode exists in the entire judgment. Despite the Apex Court's efforts to sanitise this violence, its traces remain in the legal archive which haunt this judgment's sense of 'complete justice.' Foregrounding these traces, as Khan, J. tried to do briefly, paints an alternate picture of the dispute which would not permit any easy reduction of this controversy to a mere 'title suit.' The next section evaluates the assessment of the Supreme Court in deciding the title claims in favour of the Hindu side.

IV. Structure as Mosque and Title Claim/s

In deciding the title, the first question before the Court was the fact of the existence of mosque itself. Did a mosque in fact exist at the disputed site? The Nirmohi Akhara (Suit no. 3) denied its existence arguing that 'the structure has always been a Hindu temple . . . managed by the Nirmohis at all material times.'[50] But both the Sunni Central Waqf Board (Suit no. 4) as well as the suit on behalf of the idol (Suit no. 5) accepted the presence of the mosque at the disputed site.[51] The Apex Court accepted the existence of the mosque and that

48 Since 1983, the Vishwa Hindu Parishad (VHP), a Hindu nationalist organisation, began its movement to 'liberate' the Babri masjid and mosques at Varanasi and Mathura. An ultimatum was served to the U.P. government 'to restore the birthplace of Lord Rama in Ayodhya to Hindus by Shivratri Day (Mar. 8, 1986) or face the consequences in the shape of massive agitation led by religious leaders of the country.' *Organizer* (Aug. 25, 1985), cited in Noorani, note 27 at 252–266.

49 *Allahabad High Court Judgment*, note 7 at 91. 'Before passing the judgment dated 1.02.1986 the learned District Judge first buried the second limb of the principle (appearance of justice) very deep.'

50 *Id.* at 103 (para 68). Nirmohi Akhara also denied the plantation of the idols in 1949.

51 *Ibid.* ('Hence, both in the pleading in Suit 4 and in Suit 5, there was essentially no dispute about the fact that the mosque was raised in 1528 AD by or at the behest of Babur.')

namaz was offered inside the mosque. '[I]t had been established that since 1857 until the last *namaz* was offered in the inner courtyard on 16 December 1949, Muslims had visited the mosque for worship.'[52] The argument on behalf of the deities (Suit no. 5) that the mosque was against the tenets of *Shariat* was declared by the Court to be of 'no significance' on account of 'the plural diversity of religious beliefs as they are practiced in India' where 'cultural assimilation cannot be construed as a feature destructive of religious doctrine.'[53] Also rejecting the argument of Nirmohi Akhara, the Court affirmed the presence of the mosque and that the 'last namaz . . . offered in the mosque was on 16 December 1949.'[54]

After determining the existence of the mosque, the Court went on to determine ownership and title of the entire property. According to the Court, the assessment for the purpose of determination of the title must consider the entire property one 'composite whole.'[55] It discarded the colonial bifurcation on the grounds that it never affected the 'determination of proprietary rights.'[56] To analyse the claim of possession, an assessment across historical time, governed by different sovereigns, was required. The Court proceeded on the principle that '[m]unicipal courts will only recognise those rights and liabilities which have been recognised by the new sovereign either expressly or impliedly through conduct established by evidence.'[57] Since a change in sovereignty is an act of State, in the absence of recognition of the acts of a regime by the subsequent sovereign, the 'Court cannot compel a subsequent sovereign to recognise and remedy historical wrongs.'[58]

The present dispute, the Court noted, has spanned across 'four distinct legal regimes.'[59] The regime of King Vikramaditya, who allegedly constructed a Hindu temple; the Mughal era in the sixteenth century; the British conquest of Oudh in 1856; and the constitutional regime of independent India. The Court found a continuity between the Mughal regime and the annexation of Oudh by the East India Company on February 13, 1856, 'which later became the colonial government of the British sovereign.'[60] This continuity arose from the implied recognition as 'no actions were taken by the [British] sovereign

52 *Id.* at 113 (para 74).

53 *Id.* at 115 (para 115). It was pointed out that the 'belief and faith of the worshipper in offering *namaz* at a place which is for the worshipper a mosque cannot be challenged.' *Id.* at 114–115 (para 77).

54 *Id.* at 79 (para 51).

55 *Id.* at 883 (para 771) (emphasis added). ('the nature and use of the disputed premises as a whole by either of the parties.').

56 The setting up of the railing was not a determination of proprietary rights over the inner and outer courtyards, the measure having been adopted to maintain peace between the two communities.

57 *Ayodhya Judgment*, note 1 at 765 (para 644).

58 *Id.* at 766 (para 646).

59 *Id.* at 757 (para 634).

60 *Id.* at 768 (para 650).

to exclude either the Hindu devotees of Lord Ram from worship nor (sic) the resident Muslims offering namaz at the disputed property.'[61] The line of continuity between British sovereign and independent India finds approval by the Indian Constitution itself. The Constitution specifically permits prior colonial laws to continue and 'remain in force therein until altered or repealed or amended by a competent Legislature.'[62] It is the presence of line of continuity with respect to the dispute that allowed its adjudication by municipal courts in India.

But no such continuity existed between the regime of King Vikramaditya and Mughal conquest of the territories.[63] The Court observed that the Mughal 'conquest' was a 'supra-national act between two sovereigns'[64] and perceived an absence of 'the recognition by the new sovereign of pre-existing rights.'[65] Therefore, it argued, it could not 'entertain or enforce rights to the disputed property based *solely* on the existence of an underlying temple dating to [the] twelfth century.'[66] Even if one were to surmise the destruction of the Hindu temple, this fact became irrelevant to determine the title as the 'change of sovereignty [was] an act of State and this Court [could not] compel a subsequent sovereign to recognise and remedy historical wrongs.'[67]

Once this jurisdictional proposition was accepted, the Hindu claim became one of faith and belief in the site as the birthplace of Ram. This was assessed from 1528 (when the mosque was established) till 1856 (the annexation of Oudh by the British) and from 1856–57 till India attained independence. During the latter period the grill wall, erected by the colonial government in 1857, separated the land into inner courtyard and outer courtyards. I will attempt to show how, in the assessment of historical events, the Court itself elevated Hindu faith to fill the lack of evidence of a prior Hindu temple at the site.

Worship at the Mosque During the Mughal Period (1528–1856)

The Court accepted the existence of the mosque constructed by Emperor Babur in 1528. However, it remarked 'in assessing the title of the Muslims, the physical structure of the mosque [was] one fact but a claim to possessory title [had] to be based on *exclusive and unimpeded possession* which [had] to be established by evidence.'[68] The principle of possession as both 'uninterrupted'

61 *Id.* at 768 (para 650).
62 Article 372 (1), Constitution of India.
63 *Ayodhya Judgment*, note 1 at 767 (para 648) ('no evidence has been led by the plaintiffs in Suit 5 to establish that upon the change in legal regime to the Mughal sovereign, such rights were recognised.').
64 *Id.* at 768 (para 649).
65 *Ibid.*
66 *Ibid* (emphasis in the original).
67 *Id.* at 766 (para 647).
68 *Id.* at 884 (para 772) (emphasis added).

and 'exclusive' became the cornerstone of the assessment. To establish this principle, the plaintiffs in Suit no. 4 (Sunni Waqf Board and Muslim residents) relied upon documentary evidence of 'cash grants . . . paid by royal treasury during the rule of Babur which was continued (sic) under colonial rule by the British.'[69]

However, the Supreme Court emphasised the 'crucial . . . absence of any evidence to indicate that the mosque was, after its construction, used for offering namaz until 1856–7.'[70] Why was the proof of worship required when the presence of a mosque was established? Why would a mosque be constructed in the Mughal period if not to offer prayers? If it was an abandoned mosque, then why would the subsequent British regime provide for its maintenance?[71] As there were no original grants from the pre-colonial period, how could one establish through contemporary evidence that the mosque had been in use for prayer before the nineteenth century? The counsel for the Sunni Waqf Board, Rajeev Dhavan, conceded that 'the evidentiary record essentially [commenced] with grants *which were stated to have been continued* by the British government for the upkeep of the mosque.'[72] However, this was not sufficient for the Court. It insisted on additional and specific proof that *namaz* was offered at the site. One wonders why the presence of the mosque constructed by a Muslim ruler during Mughal regime was not sufficient, on balance of probabilities, to deduce that devotees offered *namaz* there.[73]

In contrast, the Hindus were not expected to show 'exclusive' possession of the site. The evidence of Hindu 'faith and belief' in the site as the birthplace of Ram was significant to win over their counterparts. Referring to Tieffenthaler's account of 1770, the Court found his account having 'significant value when it advent[ed] to the existence of the faith and belief of Hindus in Lord Ram and of the association of the place of birth in close-proximity to the three-domed structure.'[74] In the section on 'Analysis of Title' towards the end of the judgment, the Court found both Tieffenthaler and Robert Montgomery Martin's accounts sufficient to indicate the 'existence of faith and belief of Hindus that the disputed site was the birthplace of Lord Ram.'[75] These, as against the uphill requirement of exclusive possession, were enough to serve as signposts

69 *Id.* at 791 (para 678).

70 *Ibid.*

71 A.G. Noorani, in his comment on the Supreme Court judgment, rightly asks whether the Court was presuming that 'the British spen[t] money for the upkeep of a mosque in which none prayed?' A.G. Noorani, 'Supreme Court Denies Justice' *Frontline* (Dec. 6, 2019).

72 *Ibid.*

73 The Indian Evidence Act, 1872, s. 114 (now, s. 119 of the Bharatiya Sakshya Adhiniyam, 2023) provides that the court 'may presume the existence of any fact which it thinks likely to have happened, regard being had to the common course of natural events, human conduct and public and private business, in their relation to the facts of the particular case.'

74 *Ayodhya Judgment*, note 1 at 684 (para 573).

75 *Id.* at 908 (para 788).

to the 'historical presence of worshippers and the existence of worship at the disputed site even prior to the annexation of Oudh by the British.'[76]

The Court also drew inference from a report of Archaeological Survey of India (ASI) which said that 'recoveries[were] suggestive of a Hindu religious origin comparable to temple excavations in the region and pertaining to the era.'[77] The Court was prompt to add that any 'finding of title [could not] be based in law on the archaeological findings which have been arrived at by ASI,'[78] but certainly this must have had some bearing on the Court. After all, the Court spent considerable ink, close to one hundred pages, on the discussion of the ASI report.[79] The Court also pointed out that title '[could not] be established on the basis of faith and belief alone.'[80] But the travel accounts and the ASI report were indicative of 'patterns of worship'[81] which, the Court accepted, could establish title. In the concluding part of the judgment the Court observed:[82]

> As regards the inner courtyard, there is evidence on a *preponderance of probabilities* to establish worship by the Hindus prior to the annexation of Oudh by the British in 1857. The Muslims have offered no evidence to indicate that they were in *exclusive possession* of the inner structure prior to 1857 since the date of the construction in the sixteenth century.

The evidentiary standard of the preponderance of probabilities acquires a distinct form for the two sides; while the Muslims were required to show exclusive possession in material terms, the Court accepted mere faith and belief as sufficient requirement for the Hindu claim.

Worship in the Inner Courtyard (Mosque) During the British Era (1856–1947)

The colonial wall of separation after the riots of 1856–57 limited the right to worship of the two communities within specified spheres (Muslims having the right of passage to the mosque from the outer courtyard). The Court asserted that the 'Hindu worship at Ramchabutra, Sita Rasoi . . . clearly indicated their *exclusive and unimpeded possession* of the *outer courtyard*.'[83] It is noteworthy that it was only in this context that the Court employed the yardstick of 'exclusive' possession with respect to the Hindu community. But that was limited to the outer courtyard which was exclusively granted to the Hindus. However,

76 *Ibid.*
77 *Id.* at 906 (para 788).
78 *Id.* at 907 (para 788).
79 *Id.* at 507–599.
80 *Id.* at 908 (para 788).
81 *Id.* at 908 (para 788).
82 *Id.* at 921 (para 798) (emphasis added).
83 *Id.* at 910 (para 788) (emphasis added).

following the standard mentioned by the Court, in adjudicating on the land as a 'composite whole,' possession with respect to both the outer as well as the inner courtyard was needed. Once again, the Court accentuated Hindu faith: 'Despite the construction of the wall in 1858 by the British and the setting up of the Ramchabutra . . . Hindus continued to assert their right to pray inside the three-domed structure.'[84] It is difficult to comprehend how the Hindu assertion for the inner courtyard can be understood as 'their right' when the colonial law, which the Court never contested given its constitutional continuity, would consider such an encroachment contrary to law. It is useful to mention here a few illustrations of these encroachments and their transformation in the eyes of the Court.

On November 28, 1858, Nihang Singh went inside the inner courtyard and 'erected a religious symbol'[85] according to the report of the *thanedar* (Inspector) of Oudh. An application was filed against this by the *moazzin* (Muslim priest) of the mosque, which spoke of the 'highhandedness of Hindus' in erecting religious symbols and offering worship. The Court remarked that '[e]vidently, the railing did not prevent access to the inner courtyard or to the precincts of the mosque.'[86] This was even though Nihang Singh was admonished and served a summons for his trespass.

Another skirmish between the two communities emerged in 1860, when Mir Rajjab Ali filed a complaint which stated that 'when the Moazzin recites Azaan, the opposite party begins to blow conch (Shankh/Naqoos).'[87] In March 1861, Mohd Asghar and Rajjab Ali together complained against the construction of a new *chabutra* without permission. The *subedar* sent a report for the eviction of the person. In 1866, the *mutawalli* again complained that some fresh *kothari* (small room) had been constructed by the *bairagis* inside the mosque for placing idols. This fact too had been acknowledged by the Supreme Court.[88] But all these acts of encroachment were interpreted by the Apex Court as evidence of 'contestation' by the Hindu community.

The Suit of 1885

On January 29, 1885, *Mahant* (High priest) Raghubar Das instituted a civil suit (suit of 1885) in the court of the sub-judge of Faizabad. The plaintiff described himself as 'Mahant Janmasthan at Ayodhya.'[89] The plaintiff sought an injunction that the defendant should be restrained from obstructing the

84 *Ibid.*
85 *Id.* at 64 (para 46).
86 *Ibid.*
87 *Ibid.*
88 *Id.* at 889 (para 777).
89 *Mahant Raghubar Das, Mohanth, Asthan, situate Ayodhya, plaintiff* v. *The Secretary of State for India in Council, Defendant.* Full text of the judgment is available in Noorani, note 27 at 175–188.

plaintiff from constructing a temple over the *chabutra* situated in the outer courtyard. Although the court recognised the possession and right of the plaintiff to construct the temple on the platform described in the plaint as 'Chabutra Janam Asthan' (the birthplace of Ram), it refused to grant permission due to law and order issues that might arise on such construction.[90] The appeals filed against this order were also dismissed. The Supreme Court while referring to this case only considered the limited question 'whether the findings in the suit will operate as *res judicata*.'[91] However, what was left under-appreciated was the fact that the Hindu *mahant* who instituted the suit referred to the *chabutra* situated in the outer courtyard as the birthplace of Ram. Further, there was no reference, much less any claim, with respect to the mosque or the inner courtyard as the birthplace of Ram.

Various scholars have pointed out that the claim of the central dome of the mosque as the birthplace of Ram appeared only in the twentieth century. Anupam Gupta[92] has asserted the absence of any assertion of janambhumi in the works of Swami Vivekananda, 'who visited Ayodhya in 1888, and again in 1890, as a *parivrajaka*, or wandering monk.'[93] A similar silence exists in the writing of Vinayak Damodar Savarkar, who, 'writing in 1908 on the first war of independence, 51 years earlier, devoted a whole chapter entitled "Ayodhya" to the havoc wrought by the British in Oudh before 1857.'[94] Gupta concludes that the stark 'absence of any allusion to the Ram janmabhoomi issue in their speeches and writings is an eloquent reminder of the artificiality of the main issue.'[95] A.G. Noorani has pointed out that the invention of the issue as national honour belongs to recent Hindu revivalism.[96] 'Surely, if it was a matter of "honour" for the Hindus, the founder of RSS, Hedgewar, his successor M.S. Golwalkar, and their ideological mentor V.D. Savarkar, would not have kept silent on the issue.'[97] In this light, the suit of 1888 and the description of the *chabutra* in the outer courtyard as birthplace of Ram, if alternatively read, could have furnished the documentary proof against the Hindu claim present in the judicial archive itself.

In 1934, substantial damage was inflicted upon the mosque, for which the Hindus were fined.[98] The colonial government 'sanctioned the work of repair

90 *Id.* at 181 (per Hari Kishan, Sub Judge, 'This place is not like other places where the owner has got the right to construct any building he likes . . . For this reason of breach of law and order the officers have restrained the parties from making any new construction.').
91 *Ayodhya Judgment*, note 1 at 71 (para 46).
92 He also served as a council for the Liberhan Commission, a commission of enquiry set up by the government of India ten days after the demolition of the Babri mosque.
93 Anupam Gupta, 'Dissecting the Ayodhya Judgment' 45(50) *Economic and Political Weekly*, 33–37 (2010).
94 *Id.* at 35.
95 *Ibid.*
96 Noorani, note 27, 'Introduction' and literature cited there.
97 *Id.* at xxi.
98 *Ayodhya Judgment*, note 1 at 72 (para 47).

and renovation of the damaged structure of the mosque.'[99] The Supreme Court read all of these incidents, including the damage to the mosque in 1934, as matters of 'contestation' and lack of 'exclusive possession' of the Muslims over the inner courtyard:[100]

> The riots of 1934 and the events which led up to 22/23 December 1949 indicate that possession over the inner courtyard was a *matter of serious contestation* often leading to violence by both parties and the Muslims did not have *exclusive possession* over the inner courtyard. From the above documentary evidence, it cannot be said that the Muslims have been able to establish their possessory title to the disputed site as a composite whole.

Even if one accepts the contestation argument, it remains a fact that even during the British era, the Hindu community never proved 'exclusive possession' with respect to the inner courtyard. What, then, were the legal bases on which the inner courtyard was awarded to them as a part of composite land? Also, how can trespass, aggression and violence ever qualify as matters of contestation in the legal adjudication of property rights? Can these actions not be read as evidence of historical aggression by the Hindus? The Court remained silent on the issue of Muslim contestation. The Court observed that '[d]espite the existence of the railing, the exclusion of the Hindus from the inner courtyard was a *matter of contestation* and at the very least was not absolute.'[101] The only way that the interpretation of the Court can be understood is that it placed the faith of Hindus on a higher pedestal.

Another important strand of *Ayodhya Judgment* was the status of idol as a juristic person. As we now know, Suit no. 5 was filed in 1989 by the idol of the deity itself. Obviously *de facto* it was filed by a human person, but on behalf of the deity as *de jure* an idol is a juristic person under Indian law. It is this dimension of the status of the Hindu idol as a juristic person which will now be explored historically from the limited perspective of its relevance in the *Ayodhya Judgment.*

V. Idol as Juristic Person

If there is one issue which is most unintelligible for the reader of the *Ayodhya Judgment,* then it is the status of juristic person accorded to the Hindu idol in the Indian law.[102] This is not only confusing to a reader from another

99 *Ibid.*

100 *Id.* at 892 (para 781) (emphasis added).

101 *Id.* at 892 (para 781).

102 A legal personality is the recognition of a subject in the eyes of law. It is a necessary recognition to assert any legal entitlement, claim or capability to enter in legal relations with others.

jurisdiction but also for any social scientist untrained in law in India. How can an idol file a civil suit for property rights in a court of law? This is explained by unique historical circumstances, which I will explain in this section, that led the colonial courts to introduce the notion of the Hindu idol as a juristic person in India. Thus, this issue was neither unique nor new when it emerged in the Ayodhya dispute. What was actually novel was the claim by the Hindu side that the land in and of itself is a juristic person. It was argued that since the land in this dispute has a special significance for Hindus – being the mythic birthplace of Lord Ram – this in and of itself should suffice for it to acquire juristic personality. The argument of land as juristic personality could have severe implications for the future. The Supreme Court rejected this argument. Certainly, this was one of the best moments in an otherwise convoluted and confused judgment. In this section, I will try to trace the historical recognition and innovation of new form of juristic person in Hindu idol. I will comment on the development of this notion both before and after independence in the judicial discourse.

Ascription of juristic personality to the Hindu idol is entirely a creation of judicial interpretation. The Supreme Court in *Ayodhya Judgment* observed that the 'ability to create or recognise legal persons has always varied depending upon historic circumstances.'[103] Even natural persons historically in common law were once denied the recognition of legal personhood.[104] However, soon the legal process inaugurated ways to grant personhood not only to natural persons but also to artificial entities. The ascription of legal personality to material objects which are not natural persons forms the core of artificial legal personality. Such conferring of juristic personality is possible by way of legislation or judicial interpretation.

The attribution of an artificial juristic personality to idols in India arose from a peculiar historical necessity. Large tracts of land were dedicated by Emperors in pre-colonial times for the creation of Hindu shrines or Hindu Gods,[105] and thus arose the question of what would happen to the property vested in the deity after the death of the testator. Would the property become *res nullius*, allowing the State to regulate, protect or even divest this property? Or, will the property be vested in the *purpose*, symbolised by the idol of the deity?[106] The colonial courts following the traditional Hindu law allowed the *purpose* personified by the idol to be considered as having the title of the property.

103 *Ayodhya Judgment*, note 1 at 127 (para 88).

104 The classic instance was the upholding of racial law by the US Supreme Court denying personhood to blacks as late as the nineteenth century in *Dred Scott* v. *Sandford* 60 U.S. (19 How.) 393 (1857). For a critical discussion see, Jack M. Balkin and Sanford Levinson, 'Thirteen Ways of Looking at *Dred Scott*' 82 (1) *Chicago-Kent Law Review* 49 (2006).

105 In Chapter 1, we noted, in *Nathdwara Temple* case, that Emperor Akbar had granted a *firman* for establishing the Shrinathji temple at Nathdwara.

106 See Gunthur-Dietz Sontheimer, *Essays on Religion, Literature and Law* (Indira Gandhi National Centre for Arts, New Delhi, 2004), Ch1.

These dedicated properties, for religious or charitable purposes, have a special term under Hindu law. Such property is described as *debutter* property. Those who manage or cultivate such properties are known as *Shebaits* ('managers' of property dedicated for religious purposes). *Shebaits* do not possess any ownership rights over these lands. They only have a title as managers on behalf of the deities. With the escalation in the value of endowed property, various disputes arose in the nineteenth century concerning such properties, idols and endowments.[107] The disputes with respect to ownership and management of the *debutter* property came up before the colonial courts for the first time in late nineteenth century. Three important cases decided by the High Courts of Bombay (now Mumbai), Madras (now Chennai) and Calcutta (now Kolkata) consolidated the attribution of artificial personality to the idol as a matter of convenience and practical necessity.

The Idol as a Legal Person in Colonial Times

The first case was decided by the Bombay High Court in *Manohar Ganesh Tambekar & Others* v. *Lakshmiram Govindram* (1888).[108] In this case, a temple was dedicated to the deity Shri Ranchhod Raiji. The plaintiffs (Tambekar and others) approached the High Court as 'persons interested' in the religious foundation. They accused the defendant managers of appropriating the temple offerings and income for their personal benefit and not for the benefit of the temple.[109] The defendants (*shevaks* or ministers) argued that they 'are the owners, for all secular purposes, of the idol, whom, in the spiritual sense, they serve.'[110] The offering of prayers to the deity, they argued, was in the nature of a moral duty 'which they discharge merely to satisfy their conscience . . . by their own will and judgment.'[111] The issue was whether the defendants, who were also beneficiaries of the offerings made to the temple property, can be obligated for a proper management of the temple property? And can an external third party sue them for the improper management of the temple funds?

Justice Robin West acknowledged that like Roman law, the traditional Hindu law also accepted 'the juridical persons or subjects called foundations.'[112] However, the English common law mandates the formation of a 'trust' for endowed religious property. There was no such need in Hindu law if the property was endowed by a Hindu for religious or charitable purposes. Customarily,

107 *Ayodhya Judgment*, note 1 at 148 (para 106).
108 (1888) ILR 12 Bom 247.
109 *Ibid.* (per Robin West, J.) ('The income of the temple having, as they say, largely increased, and being wrongly or unduly appropriated by the defendants, called generally the *shevaks* (or ministers), to their personal purposes, they pray for the appointment of a receiver for the exaction from the defendants of accounts of their management.').
110 *Id.* para 3.
111 *Ibid.*
112 *Id.* para 11.

the rulers and emperors maintained an endowment in accordance with the will of the person who endowed the property. They were required to safeguard the property 'as it [was] consistent with his own dharma or conception of morality.'[113] Endowing a judicial personality to an idol under Hindu law and accepting the claim of the plaintiff, the Court observed:[114]

> [I]f there is a juridical person, [which is] the ideal embodiment of a pious or benevolent idea . . . this artificial subject of rights is as capable of taking offerings of cash and jewels as of land. Those who take physical possession . . . incur thereby a responsibility for its due application to the purposes of the foundation . . . They are answerable as trustees even though they have not consciously accepted a trust, and a remedy may be sought against them for maladministration.

The Bombay High Court was not inventing the idea of idol as an artificial legal person. It was only consolidating the position and reverence given to property under traditional Hindu law dedicated for religious purposes. The Bombay High Court equated the notion of attributing juridical personhood with embodiment of a pious or benevolent purpose in the category of the Hindu idol. The classical Hindu law received a judicial approval by colonial courts in accepting the Hindu idol as a juridical person. By conferring personhood on the Hindu idol, the following aims were achieved. First, it provided legitimacy to any third party (worshipper) interested in the idol or *debutter* property to check and control any corrupt *shebaits* who might go against the purpose of the endowment. The corollary of this legal fiction was that even in the absence of a trust (as required under English common law), it mandated duties and responsibilities on managers of *debutter* property who were receiving benefit from the property. Second, it provided an adjudicative framework to determine the rights, responsibilities and duties of managers in cases where the endowment's original founder was not alive as the *shebaits* lacked legal ownership.

Creation of any endowment with a pious intent/purpose thus became sufficient to attribute legal personality to the idol. The High Court clarified that the legal personality was not rendered to divinity itself but to one or other form of its manifestation.[115] The polytheistic nature of Hindu religion made the consideration of the idol to be granted legal personality more conducive, because the property was generally dedicated in the name of some deity.[116]

113 *Ibid.*

114 *Ibid.*

115 *Ibid.* This distinction between divinity which is formless or abstract from its physical and tangible manifestation has been reiterated by the Supreme Court in the *Ayodhya Judgment.*

116 As the Supreme Court observed in its survey on the subject in *Ayodhya Case*: 'Legal personality is conferred on the pious purpose of the individual making the endowment. Where the endowment is made to an idol, the idol forms the material representation of the legal person.' *Ayodhya Case*, note 1 at 152 (para 111).

The juristic personality given to the idol or deity was to safeguard the purpose for which the religious grant was originally made.

The next case on this issue came before the Madras High Court in 1904. In *Vidyapurna Swami* v. *Vidyanidhi Swami* (1904),[117] the Madras High Court reiterated the important social function served by investing an idol with artificial personality. The social function was empowering the devotees as interested persons who, as 'next friends of the idol,' could sue the *shebaits*. This result could also have been attained, the High Court noted, by granting an artificial personality to 'devotees as a collective' or a 'community of worshippers.'[118] However, on grounds of practicality and convenience, the idol itself was considered a juristic person. The attribution of juristic personality, therefore, was based on reasons of pragmatism and convenience of adjudication by secular courts.[119]

The next decision on this issue was delivered by a five-judge-bench decision of the Calcutta High Court in 1910. In *Bhupati Nath* v. *Ram Lal Maitra* (1910),[120] a complex question came before the Calcutta High Court. The testator (Umesh Chandra Lahiri) bequeathed his property to various trustees; one provision in his testament dedicated the property to the goddess Kali for the establishment of her idol. After his death, the plaintiff (Bhupati Nath) argued that this provision of the testament was void and invalid on account of the absence of the idol at the time of the testator's death. Part of the argument of the plaintiffs was based on a previous precedent: that in case of an idol, its presence was not enough because its consecration (*pran-pratishtha*) was imperative.[121] In the present case, both the establishment as well as the consecration of the image of goddess Kali took place after the death of the testator.

The Calcutta High Court, however, upheld the validity of the dedication to safeguard the pious purpose intended by the testator. It observed that 'this manifestly was a disposition for religious purposes and favoured by Hindu law.'[122] Conceding the nature of the property, it was pointed out that despite

117 (1904) ILR 27 Mad 435.

118 *Ibid.*

119 The *Ayodhya Judgment* reviewed and reiterated the law relating to idols as juristic persons, the Apex Court reiterated that the evolution of the concept was 'not based on strict legal principle but is an outcome of historical circumstances, legal necessity and convenience.' *Ayodhya case,* note 1 at 139 (para 98).

120 (1910) ILR 37 Cal 128 [Hereafter, '*Bhupati Nath*'].

121 The precedent which laid down this proposition was *Dourga Proshad Dass* v. *Sheu Proshad Pandah* (1880) 7 C.L.R. 278. It was decided, by the Calcutta High Court, that for an idol to have juridical existence, its consecration following proper rituals and ceremonies is required. This decision along with various others, that observed that a gift made to a Hindu deity is void if the idol of the deity came into existence in the future, were overruled by the five-judge bench judgment.

122 *Bhupati Nath*, note 120. In his opinion, H. Lawrence Jenkins, CJ., makes a reference to *Vyavahara Adhyay* of *Mitakshara* and *Mahanirvana Tantra* to elucidate this point.

the testator's death 'the pious purpose is still the legatee, the establishment of the image is merely the mode in which the pious purpose is to be effected.'[123] The High Court clarified that an idol was a juristic person in law but 'it is only in *an ideal sense* property can be said to belong to an idol.'[124] Another judge who wrote a separate concurring opinion, James Stephens, J., compared the position of the idol to a minor and observed that the managers or 'the ministers of an idol have . . . the same rights that they would have if they were trustees for his benefit, or if he was an infant and they managers on his behalf.'[125]

A few important propositions emerged from this decision. The first was the attempt of the colonial courts to protect the original intended *purpose* of the endowment which was central in conferring an artificial personality to the idol. This was in tune with the classical Hindu law where a dedication of property made to the deities was greatly valued. The idol was considered the physical or corporeal manifestation of a divine purpose. Second, a consolidation of the traditional viewpoint that pious gifts made to deities stood on a different footing than ordinary gifts of corporeal property.[126] When a gift is made, the donor is divested of his rights over the tangible property (moveable or immovable). But where the gift is made to divinity, the person to whom the gift was made did not exist. This lacuna was filled by ascribing an artificial juridical personality to the deity. This explains the third important point made by the Court that the property is vested in the idol in an 'ideal sense,' which means that the actual beneficiaries of the property were natural persons. As already mentioned, any individual devotee can sue as a 'next friend' on behalf of the idol for maladministration by managers. This formulation provided legal certainty with respect to ownership and possession of the property endowed for religious purposes (*debutter*).

The point was again reiterated in a later case of *Mohatap Bahadur* v. *Kali Pada Chatterjee* (1914),[127] where the dedicated idol had been washed away by floods and another idol had been established by the Maharaja of Burdwan.[128] The Calcutta High Court directed the *shebaits* to fulfil their duties and continue to perform religious rites, as the destruction of the original idol did not extinguish the 'pious purpose' for which it had been originally established.

123 *Id.* para 8 (per Lawrence H. Jenkins, C.J.).

124 *Id.* para 15 (per Lawrence H. Jenkins, C.J., emphasis added). ('[T]he rule which requires relinquishment should be to a sentient person does not forbid the gift of property to trustees for a religious purpose, though that purpose cannot in strictness be called a sentient person . . . this at least seems clear that the rule which requires relinquishment should be to a sentient person does not forbid the gift of property to trustees for a religious purpose, though that purpose cannot in strictness be called a sentient person.').

125 *Id.* para 22 (per James Stephen, J.).

126 *Id.* para 62 (per Mookerjee, J.). ('[I]t is established beyond the possibility of dispute that the ordinary conception of a gift is not applicable to the case of dedication to the deity.').

127 AIR 1914 Cal 200.

128 The respondent was the *shebait* of the idol of 'Trilokeshvar Shiva' for whose worship certain land was dedicated by the Maharaja of Burdwan.

This underscored the law's intent to protect the pious purpose for which the property is endowed to religious deities.

The Position of the Idol After Independence

This position of the religious idol as a juristic person was consolidated in the early decisions of the Supreme Court in independent India. In 1956, in a four-judge bench decision in *Deoki Nandan* v. *Murlidhar*,[129] a Hindu ceremoniously installed the idol of 'Shri Radhakrishnaji' on a piece of land called Thakurwada in Sitapur district. After his death, the property, which was in the name of the idol, got transferred and was managed by his nephew Murlidhar. A distant agnate of the original founder filed a case on the grounds of gross mismanagement of the dedicated property. The lower court and first appellate court refused to interfere on the grounds that the property was private and built for worship within the family. The Supreme Court, allowing the appeal, explained that the property dedicated to divinity must be seen as 'abandoned' by the true owner and thus cannot be considered as private property. It is vested symbolically in the gods themselves and therefore an action against the maladministration of such property was maintainable.[130] Once again, the idea of fictional legal personality ensured that the original purpose of the dedicated land was restored.

Yogendra Nath Naskar v. *Commissioner of Income Tax, Calcutta* (1969)[131] posed an interesting issue of taxation before the Supreme Court for the income tax assessment of the deities through *shebaits*. Ram Naskar left property as *debutter* for two deities in the land beside his residential home at Calcutta. His two adopted sons were appointed as *shebaits*. The appellant was one of the adopted sons who argued that *debuttar* property, in the absence of an express trust, was not amenable for tax assessment. Justice V. Ramaswami, referring to the work of B.K. Mukherjea on Hindu religious and charitable endowments, observed:[132]

> With regard to Debutter, the position seems to be somewhat different. What is personified here, is not the entire property which is dedicated to the deity but the deity itself which is the central part of the foundation and stands as the material symbol and embodiment of the pious purpose which the dedicator has in view.

129 AIR 1957 SC 133.

130 *Ibid.* Referring to the classical texts of Hindu laws, the Court pointed out that 'according to the texts, the Gods have no beneficial enjoyment of the properties, and they can be described as their owners only in a figurative sense (*Gainartha*), and the true purpose of a gift of properties to the idol is not to confer any benefit on God, but to acquire spiritual benefit by providing opportunities and facilities for those who desire to worship.'

131 AIR 1969 SC 1089.

132 *Ibid.*

The Court held that the dedicated property was owned by the religious foundation, and the *shebaits* who carried out the maintenance and acquired the benefits from the property were amenable to be assessed under income tax law.[133] The Hindu idol or deity, the Court observed, is an individual within the meaning of Section 3 of the Income Tax Act and can be assessed for tax purposes, and the exemption claimed for Hindu deities was rejected.

Pious Purpose in the Context of Non-Hindu Religious Structures

An important question that arose to be decided by the Indian Supreme Court was whether '*Guru Granth Sahib*,' the sacred book of Sikhs, can acquire the status of a legal person? The factual question that arose in *Shiromani Gurdwara Prabandhak Committee, Amritsar* v. *Som Nath Dass* (2000)[134] was whether the land under dispute was a Sikh gurdwara, *dharamshala* or *dera*. The ownership column of the land in official records indicated the '*Guru Granth Sahib*' as the owner. It is the prominent religious book, considered as a master/guru in Sikhism after the demise of the last living guru, Guru Gobind Singh. The revenue officer had permitted the transfer of title (mutation) of the land in the name of the religious book.

The tribunal and the Punjab High Court invalidated the mutation on the ground that *Guru Granth Sahib* was not a juristic person and therefore cannot acquire immovable property. The Supreme Court, setting aside these decisions, declared the book itself as a juristic person. Following the logic of a benevolent endowment for the religious purpose, it observed that the faith of the Sikhs in the book 'necessitated the creation of a unit to be recognised as a *juristic person*.'[135] When the 'donor endows for an idol *or for a mosque* or for any institution, it necessitates the creation of a juristic person.'[136] This reinstated the notion that by virtue of a juristic personality, the legal apparatus ensures that the divine purpose for which the original grant was intended is protected and the original intent of the donor is executed.

The Supreme Court distinguished Hinduism and Sikhism and clarified that the *Guru Granth Sahib* 'cannot be equated with an "idol" as idol worship is contrary to Sikhism.'[137] Nevertheless, despite different contexts, the Court

133 The Court also referred to the origin of this principle from the doctrine of *pia causa* (pious cause) in Roman law. What distinguishes Indian law from its Roman counterpart is the fact that the Roman law 'took the view that the endowments of charitable foundations were a species of Church property. *Piae cause* were subjected to the control of the church, that is, of the bishop or the ecclesiastical administrator, as the case might be. A *pia causa* was regarded as an ecclesiastical, and consequently, as a public institution, and as such it shared that corporate capacity which belonged to all ecclesiastical institutions by virtue of a general rule of law. A *pia causa* did not require to have a juristic personality expressly conferred upon it.' *Ibid*.

134 (2000) 4 SCC 146 [Hereafter, '*Guru Granth Sahib*'].

135 *Id*. para 28.

136 *Id*. para 19 (emphasis added).

137 *Id*. para 34.

conferred an artificial juristic personality upon the *Guru Granth Sahib*. It is because of the 'legal recognition as a juristic person, the followers of both the religions give them respectively the same reverential value.'[138] The absence of the phenomenon of idol worship did not limit the judiciary from ascribing a distinct legal personality to the sacred book. It is this legal expediency and the underlying premise (that public interest was served by the benevolent dedication of religious or charitable property) that became central in deciding the question of artificial personality.[139] On this register, and as specifically mentioned in the *Guru Granth Sahib* case, it would seem that there is actually no limitation on attributing a juristic personality to a mosque in India. It is significant, then, that the mosque in the Babri Masjid case was not granted a juristic personality[140] by the colonial courts. This was because in the pre-colonial judgment that formed the basis of the proposition, the question was framed in unique terms, seeking judicial personality for the mosque *as* land in and of itself.

Land as a Juristic Person in and of Itself

As already noted, the issue of land or place of birth in and of itself (Asthan, Shri Ram Janambhumi, Ayodhya) as a juristic person arose for the first time in post-independent India in the *Ayodhya Judgment*. If the land itself were to be accepted as a tangible manifestation of divinity and in turn a juristic person, all competing claims against it would have stood extinguished since it would have ceased to have the character of an immovable property and would have become an owner in and of itself.

It was urged before the Supreme Court (in Suit no. 5, filed in 1989) that the spot under the central dome of the mosque where the idols were placed was Lord Ram's birthplace, which should be conferred a juristic personality. It was contended that since the presence of an idol was not necessary in Hinduism for ascription of legal personality (as other forms of *manifestation* of the deity were equally acceptable),[141] the land which was worshipped as a deity could itself be granted the status of a juristic person.[142]

138 *Id.* para 34.

139 In the *Ayodhya Judgment*, the Court consolidated this position: 'The State will therefore protect property which stands vested in the idol even absent the establishment of a specific or express trust. The pious purpose, or "benevolent idea" is elevated to the state of a juristic person and the idol forms the material expression of the pious purpose through which legal relations are affected.' *Ayodhya case*, note 1 at 156 (para 115).

140 This was held in *The Mosque, Masjid Shahid Ganj* v. *Shiromani Gurdwara Parbandhak Committee, Amritsar*, AIR 1940 PC 116.

141 'It is conceivable that in certain instances the land itself would possess certain unique characteristics. For example, it may be claimed that certain patterns on a sea-shore or crop formations represent a manifestation of the divine. In these cases, the manifestation is inseparable from the land and is tied up to it.' *Ayodhya Judgment*, note 1 at 215 (para 193).

142 *Id.* at 192 (para 160). This argument was accepted by two of the three judges in the Allahabad High Court – V. Shama & Sudhir Aggarwal, JJ – who accepted that the land in Ayodhya itself constitutes a juristic person.

The Supreme Court rejected this contention. It noted that idols were granted legal personality to safeguard the benevolent purpose of religious dedication, which was not the case in the present instance because there is no express dedication to the land which had ever been made. The Apex Court rejected and overturned the verdict of the Allahabad High Court in this regard. According to the Supreme Court, this contention, if accepted, had the potential to stultify the very purpose of attributing juristic personality to material objects:[143]

> [In the absence of any clear] manifestation, recognising the land as a self-manifested deity would open the floodgates for parties to contend that ordinary land which was witness to some event of religious significance associated with the human incarnation of a deity (e.g. the site of marriage, or the ascent to a heavenly abode) is in fact a Swayambhu deity manifested in the form of land.

The Supreme Court distinguished property vested in a religious foundation or deity from property in and of itself as a juristic person. The latter would amount to altering the character of immovable property and making all the legal principles inapplicable to it. Accepting such a proposition would amount to legitimising all the 'claims to "absolute title" sustained merely on the basis of the faith and belief of the devotees.'[144] Accepting this argument would have amounted to elevating subjective faith and belief of devotees beyond the legal framework and its categories – limitation, ownership, possession, etc. It seems that the Supreme Court did not wish to open the floodgates for all kinds of religious claims by declaring the *spot* of Ram janambhumi as a legal personality, because its purpose for securing the janambhumi to the Hindu side was better served in this case by declaring the idol itself a juristic person. Nevertheless, this proposition as laid down in the *Ayodhya Judgment* is important to stultify any future claims that would have arisen had the Court declared the land in and of itself a juristic person. But the contentious point, for this chapter, is that if the juristic personality of the idol was meant to protect the pious purpose, then how and where did the Supreme Court locate that purpose in this dispute where the idols were placed in violation of the rule of law?

Maintainability of the Deity's Plaint of 1989

With respect to the Nirmohi Akhara (Suit no. 3), the Supreme Court clarified that the plaintiffs had claimed the management rights of the temple as *shebaits*. They were not *de jure shebaits*, as they did not have deed of dedication.[145] Their assertion was one of *de facto shebaits* 'by virtue of their long-standing presence

143 *Id.* at 215 (para 192).
144 *Id.* at 221 (para 201).
145 *Id.* at 406 (para 360).

at the disputed site.'[146] They pleaded the absence of any mosque at the site and claimed that they had managed the inner courtyard at all times. Both assertions, however, were made without any evidence and were rejected by the Supreme Court.[147]

The Nirmohi Akhara's attempt to claim title of the land adversely affected their case. It gave an impression of dereliction of duty on their part. The Court accepted the argument pleaded on behalf of the deities that the Nirmohi Akhada had failed to fulfil its managerial duties as it claimed the title to the land. In the Court's words:

> Suit 5 is founded on the plea that the needs and concerns of the deity of Lord Ram were not being protected and that the parties to the earlier suits were pursuing their own interests. This apprehension as the basis of Suit 5 is not without substance.[148]

It was only on account of Nirmohi Akhada's 'historical presence' and 'role' at the disputed site that the Court directed that they must be given 'an appropriate role in the management' of the trust to be made for the construction of the temple.[149]

The suit on behalf of the deities (Suit no. 5) was filed in 1989. There was an issue regarding the limitation period, as the cause of action had arisen in 1949. On principle, the Supreme Court rejected the argument that the deities could be treated as *perpetually minor* and the law of limitation applied to the deities as it did to any other natural person.[150] However, the Court accepted the suit on two grounds. First, that the worship or *seva-puja* of the deities continued even after the attachment of property in 1949. Therefore, it observed, one could not suggest that 'the cause of action in Suit 5 arose on 29 December 1949.'[151] The second ground was that the dereliction of the duty by the *shebaits* (the Nirmohi Akhada) has given sufficient reason for a 'next friend' to sue on behalf of the idols.

The Supreme Court itself acknowledged the illegality of the act of idol installation in 1949, but at the same time it stretched the time period for the

146 *Ibid.*

147 *Id.* at 426 (para 385). ('Nirmohi Akhara has failed to prove that at the material time, the disputed structure was a temple which was in its possession and that no incident had taken place on 22/23 December, 1949. Absent exclusive possession of the inner courtyard, the claim that Nirmohi Akhara was managing the inner courtyard as shebaits does not arise.').

148 *Id.* at 479 (para 428).

149 *Id.* at 925 (para 804). This was an extraordinary direction in which the Court justified taking recourse to Article 142 which allowed it to pass orders and decrees beyond the claims in order to effectuate 'complete justice.'

150 *Id.* at 473 (para 425) ('it is an established position that a deity cannot on the ground of being a perpetual minor stand exempted from the application of the Limitation Act.').

151 *Id.* at 477 (para 428).

cause of action for the purposes of limitation in favour of the Hindu community.[152] The continuation of worship of illegally transplanted idols, by administration and judicial order, instead of inviting the Court's condemnation, functioned to the benefit of the Hindu party in Suit no. 5. As to the second reason for allowing the suit instituted by the idols, the Supreme Court indicated that the Nirmohi Akhada failed to perform its managerial functions satisfactorily. Instead of focusing on their managerial functions they 'travelled beyond the claim of management' in their plaint and claimed the 'alleged "right and titles" and its "title and interest".'[153]

The Supreme Court also accepted the deity's suit on the ground that they were juristic persons. However, this presumption of juristic personality of idols was made without any evidence for their dedication for a specific religious or benevolent purpose (which, as we have seen in the survey of aforementioned cases, had been the pre-requisite for conferring juristic personality to idols in previous decisions). On the contrary, the Supreme Court itself accepted that the purpose for instituting the idols had been malevolent and *mala fide*. In this sense, the argument that applied to *Asthan Sri Ramjnambhumi*, i.e. the land (second plaintiff in suit no. 5) applied equally to *Sri Ram Lalla Virajman* (first plaintiff), the idol. These flaws in the Court's reasoning appeared at least two levels. One, the entire jurisprudence of pious purpose and historical necessity fell flat. The acceptance of the illegally placed idols flew in the face of the entire jurisprudence of a pious purpose and historical necessity thus far. By allowing the deities to sue for title to that land, the Court turned the idols themselves into annexationist gods. Second, this encouraged the violation of the law by justifying the Hindus trespassing into premises delineated for the Muslims.

In denying a legal personality to land as birthplace, the Court observed that the 'adjudication of civil claims over private property must remain within the domain of the secular if the commitment to secular values is to be upheld.'[154]

152 One can notice the hesitation and reluctance of the Supreme Court in discussion and simultaneous denial of the events of Nov. 22/23. At various points, it accepted and condemned the plantation of idols inside the mosque. Commenting on the maintainability of Suit no. 4 (filed by Sunni Waqf Board), the Court observed that their 'cause of action . . . is founded on the events which took place on 23 December 1949 [when] . . . idols were placed inside the mosque by a crowd of Hindus. The intent of doing so was to destroy, damage and defile the mosque.' *Id.* at 737 (para 612). Yet the Court, while evaluating the testimonies of Hindu and Sunni Muslim witnesses, mentions that the 'possibility of any idol under the central dome prior to 22–23 December 1949 stands excluded on a *preponderance of probabilities*.' *Id.* at 630–631 (emphasis added). This transformation of an established fact into the realm of 'probability' in the same judgment shows how the Court wanted to *deny* this established fact, something they could only suggest in a weak manner due to the historical evidence, even in the form of a first information report (FIR) lodged in the local police station available for this criminal act by the Hindu mob. But this minor detail explains a lot about the eventual outcome arrived at by the Court.

153 *Id.* at 479–480 (para 428).

154 *Id.* at 223 (para 204).

It further stated in strong words that 'our courts cannot reduce questions of title, which fall firmly within the secular domain and outside the rubric of religion, to a question of which community's faith is stronger.'[155] But in allowing the deities' claim, in the absence of any dedication or benevolent purpose, it acceded itself to the subjective faith of the Hindu community.

VI. The Addendum as Judicial Unconscious

Making sense of the *addendum* at the end of the judgment is a profoundly difficult task given the secrecy of authorship (of the main judgment as well as the *addendum*), an unprecedented practice inaugurated by the *Ayodhya* judgment. The judgment's anonymity reveals the temptations of the judiciary to hide behind the veil of secrecy. The deliberate obfuscation of the authorship of the judgment demonstrates that judicial transparency perhaps is no more a democratic virtue for the Supreme Court of India.

We are given to understand by the Supreme Court that one of the judges 'while being in agreement with the above reasons and directions has recorded separate reasons.'[156] The separate elaboration, running into more than a hundred pages of the *addendum*, addresses the following issue: 'whether the disputed structure is the birth-place of Lord Ram according to the faith and belief of Hindu devotees.'

This concern is strange since the anonymous author, signatory to the main text, must have also shared the unanimous view that the issue of the site being or not being the birthplace of Ram is irrelevant to decide the title suit. This leaves one wondering how and why this hypothesis, shrouded in mythology and receding in space and time, even further back from the times of King Vikramaditya, found such elaboration in the *addendum*? The question posed is answered affirmatively with extensive iteration of Sanskrit *slokas* and references to the *puranas*, among other things.

One might characterise the *addendum* as irrelevant or impermissible.[157] But that would be covering up what disrupts the unity of the judgment. The crack it uncovers exposes the original wound. The oddity of the *addendum* is apparent from its different *form* (a distinct font) in which it is written, as if denying any continuity with the main text. In terms of its content, it provides clues to the crisis and contradictions that are at the heart of the judgment itself.

All five judges, after all, agree that the reasons recorded in the *addendum* are separate, but they insist that they are not in disagreement with it. This,

155 *Id.* at 224 (para 205).

156 *Ayodhya Judgment*, note 1 at 929.

157 As learned a scholar as Upendra Baxi, in a short article demonstrating his extraordinary capacity to get everything wrong about the judgment, does not see the addendum as a part of the judgment. 'This, clearly, cannot be part of the judgment because anonymous judicial opinions are constitutionally impermissible.' Upendra Baxi, 'Award of Five Acres for Masjid in Ayodhya Is an Effort to Do Complete Justice' *The Indian Express* (Nov. 12, 2019).

then, is not a dissent. But its attempt to answer the question unworthy of consideration in the main text leaves it split. This outburst is at once in agreement and at odds with the main text. In this strange attempt, the judgment reveals its own crisis. It unravels the uncritical stitching together of faith and fact, tradition and history in both itself and the judgement as a whole.

Mythology as/of the Judicial Discourse

The ***addendum*** in no uncertain terms declared that '[f]aith and belief foster and promote the spiritual life of the soul.'[158] Then it clarified that the faith, trust and belief of the Hindus in the birthplace of Ram was the central inquiry of the ***addendum***. The ***addendum*** scanned and cited centuries-old Hindu texts in original Sanskrit and their English translations. A reference to mythology to appreciate the Hindu belief was one thing but the fusion of mythology into history is quite another. It is the latter which turned the judicial reasoning into ecclesiastical elaboration.

In paragraph 32, the anonymous judge provided the necessary impetus and trigger to the sacred geography argument of the Hindu nationalists when he recited from ***Brihad Dharmottara Purana***, a passage where Ayodhya was one of the sacred cities for the Hindus: 'Ayodhya, Mathura, Maya (Haridwar), Kashi, Kanchi, Avantika (Ujjain) and Dvaravati (Dwarka) are seven most sacred cities.'[159] In one stroke, the judicial discourse far surpassed the claims of the Ram janambhumi movement. The astrological preciseness and 'planetary situation' at the birth of Ram was also inferred from the Valmiki Ramayana.[160] After referring to the visit of Guru Nanak, the founder of Sikhism, who visited the birthplace sometime during 1510–11, the Court found this as corroborating 'the faith and beliefs of the Hindus' which '[could] not be held to be groundless.'[161]

The most fateful part of the ***addendum*** was when the illegal trespass by the Hindu parties found mention as forms of persistent protest, as actions of worship of the Hindu devotees. The context of this comment was the reference to the 1934 demolition of the mosque. The documents of the repair of the mosque were put on record by the plaintiffs of suit no. 4 to show their possession prior to 1949. The ***addendum*** turned them on their head by describing them as 'testimony of ***differences and disputes*** between the parties which took place in 1934 damaging the Mosque.'[162] The silencing of violence, also the hallmark of the main text, was not the only sin of the ***addendum***, as the

158 *Ayodhya Judgment*, note 1, ***Addendum***, at 16 (para 28).

159 *Id.* at 19.

160 *Id.* at 31.

161 *Id.* at 65. 'It can, therefore, be held that the faith and belief of Hindus regarding location of birthplace of Lord Ram is from scriptures and sacred religious books including Valmiki Ramayana and Skanda Purana, which faith and belief (sic.), cannot be held to be groundless.' *Id.* para 72.

162 *Id.* at 99 (emphasis added).

documentary evidence of the mosque destruction metamorphosed into evidence of proof 'that within the premises of Mosque which premises is (sic.) bounded by boundary wall (sic.) the Hindus were visiting and worshipping in the period in question.'[163] The *addendum* concluded the section in the following words:

> The above documentary evidence are testimonials of faith and belief of the Hindus that the Mosque was on the janamsthan of Lord Ram. Their *protests, persistence and actions to worship* within the Mosque is testimony of their continued faith and belief that premises of the Mosque is Janmasthan of Lord Ram.[164]

Conclusion

At one place in the judgment, the Supreme Court observed that 'in matters of faith and belief, the absence of evidence may not be evidence of absence.'[165] But there exists an ineffable and inevitable lack of evidence in the deference of the Court to faith and belief. Besides the erasure of the violence of the 'official' representatives of the rule of law, there were myriad other absences that scar the text of the judgment.

In the last pages of the judgment, the Apex Court decreed the entire disputed land in favour of the deities in Suit no. 5. The central government was asked to 'formulate a scheme' for various things 'including the construction of a temple and all necessary, incidental and supplemental matters.'[166] Along with this, the Court also asked for the allotment of 'a suitable plot of land admeasuring 5 acres'[167] to the 'Sunni Central Waqf Board, the plaintiff in Suit 4.'[168] These directions, the Court continued, 'were issued in pursuance of powers vested in this Court under Article 142 of the Constitution.'[169] This Article of the Constitution empowers the Supreme Court to 'pass such decree or make such order as is necessary for doing complete justice in any cause or matter pending before it.'[170]

163 *Ibid.*
164 *Id.* at 99–100.
165 *Id.* at 215 (para 192).
166 *Id.* at 926 (para 805).
167 *Id.* at 926–927.
168 *Id.* at 927 (para 805).
169 *Ibid.*
170 Article 142, Constitution of India. The Court also asked the government to provide 'appropriate representation . . . to the Nirmohi Akhara in such manner as the Central Government deems fit.' *Ayodhya Judgment*, note 1 at 927 (para 805). This too was strange given that the Supreme Court indicted the Nirmohi Akhara for dereliction of duty in acting contrary to the claims of the deities.

In 1985, the *Organiser*, the mouthpiece of the Hindu nationalist organisations, pointed to the 'display of generosity' of the

> offer of the Hindu religious bodies to Muslims to allot them a different land and get a mosque of their choice design (sic.) constructed through donations raised by Hindus, if they withdraw their claim . . . over the birthplaces of Shri Rama in Ayodhya, Shri Krishna in Mathura and the Vishwanath temple in Varanasi.[171]

In 2019, this language of 'great Hindu generosity' found the constitutional vocabulary of 'complete justice.'

171 *Organiser* (Aug. 25, 1985), cited in Noorani, note 27 at 258.

5 In Lieu of a Conclusion

This book has tried to highlight the functional dimension of law and argue that the technocratic doctrines and interpretive tools exhibit a form of mythology where law becomes a sacred site insular from history or society. Focusing on judicial interpretation(s) in Supreme Court and High Court cases on essential versus secular practices of religion, debates on anti-cow slaughter laws, election law and religious electoral appeals, and the *Ayodhya Judgment,* I have traced the developments in laws and their interpretations and excavated the details wherein lie the deeper mythical structures of secular law. The limited scope of this study has revealed that while interpreting and adjudicating on religious disputes, the modern law most acutely exposes its own mythology.

While adopting the methodology of studying the interpretive processes of the judiciary, with statutes and case law as the primary archival material, I remain aware that the mythological character of the modern/secular law, could be excavated with other methodological approaches, such as looking at biographies – the intellectual or political makeup – of individual judges who delivered the verdicts. One could also undertake a purely 'internal' study of the judicial process (within legal precedents and the language of the law) as distinguished from an 'external' study of law (entirely shaped by political considerations). However, for a historicised account of the jurisprudence of constitutional secularism and religious freedom, it is imperative to situate the 'legal' text within the 'social,' 'political' and 'cultural' context. I have attempted to take a middle path, between the two extremes – 'legal formalism' on the one hand, and instrumentalist view of law on the other[1] – to understand the evolving history of legal judgments. Thus, for this study, the legalese, technocracies and the internal workings of the logic(s) of law have been as important as the social and political forces that shaped its ever-evolving face.

In what follows, I will map a few recent developments that have taken place since some of the major pronouncements discussed in this book. Reflecting on some pressing issues which have been discussed (and are again before the Court demanding judicial intervention and resolution), I maintain that,

1 Upendra Baxi, *Marx, Law and Justice* 16–30 (N.M. Tripathi (P) Ltd., Bombay, 1993).

DOI: 10.4324/9781003398561-6

despite the temptation of viewing the judiciary as an instrument of political class to evaluate its decisions, one must remain focused on the judicial process as well as legal technicalities that construct the logic of these outcomes. In lieu of a conclusion, I will highlight frontiers which could not be pursued in this work but which pave the way for further possibilities in research.

Challenge to the Supreme Court Verdicts

Against the verdicts in the Sabarimala case and the Ayodhya case, review petitions were filed in the Supreme Court in 2018 and 2019, respectively. In *Ayodhya Judgment*, review petitions were filed in the Supreme Court in 2018 and 2019, respectively. The review petition in the Ayodhya case was dismissed by the Supreme Court, while in an awkward turn of events described here, the *Sabarimala* review petition was accepted. The Court, in accepting the review, proposed for a larger bench to decide certain questions of law, such as the essential practices test. This larger bench has not yet been constituted and the issue is pending before the Court. In what follows, I will show how the very acceptance of the review petition was full of errors and ironies within the judicial process. The procedure for the review petition is specified in the Supreme Court Rules, 2013. These rules relating to practice and procedure are made by the Supreme Court with Presidential approval.[2] More specifically, the Indian Constitution has empowered the Supreme Court to review its own judgments or orders under Article 137.[3] The Supreme Court in various precedents has iterated on the limited and narrow scope of its review jurisdiction. This proposition had found its clearest expression in the words of one of India's most prominent judge, V.R. Krishna Iyer, J.:[4]

> A review of a judgment is a serious step and reluctant resort to it is (sic.) proper only where a glaring omission or patent mistake or like (sic.) grave error has crept in earlier by judicial fallibility. A mere repetition,

2 Article 145 (1) of the Constitution of India empowers the Supreme Court to make its own rules 'for regulating generally the practice and procedure of the Court' after an approval from the President of India.

3 Order XLVII (Part IV) of Supreme Court Rules, 2013 lays down the procedure for review. The review petition must be filed within 30 days of the judgment, and once dismissed no other review petition can be entertained. The grounds of review of a judgment are restricted by Order XVIII of the Supreme Court Rules, 2013 read along with Order XLVII, Rule 1 of the Civil Procedure Code, 1908. The grounds for seeking review are limited to (1) discovery of new evidence which was either not found earlier or could not be produced, (2) the existence of an error apparent on the face of the record, or (3) any other sufficient reason which is analogous to the previous two reasons. A review application, according to the Rules, must 'as far as practicable be circulated to the same Judge or Bench of Judges that delivered the judgment or order sought to be reviewed.' Available at: https://main.sci.gov.in/sites/default/files/Supreme%20Court%20Rules%2C%202013.pdf.

4 *Sow Chandra Kante and Ors.* v. *Sheikh Habib* (1975) 1 SCC 674 (emphasis added).

> through different Counsel, of old and overruled arguments, a second trip over ineffectually covered ground or minor mistakes of inconsequential import are obviously insufficient.

Only a conspicuous and glaring error, therefore, on account of judicial fallibility invites a review. This procedural background is important to fully appreciate the reviews of *Ayodhya Judgment* and *Sabarimala Judgment*. The review petitions in the *Ayodhya* case were summarily dismissed in an 'in-chamber' hearing, whereas the Sabarimala review took a long course of hearings eventually leading to a review verdict delivered one year later. The *Sabarimala* review decision asked a larger bench to clarify and settle certain legal questions which arose in the *Sabarimala Judgment*.

The Ayodhya Review

A five-judge bench[5] dismissed 18 review petitions which were filed against the Supreme Court verdict in the *Ayodhya Judgment*. The first review petition was filed on December 2, 2019, by Maulana Syed Ashhad Rashidi, legal heir of original litigant M. Siddiq and U.P. President of Jamiat Ulama-e-Hind,[6] who argued that the use of 'complete justice' under Article 142 of the Constitution by the Supreme Court was erroneous.[7] On December 9, another petition was filed by Hindu Mahasabha questioning the grant of five-acre land to the Muslim side and against the refusal of the Supreme Court to grant juristic personality to the 'land' at Ayodhya.[8] On the same day, 40 academics and activists such as Irfan Habib, Sabnam Hashmi, Jayati Ghosh and Nandini

5 The judges who heard the review petitions were same as those who delivered the original judgment. However, Sanjiv Khanna, J. replaced Ranjan Gogoi, CJ. who retired soon after delivering the *Ayodhya* judgment.

6 'President of Jamiat Ulama-e-Hind Files Review Plea Against Supreme Court's Ayodhya Verdict,' available at: https://theprint.in/judiciary/president-of-jamiat-ulama-e-hind-files-review-plea-against-supreme-courts-ayodhya-verdict/329121/. Full text of the petition is available at: https://scobserver-production.s3.amazonaws.com/uploads/case_document/document_upload/1081/Review_Petition_-__Final_.pdf. All India Muslim Personal Law Board (AIMPLB) was also one of the review petitioners. '10 Key Arguments in 18 Ayodhya Review Petitions Before Supreme Court Today' *Hindustan Times* (Dec. 12, 2021), available at: www.hindustantimes.com/india-news/10-key-arguments-in-18-ayodhya-review-petitions-before-supreme-court-today/story-KYhEw2k3JhDDsJatei9heL.html. Uttar Pradesh Sunni Central Wakf Board, one of the original parties to the dispute, decided against challenging the verdict.

7 The problems of invoking Article 142 in *Ayodhya* judgment are discussed in Chapter 4. Also see Amit Bindal, '"Complete Justice"? Silences and Erasures in the Ayodhya Judgment' 11 *Journal of Indian Law and Society* 48 (2020).

8 'Ayodhya Verdict: Hindu Mahasabha Files Review Petition Over 5-Acre Land to Muslims' *The Indian Express* (Dec. 9, 2019), available at: https://indianexpress.com/article/india/ayodhya-verdict-hindu-mahasabha-files-review-petition-over-five-acre-land-to-muslims-6158509/.

Sundar, among others, filed a review on the ground of framing of the dispute by the Supreme Court as strictly between two religious communities.[9] All these appeals were dismissed.[10] The Supreme Court did not find any substance in the review petitions filed by the parties to the suit. It dismissed the other petition (filed by academics and activists) on the ground that those who were not a party in the original dispute cannot file petitions for review of the final verdict.

The Sabarimala Review

After the *Sabarimala Judgment*, more than 50 review petitions were filed by various individuals and institutions. The first petition was filed by National Ayyappa Devotees Association and the Nair Service Society on October 8, 2018. A five-judge bench heard all the review petitions and delivered the judgment one year later on November 14, 2019, in *Kantaru Rajeevaru* v. *Indian Young Lawyers Association* (2019).[11] The review petitions were heard along with 'several fresh writ petitions [that were] filed as a fall out of the judgment.'[12] The Supreme Court, by a majority of 3:2,[13] decided to keep the review (and fresh writ) petitions pending while referring the same to a larger judge bench.[14]

Two unique and unprecedented aspects of the review judgment are noteworthy. One, that A.M. Khanwilkar, J. who was in favour of the entry of women in the Sabarimala temple in *Sabarimala Judgment* and had concurred with Dipak Misra, C.J., reversed his position in the *review*. Khanwilkar's, J. change of position – he now concurred with Ranjan Gogoi, C.J., and Indu Malhotra, J. – remains unexplained, as he did not write a separate opinion either in the original judgment or its review. Even though one of the justifications given by the majority judges for deferring the petitions was to 'ensure consistency in (judicial) approach for posterity,'[15] this inconsistency in

9 The petition challenged the very opening paragraph of the *Ayodhya* judgment, which reads: 'These first appeals center around *a dispute between two religious communities*' (para 1, emphasis added). For the details of review petition, see 'Academics, Activists File Review Petition Against Ayodhya Verdict' *The Wire* (Dec. 11, 2019), available at: https://thewire.in/law/ayodhya-review-petition. Full test of the review petition is *available at*: www.livelaw.in/pdf_upload/pdf_upload-367790.pdf.

10 'Ayodhya Verdict Is Final. Supreme Court Dismisses 18 Review Petitions' *Hindustan Times* (Aug. 4, 2020).

11 *Kantaru Rajeevaru* v. *Indian Young Lawyers Association* (2020) 2 SCC 1, available at: www.sci.gov.in/pdf/JUD_6.pdf (Hereafter, '*Sabarimala Review*'). All the judges on the bench were same except Dipak Misra, C.J. who retired and was replaced by Ranjan Gogoi, CJ.

12 *Id.* para 1.

13 The majority opinion of *Sabarimala Review* was written by Ranjan Gogoi, C.J. (on behalf of A.M. Khanwilkar and Indu Malhotra, JJ.). The dissent was written by R.F. Nariman, J. (on behalf of D.Y. Chandrachud, J.).

14 *Sabarimala Review*, note 11, para 9.

15 *Id.* para 4.

Khanwilkar's J., opinion remains unexamined. The second procedural uniqueness was the clubbing of the review petitions with 'fresh writ petitions.'[16] The review of a judgment has a limited task to adjudicate on the correctness of the given verdict. Enveloping additional petitions to pose a legal question to be decided by a larger bench is both unwarranted and surprising. In this regard, one can also notice the disparity in judicial approach: rejecting the review petition filed by third parties in the *Ayodhya Review*, while entertaining new writ petitions along with the review petitions in the *Sabarimala Review*. Legal commentators and newspaper editorials rightly decried the majority judgment in the *Sabarimala Review*, calling it 'unnecessary,' leading to an 'irresolution'[17] and 'open[ing] up for abuse the limited jurisdiction for review.'[18]

The majority opinion referred to the pending cases of entry of Muslim women in Durgah/Mosque,[19] the inter-religious marriage of Parsi women[20] and female genital mutilation in Dawoodi Bohra Muslims[21] and observed that the 'prospect of the issues arising in those cases being referred to larger bench cannot be ruled out.'[22] Simply put, the majority foresaw (and listed)[23] the issues that could potentially arise in these pending cases, which overlapped with the review petitions, and thus justified its decision of calling for constitution of a larger bench. The dissent written by R.F. Nariman, J. rebuffed this judicial approach of the majority judges, explaining that

> if and when the issues that have been set out in the learned Chief Justice's judgment arise in future, they can appropriately be dealt with by the bench/benches which hear the petitions concerning Muslims, Parsis and Dawoodi Bohras. What is before us is only the narrow question as to whether grounds for review and grounds for filing of the writ petitions have been made out.[24]

16 While a review petition is filed against a judgment of the Court, writ petition is filed under Article 32 of the Constitution against the violation of any fundamental right. '[B]y virtue of Order VI Rule 1 of the Supreme Court Rules, the "fresh writ petitions" should have been heard by a division bench of the court. If the division bench had any "doubt" regarding the 2018 verdict, they could have invited the attention of the Chief Justice, who could have then referred the matter to a bench of appropriate strength. A reference to a larger bench – if made – could have only been through the writ petitions and not while exercising the review jurisdiction under Article 137.' See K. Nivedhitha, 'Sabarimala Review: The Curious Case of Review Petitions' Adjudication' (Nov. 21, 2019), available at: www.theleaflet.in/sabarimala-review-the-curious-case-of-review-petitions-adjudication/.

17 See Editorial, *The Hindu* (Nov. 15, 2019).

18 A review to the judgment of the Supreme Court is maintainable only if there is an error which is apparent and significant enough to jeopardise the interests of justice. See Suhrith Parthasarathy, 'A Revival of Battle Already Fought and Lost' *The Hindu* (Nov. 28, 2019).

19 Writ Petition (Civil) No.472 of 2019.

20 Special Leave Petition (Civil) No. 18889/2012.

21 Writ Petition (Civil) No.286 of 2017.

22 *Sabarimala Review*, note 11, para 5.

23 *Ibid.*

24 *Id.* para 2 (dissenting opinion).

This was a reminder that the speculative questions and concerns were not in issue even in the original judgment, much less in the review petition. The dissent also noted that most of the arguments in the review were 'reargued' or were a 'mere rehash' of the original case and thus did not constitute 'an error apparent on the face of record.'[25] Responding to the contention of lawyer K. Parasaran (who led the arguments on behalf of the review petitioners) that the sole observations of D.Y. Chandrachud, J. on Article 17 were a 'material error,' Nariman remarked that Chandrachud's opinion was 'a possible view' and thus 'cannot be a subject matter of review.'[26]

Sabarimala Review is unsatisfactory on both procedural and substantive evaluation. One cannot rule out the instrumentalism of the verdict, succumbing to the difficulties that were faced in the execution of the *Sabarimala Judgment*. However, an easy instrumentalist reading does not take us very far. Instead, I suggest that this reveals the *internal* failure of the judicial process. We may find the reason behind the 'irresolution' of the review is the lack of conversation between the majority judges in the *Sabarimala Judgment* and their failure to work through the issues arising from the concept of constitutional morality. To illustrate, one of the issues which *Sabarimala Review* has proposed for resolution to a larger bench concerns the meaning of constitutional morality: 'Is it [constitutional morality] over arching morality (sic.) in reference to preamble or limited to religious beliefs or faith. There is need to delineate the contours of that expression, lest it becomes subjective.'[27]

I have argued in Chapter 1 that constitutional morality in the majority opinion of the *Sabarimala Judgment* was expressed in universalist and transhistorical terminology. This was perhaps the reason why K. Parasaran's argument that constitutional morality was a 'vague' concept found resonance with most of the judges (including Khanwilkar, J., who had previously endorsed it in the *Sabarimala Judgment*). Another issue raised for reconsideration was whether what was 'essential' or integral to religion should be 'left exclusively to be determined by the head of the section of religious group.'[28] This again, as I have argued, was an issue that had not been satisfactorily resolved by the majority opinion in *Sabarimala Judgment*. A closer reading of the interpretive process, therefore, reveals deeper conceptual and procedural issues in understanding the outcomes and implications of critical Supreme Court judgments.

These two questions, posed to a larger bench, are pertinent as they expose the deeper linkage between religious and judicial faith. On the one hand, we find judicial reticence in answering the question of 'religious faith,' ostensibly on the grounds that the Court as a secular institution was incompetent to deal with theology. But on the other hand, we see a form of judicial faith appearing

25 *Id.* paras 18, 19 (dissenting opinion).
26 *Id.* para 14 (dissenting opinion).
27 *Id.* para 5 (majority opinion).
28 *Ibid.*

in the form of universal doctrines and principles which transcend all historical, political or social contexts. The judicial distancing from religious faith illustrated a constitutionalism arising out of liberal political philosophy with modernity defining itself in opposition to myth. But the interpretive process of several critical cases that had, in different ways, to do with religion in one way or another did bring questions of religious faith into the judicial domain, leading the Court to investigate and pronounce on religious faith and its essential practices. This interpretive process, combined with the formal reluctance of the judiciary to confront the religious, has ceded ground to an authoritarian religious orthodoxy, permitting the community leaders to determine the contours of 'essential' religious faith, which also potentially undermines the liberal value of preserving individual autonomy. This conundrum thus calls for a robust engagement with religion without relinquishing the useful elements of liberal constitutionalism as suggested in this study. The judicial discourse must relinquish and abandon the strict opposition between the religious and the secular.

The 'judicial faith,' or what I have described as 'secular mythology,' appearing in concepts like constitutional morality constitutes a blind spot of the legal process. The judiciary needs to recognise the difference between these idealised conceptions and the way they are actualised or developed concretely in particular historical moments. These ideational forms take the shape of judicial faith/mythology unless put under scrutiny with respect to their origins, moves and shifts in different historical periods. As I have analysed in this book, the notion of constitutional morality and the doctrine of presumption of constitutionality of laws enacted by a competent legislature have acquired the shape of judicial faith in their articulation by the judiciary. In this sense, this work encourages critical accounts of standards, norms and doctrines evolved by judicial interpretation by continually putting them to contextual scrutiny.

The Terms of the Cow Protection Debate and the Way Forward

In the cow protection debates, I have tried to rethink the framing of the debate in terms of religion versus economy. This binary was adopted not only by the Hindu nationalists who couched their cow protection position in economic terms but also by scholars who argued that the economy claim was merely a tactic of Hindu nationalists to camouflage the real religious motives. However, the dominant scholarship bypasses the fact that the cow protection cause has been consolidated by the judiciary relying on economic and not religious arguments. Indeed, the argument that convinced the Supreme Court for this total ban on cow slaughter including bulls and bullocks in 2005 was the claim of scientific reasoning linked to improvement of breed, the utility of the cow for the national economy and the argument of compassion for creatures. The Supreme Court did not mention the religious reverence of the cow even once in the majority opinion of *Mirzapur*. It applauded the parties of the dispute for staying away from religious sentimentalism and adhering to economic objectivity. Adcock has demonstrated that scientific advancement and breed improvement was an old trope for the cow protectionists:[29]

> [The state] endorsement for cow protectionist institutions did not begin, but rather continued, after Independence. When colonial cow protectionists embraced the language of breed improvement and focused attention on the slaughter associated with the urban milk supply, they succeeded in securing state endorsement of cow protectionist *gaushalas* as institutions working for the material good of all Indians.

She argues that this connection between economic utility and national development sat well with the rhetoric of Hindu nationalists. Enlisting the utility of the cattle for agricultural draught labour, manure and milk products enabled cow protection to acquire the form of a national cause.[30] The underlying message of such formulation was 'that those who insist on slaughtering cattle are, at best, selfish and short-sighted, and cause significant harm to the national interest.'[31] I agree with Adcock that the economic-religious binary debate has helped little in fighting the militant cow protectionist lobby. She argues that the historical scholarship must note the protesting voices of Dalits who bear the brunt of the cow protection cause.[32]

Also of significance is the work of James Staples who, in his ethnographic analysis of beef trading in South India, challenges the commonly held assumption that the beef trade is primarily conducted by non-Hindus, Dalits or tribals and that 'respect towards cattle, cows especially, and the application of the logic of kinship to human–bovine relations are the near-exclusive preserve of high caste, mostly vegetarian Hindus.'[33] Staples illustrates the role played by wilful ignorance at all levels of the beef trade in Andhra Pradesh and Telangana. His conclusions, based on two decades of work in the field, are important

29 Cassie Adcock, '"Preserving and Improving the Breeds": Cow Protection's Animal-Husbandry Connection' 42(6) *South Asia: Journal of South Asian Studies* 1141–1155, 1152 (2019).

30 In the election campaign of 2014, two slogans used by Hindu nationalists were: '*Modi ko Matdaan, Gai ko Jeevan Daan*' (Vote for Modi, give life to the cow) and '*BJP ka sandesh, bachegi Gai, bachega Desh*' (BJP's message, the cow will be saved, the country will be saved). See Iqtidar Karamat Cheema, *Constitutional and Legal Challenges Faced by Religious Minorities in India* 7 (United States Commission on International Religious Freedom, 2017).

31 Cassie Adcock, 'Cow Protection and Minority Rights in India: Reassessing Religious Freedom' *Asian Affairs* 7 (2018).

32 *Id.* at 9. In July 2016, various Dalit family members were spanked for skinning a cow in Una, Gujarat. This led to a protest by the Dalits involved in carcass removal in the state of Gujarat. See, Shivani Kapoor, '"Your Mother, You Bury Her": Caste, Carcass and Politics in Contemporary India' 3(1) *Pakistan Journal of Historical Studies* 5–30 (2018). Also see Kathryn C. Hardy, 'Provincialising the Cow: Buffalo–Human Relationships' 42(6) *South Asia: Journal of South Asian Studies* 1156–1172 (2019).

33 James Staples, 'Blurring Bovine Boundaries: Cow Politics and the Everyday in South India' 42(6) *South Asia: Journal of South Asian Studies* 1125–1140, 1127 (2019).

not only to challenge the commonly held assumptions about beef eating and trading practices, but also to address the increasing incidents of 'cow vigilantism' which have led to the lynching of people (especially from minority and marginalised communities) on the suspicion of eating beef.[34] Summing up his essay, Staples writes:[35]

> Brahman cattle owners, for example, appear no less likely than their lower-caste or Muslim counterparts to sell their no-longer-useful cattle into the beef market, even if they work hard to maintain ignorance of their involvement. Those who eat beef, too, relate to their own cattle via the same kinship idioms as vegetarian Hindus, in some cases even keeping their own animals out of the market. Such knowledge might be used to challenge a vigilantism which . . . is often less about meat per se and more about the identities of those targeted.

If law is a social discourse, then legal scholarship must find ways for these forms of knowledge to find their way in the judicial discourse. Such a possibility would begin by debunking the modern law's self-assessment as a fully autonomous institution unmindful of the prevalent sociological and historical realities. Staples' work provides a necessary change in orientation for historical and legal scholarship on this issue, which is yet to account for 'the concrete, everyday relationships, exchanges, networks and processes through which buffalo and cows are transformed into one of the most contested components of the Indian diet.'[36]

The Anthropocene and Species Best Interest

Following the methodology of extensive analysis of the judicial precedents and the Court's reasoning, this book could not attend to some important issues which require deliberation in a separate monograph. I will briefly touch upon them here. One such issue with respect to cow protection debate is the concern with the ethical treatment of animals. The cow protectionists (*gau rakshaks*) do not pursue their cause as a political one, but one which is driven by the impetus of ethical commitment towards the cow. This has led to the argument that the Hindu Right, in juxtaposing its religious reverence with the

34 See Shabnum Tejani, 'Cow Protection, Hindu Identity and the Politics of Hurt in India, c.1890–2019' 3 *Emotions: History, Culture, Society* 136–157 (2019). Tejani describes the killing of Mohammad Akhlaq near Dadri in the state of U.P. and merciless beating with iron rods of Dalit youth in Una, Gujarat. *Id.* at 136–138; Vatsa Aditi, 'Dadri Lynching: Delhi CM Arvind Kejriwal Claims He was Initially Stopped from Entering Bisara' *The Indian Express* (Oct. 4, 2015), available at: http://indianexpress.com/article/india/india-news-india/kejriwal-stopped-from-entering-dadri-village-asks-why-me/.

35 Staples, note 33 at 1140.

36 *Id.* at 1127–1128.

ethics of care, stands on the side of animal rights activists.[37] Undoubtedly this claim is false, as the exclusive focus on cows betrays the claim of universal ethics in the Hindu nationalist imagination. Nevertheless, one must acknowledge the strategic use of the argument and challenge it seriously. For legal scholarship, this became a pressing issue as the 2005 *Mirzapur* decision accorded its approval for total ban on cow progeny by evoking the fundamental duty of all citizens under Article 51-A (g) to 'protect and improve the natural environment including forests, lakes, rivers, and wildlife, and to have compassion for living creatures.'[38]

In a different but not unrelated context, a recent Supreme Court decision in *Animal Welfare Board of India* v. *A. Nagaraja & Ors*, delivered on May 7, 2014, is noteworthy.[39] The judgment examined the question of *Jallikattu* (a traditional event with a ceremonial bull-man tussle that has cultural and ritual meanings), bullock cart races in the states of Tamil Nadu and Maharashtra from the vantage point of animal rights. The Supreme Court in its interpretation of the Prevention of Cruelty to Animals Act, 1960 (PCA), articulated the concern for non-human species. It declared that it is the duty of the Court to protect animals as 'they are unable to take care of themselves as against human beings.'[40] The Court upheld the ban on *Jallikattu* on the grounds of cruelty meted out to animals such as bulls and bullocks. Abhayraj Naik, an environmental activist and lawyer applauded the decision of the Supreme Court as the 'legal recognition of nature' and noted that the rights granted to the animals 'unlike the earlier judgements, apply to individual animals and not just to the species of animals.'[41]

The ontological imaginary of this judicial interpretation was guided by what the Court described as 'Species Best Interest.'[42] This certainly was a judicial step beyond a utilitarian and anthropocentric imagination of modernity. One important point to note about the *Jallikattu Judgment* was that despite its citations from Isa Upanishad and struggle for an alternative imagination, its eventual decision follows the rights-based framework in imagining justice for non-human species. Even Naik, who celebrated this judicial endeavour, notes that the judgments on environmental protection exhibit 'a liberal, rights-centric, individualistic frame struggling to contain the seeds of non-Socratic, non-Cartesian, eastern philosophies and lived experiences on the interconnected nature of life.'[43] It prompts the question about whether the liberal vocabulary

37 Cassie Adcock and Radhika Govindrajan, 'Bovine Politics in South Asia: Rethinking Religion, Law and Ethics' 42(6) *South Asia: Journal of South Asian Studies* 1095–1107 (2019).

38 Article 51-A (g), Constitution of India.

39 (2014) 7 SCC 547 [Hereafter, '*Jallikattu Judgment*']. The judgment was written by K.S. Radhakrishnan, J. on behalf of Pinaki Chandra Ghose, J.

40 *Id.* para 26.

41 Abhayraj Naik, 'Law's Nature' 721 *Seminar* (2019), available at: www.india-seminar.com/2019/721/721_abhayraj_naik.htm.

42 *Jallikattu Judgment*, note 39, para 12.

43 Naik, note 41.

of rights is sufficient and adequate for alternative ontological imaginaries. This question troubles, and limits, the transformative potential of the judgment and requires scholarly attention.

Another aspect that requires deliberation is the near-monolithic discursive distinction created between animal lovers and animal haters/killers which feeds into the language of Hindu nationalists. Staples introduces the notion of ambivalence of love as he notes that beef eaters and cattle traders baulk at the idea of eating their own animals or even selling them in the market for consumption: '"They are like brothers and sisters to us", or "they are our children!", people routinely claimed of their livestock, invoking kinship as the logic that prevented them from eating them.'[44] He acknowledges the limits of this kinship-tie, as the animals are not always treated well and demands of excessive labour on them were commonplace. He describes this as mirroring the image of all forms of kinships and familial relations. It is this ambivalence of love that challenges the simplistic opposition between animal-lovers and animal-haters.[45]

Aarti Sethi pursues this argument in distinguishing social embeddedness from the rights-bearing individuality of non-human species in an agrarian social order.[46] Acknowledging that violence was a marked feature of this social co-existence, Sethi seeks to examine its signification or meaning from within the social order. Sethi argues that in the festival of Pola in western India 'the ritual enactment of domination [was] thus not only, or . . . not centrally, the mark of the taming of an animal by humans, but rather the mark of the bull's inclusion into social relations.'[47] She examines the rituals, mythology in folklore and official Gazettes of Maharashtra, associated with Pola: washing of feet, adorning of the bull, its treatment as a gift from Lord Shiva/Mahadeva etc. The Chandanpur Gazette of 1909 records the lore of origin of the festival: how Lord Shiva on the complaint of bullocks of not being treated well decided to appear to enquire into the situation himself, '[m]en got to know of this and that day treated the bullocks so well that when Mahadeo came he found their complaint utterly groundless. The bullocks were outwitted but they still claim their day.'[48]

From a legal perspective, Sethi's claim undermines itself as she recounts the associated violent practices, on the day of the duel, of inebriating the bull, rubbing substances into its eyes and many other cruel manifestations which find mention in the *Jallikattu Judgment*.[49] She also notes the gendered nature

44 Staples, note 33 at 1135.

45 For a psychoanalytic exploration on the point of ambivalence in the context of the death penalty debate, see Judith Butler, 'On Cruelty' 36(14) *London Review of Books* (2014).

46 Aarti Sethi, 'Mahadev's Gift: Men, Bullocks and the Community of Cultivation in Central India' 42(6) *South Asia: Journal of South Asian Studies* 1173–1191 (2019). Sethi pursues an archival and ethnographic study of Maharashtra's Pola festival of bullock fights and bullock races, which are specifically noted in the *Jallikattu Judgment*.

47 *Id.* at 1178.

48 Cited in Sethi, *Id.* at 1183.

49 *Jallikattu Judgment*, note 39, para 12.

of the event and the 'masculine excess spiralling into violence that is a feature of Jallikattu and Pola [was] performatively also indexed to the social body of caste.'[50] Despite this, against the *Jallikattu Judgment*, she maintains:[51]

> In the ritual, while violence is certainly present, animality is not the mark of an exception to socio productive and ethical recognition, where 'the bulls involved are physically and mentally tortured for human pleasure and enjoyment'. Rather, the animal marks the order of the normative. The animal is a participant in rites that represent the domains and practices of normative prescriptions, divine and ancestral debts, familial and social exchanges, relations of domination, hierarchy and violence, which compose agricultural life.

What Sethi describes as 'social personhood' is also an offshoot of the utilitarian anthropocentric imaginary and hardly sensitive to the 'Species Best Interest' standard evoked by the Supreme Court in *Jallikattu Judgment.* While it remains difficult to advocate uncritically for these performances and performative excesses for the reasons mentioned earlier, Sethi reminds us that an inquiry into social embeddedness of meaning is needed for legal justice to become more grounded. This would also interrogate and debunk the ethical claim of cow protectionists as one of 'compassion.'[52]

Mother, Myth and History

One theme I have attempted to pursue is the way in which the technical legal process's conflating of Hinduism with Hindutva ignores the historical and political differences in these categories and bolsters the conflation of myth and history in arriving at the final verdict in Ayodhya. Here, I wish to draw upon this argument of personification of the land and its association with the Hindu nationalist agenda. Gyanendra Pandey notes the recurring theme of 'timelessness' in what he calls the 'Hindu History' that is circulated by Hindu nationalists in various forms.[53] 'The monument (Hindu Temple) and the struggle (for avenging the wrongs) are always there – like God or the nation, eternal and immutable.'[54] In variety of vernacular literature reviewed by Pandey, what is notable is the absence of any concrete historical moment of *construction* of the birthplace. Only the theme of *destruction* follows the logic of historical time

50 Sethi, note 46 at 1190.

51 *Id.* at 1184.

52 Also see Shaheed Tayob, 'Disgust as Embodied Critique: Being Middle Class and Muslim in Mumbai' *South Asia: Journal of South Asian Studies* 1–18 (2019).

53 Gyanendra Pandey, 'The Appeal of Hindu History' in Vasudha Dalmia and Heinrich von Stietencron (eds.), *Representing Hinduism: The Construction of Religious Traditions and National Identity* 369–388 (Sage Publications, New Delhi, 1995).

54 *Id.* at 378.

as firmly fixed. History, framed this way, becomes an endlessly repeated tale of aggression by 'foreigners and resistance by "the Hindus" . . . the identity of "foreigners", like that of "natives", is (permanently?) fixed.'[55] It was this 'permanence' or eternal fixity of identity that formed the hallmark of mythologisation of 'Hindu history' writing. The Ram janambhumi, Pandey notes, on this account was always present, at times 'smiling,' despite its alleged destruction by Babur! On this formulation, there never was any mosque but eternally the sacred land of Lord Ram, an argument central in the review petition filed by Hindu Mahasabha against the *Ayodhya Judgment*. Further, this narrative is useful in discerning the tone, tenor and framing of the 'addendum' of the judgment which also slipped into this form of mythic importance of the land in establishing the faith and belief of the Hindus.

More worrying is the future threat that this discourse of permanent hurt can lead to. A city civil court of Varanasi ordered a survey of the site at Kashi-Vishwanath Temple-Gyanwapi Mosque by a five-member committee of the Archeological Survey of India (ASI).[56] Some lawyers who are inclined towards the cause of Hindu nationalism have celebrated this move as a 'glimmer of hope.'[57] Curiously, they claim that such an order was a logical fallout of the Ayodhya judgment of the Supreme Court,[58] even though the Supreme Court had categorically rejected such opening up of the 'historical' claims. Recently, the All India Muslim Personal Board (AIMPB) approached the Supreme Court to stop the lower courts from entertaining petitions alleging the presence of ancient Hindu temples under Islamic places of worship.[59] The context of this anguish was an Ajmer civil court issuing notices in a petition alleging existence of a Mahadev temple underneath the Ajmer Sharif Dargah. This is clearly in direct contravention of the Places of Worship Act, 1991;[60] however, selective/(mis)readings of previous precedents as seen in the discussion of

55 *Id.* at 379.

56 Radhika Rameseshan, 'Will Varanasi's Gyanvapi Mosque Go the Babri Masjid Way?' *Times of India* (Apr. 13, 2021).

57 Yasowardhan Tiwari and Anujay Srivastava, 'Kashi Vishwanath vs Gyanvapi Mosque: Resolving Battles Over "Sacred Spaces"' *The Daily Guardian* (Apr. 24, 2021).

58 'The present legal tussle could be adjudicated by the court in line with the Ayodhya decision, by recognizing and allowing the claims of the hindu deity, i.e., Lord Vishveshwar or Lord Shiva, over the disputed land and providing adequate compensation and an alternate land for the building of a mosque for the representatives of Gyanvapi Mosque in accordance with the precedent set by the Ayodhya judgment.' *Ibid.*

59 See 'Direct Courts to Not Open Doors to New Disputes': Muslim Body AIMPLB to CJI on Ajmer Row' *Hindustan Times* (Nov. 28, 2024).

60 Curiously, on Dec. 19, 2024, Mohan Bhagwat, the Chief of Rashtriya Swayamsevak Sangh (RSS), an organisation which stands for Hindu nationalism, remarked that 'it is not acceptable to resort to extreme hatred, malice, enmity, suspicion and rake up such new issues on a daily basis.' See Gulam Jeelani, 'RSS Chief Mohan Bhagwat Warns Against Fresh Temple-Mosque Disputes – "Not Acceptable to Resort to Extreme Hatred"' *mint* (Dec 21, 2024), available at: www.livemint.com/politics/rss-chief-mohan-bhagwat-warns-against-fresh-temple-mosque-disputes-not-acceptable-to-resort-to-extreme-hatred-11734751895570.html.

Hindutva judgments is an ever-present possibility in the discursive realm of law. The question of judicial process and the Supreme Court speaking as an institution becomes important in this respect. Equally compelling is the issue of confronting the appeal of mythological history which is increasingly gaining prominence despite its imaginary formulation.

These issues also acquire significance from a feminist perspective. For instance, the concern around protecting the cow, which is imagined as the 'mother' of the nation requires deeper exploration with regard to the implications of such gendered vocabulary and reliance on the maternal metaphor.[61] This would perhaps make the connection between the masculine/militant discourses of cow protection and the protection of the-land-seen-as-mother, the *Asthan Sri Ram Janambhumi*, through the grant of juristic personality more pronounced. Urvashi Butalia had anchored the idea that the role of women and their mythological framing was used by the Hindu nationalists to keep the 'myth' of 'permanent rape' alive around the discourse of 'abducted women' after partition.[62] The nationalist discourse of the newly formed Indian State was keen to bring them back as a question of national honour and virility. In doing so it entirely denied the agency of the abducted women. But for the Hindu nationalists, the desire was quite the opposite:[63]

> The abducted and raped women must stay where they are, in a state, if you like, of *permanent* rape because it is this that will enable Hindu men to avenge themselves on those responsible for this condition of their 'sisters', every Sita and Draupadi.

This eternal identification of permanent victimhood (arising from the discourse of permanent or eternal hurt), Butalia showed, made various men turn towards militant Hinduism during the Ram Temple movement in the nineties.[64] Thus, the Ayodhya dispute and what will follow must also be examined from a gender perspective.[65] Butalia points to the gendered dimension of linking women with property in communal disputes including Ayodhya: 'This is a motif that recurs in almost all communal rhetoric today . . . In much sectarian violence in India today the 'losses' of partition, in terms of women and property provide powerful

61 See generally Tanika Sarkar, 'Nationalist Iconography: Image of Women in Nineteenth Century Bengali Literature' 22(47) *Economic and Political Weekly* 2011–2015 (Nov. 21, 1987).

62 Urvashi Butalia, 'Muslims and Hindus, Men and Women: Communal Stereotypes and the Partition of India' in Tanika Sarkar and Urvashi Butalia (eds.), *Women and the Hindu Right* 58–81 (Kali for Women, New Delhi, 1995).

63 *Id.* at 76 (emphasis in the original).

64 *Ibid.*

65 In this context, the work of British psychoanalytic feminist Jacqueline Rose is worth mentioning. For her scathing indictment of Zionism and the construction of Jewish victimisation as a fixed identity, see Jacqueline Rose, *The Question of Zion* (Princeton University Press, 2005).

referrents (sic).'[66] The *Ayodhya* judgment from this perspective requires a clarion call for thinking about the appeals and strategies of the agenda of Hindu nationalism and how they play out on the legal register.

However, the Supreme Court has stripped Hindutva of all political ascriptions and entrenched it with Hinduism sidestepping the complex history of these notions. This insular and ahistorical judicial attitude demonstrates how the Indian Constitution has been increasingly read as a scripture with its sacred text, institutional hierarchies and morality guiding the judicial interpretive practices. The insistence of this study is not to separate the realms of constitutionalism and religion, or law and myth, but to understand and engage with the close affinities between the two. Such an acknowledgment would make the law less amenable to violent appropriation by the sectarian ideologies of religious politics.

66 Butalia, note 62 at 77.

6 Epilogue

This book advocates a serious engagement with religion, considering it as a real factor in human events, imagination and interactions within the social space. The law and legal institutions cannot discount its impact or relevance. For this, it is important that we understand the meaning of what is it to 'engage' and what is 'religion' or religions. The plural is used not only to refer to many religions, but the myriad possibilities enwombed within a certain religious tradition or text. I have tried to argue that the desire to flush out religion as insignificant in law is driven by the impetus of European modernity, the reverberations of which flash in the attitude and discursive logics of the courts and legal scholars. The deep desire to expunge religion from public affairs is a myth of European modernity.

Nevertheless, every chapter of this book presents a sketch where religion appears to beset all conflicts and make things go awry on the social plane. Specifically, Chapter 3 can be read as a defence of the provision which in plain terms negates the appeal of religion during elections. Then, how are we to understand my plea *against* the exclusion of religion? This requires explanation. I wish to suggest that religion permeates every fabric of social and individual life. By this I do not mean religious rituals, marks or symbols or even a theological lens to view the world as the only possible way to see. Theologically, one cannot entirely separate rituals from religion. Nevertheless, reducing religion simply to the outward performances or a social identity misses the multiplicity which exists in the idea of religion. An over emphasis on religious rites and rituals has cruelly limited the idea of religion to its marks and markers, church and temples. This has reduced religious yearning to empty postures requiring unbearable dumbness of the being to meekly follow and accept, which is why a reluctance towards such meaningless rituals rightfully persists. But this form of religion is only one half of the story, or more accurately, it is only the proverbial tip of the iceberg beneath the horizon.

There is another religion which strives beyond and leaps above the crude materialist view of the world. Other than providing the wonder to the temporal world, it proffers an opportunity to fly with wings beyond the obtuse

DOI: 10.4324/9781003398561-7

confines of mundane reality.[1] A modern ear would be strongly tempted to dismiss such an idea as an individualistic escapism into fantasy. But this *other scene* of religion has provided a beacon light to the struggle against rigid social structures, ideologies of the State or 'mind forged manacles'[2] of rigid theological structures. One must recall that the initial European resistance against the corrupt Catholicism in Germany, where the church issued indulgences and passports for the living and the dead to escape purgatory, found the most formidable resistance from within religion. One notable voice was echoed by a graduate student in liberal arts and an aspiring law student who gave up his legal studies to become a Catholic monk of St. Augustinian order, Martin Luther. He textually opposed the Catholic church by inaugurating another reading of the Bible. His opposition was rooted in a careful re-reading of the scripture, which he translated in German despite the opposition of clerics and Pope Leo X. Luther's entire programme was based on another reading of the New Testament, *sola scriptura*, to demonstrate how the Church and its councils have gone against the scriptural mandates. Even the staunchest critics of Luther cannot deny that religion played a key role in German reformation against the Romish priesthood.[3] Despite the conservative and defensive utterances from Luther entirely dismissing the external change,[4] his radical Biblical interpretations gave effect to a rebellion against the status quo in Germany and Europe. This *detour* into Lutherian reformation only indicates the emergence of modernity as a radical reinterpretation of the scripture.

It is an unfortunate truth that Western modernity in its emphasis on disenchantment has *necessarily* taken away this other side of religion. I emphasise necessarily because the discourse of modernity leaves little space for anything which goes 'beyond' the closed, confined and constricted zones of acceptable

1 The term 'fly' is not merely used metaphorically, as Carlos Eire has demonstrated the issue of 'levitation' historically in a certain cultural context, leaving open the idea of 'impossible' and 'possible' on the historical crossroads. See Carlos Eire, *They Flew: A History of the Impossible* (Yale University Press, Yale, 2023).

2 Borrowing from Wiliam Blake, 'London' in A.S. Hamilton (ed.), *William Blake: The Complete Poems* (Pearson Education, 2008).

3 A historical sketch of Martin Luther from his student years till he was labelled a heretic can be found in Carlos M.N. Eire, *Reformations: The Early Modern World* 133–184 (Yale University Press, Yale, 2016). The initial attack of Luther was framed in defence of faith (*sola fide*) in opposition to the purity of behaviour accented by the Roman church. Luther was remarkably reading St. Paul, a new way to interpret the New Testament. Marxist historians such as Abraham Friesen have dubbed Luther as harbinger of an early bourgeoisie revolution (especially due to his opposition of Peasants Revolt of 1524–1525). But Eire correctly notes that the 'prominent role played by religion in this uprising cannot be attributed solely to the upheaval sparked by Luther, but by the same token religion cannot be totally dissociated from it.' *Id.* at 200.

4 Luther's tirade in April 1525 against the demand by peasants in Swabia to abolish serfdom was the following: 'This article is dead against the gospel . . . This article would make all men equal, and turn the spiritual kingdom of Christ into a worldly external kingdom.' Martin Luther, cited in Eire, *Id.* at 206.

knowledge systems.[5] There is no serious work on the intersection of this other side of religion and law. The closest that we come in law to this other side of religion is in the writings dealing with mythology and law (as discussed in the introduction), where it also appears only as a fleeting glimmer. However, an even more rebellious aspect of religion requires an evaluation of that strand of religion which rebels against religion itself.

One exemplary opening in this direction can be seen in the work of Jacques Derrida. In his later seminars on the *death penalty*, he offers the provocation to read jurisprudence as theology. Derrida deconstructs the taken-for-granted distinctions between law and theology.[6] In the first session of his Death Penalty Seminars (1999–2000), Derrida invokes four mystics and their theological distance with the clerics and ecclesiastical authority: Socrates, Jesus Christ, Joan of Arc and Al Hallaj Mansoor, who were all condemned to the death penalty in Athens, Jerusalem, France and Iraq, respectively.[7] Carefully selecting these figures from different geo-political spaces and times, he focusses on the divine visions or direct communication with divinity of these figures, which in turn made them the enemies of the State. Derrida argues that these figures were condemned for heresy on theological grounds, even though their message was neither secular nor against theology but precisely formulated in terms of theology, which Derrida calls *another* theology which is at odds with itself:[8]

> what is condemned, in all four cases, what sees itself theologico-politically condemned is not the non-theologico-political but another political theology that is visibly promised or announced or demanded or attested to by the four who are condemned to death. All four have a theological and political message, another message.

5 The reluctance of the modern academy to anything remotely superhuman is conspicuous. Scholars are shunned for expanding the horizons or thinking and exploring into anything like psychokinesis, telepathy, clairvoyance or anything which comes within parapsychology. See Stephen E. Braude, *The Limits of Influence: Psychokinesis and the Philosophy of Science* ix–xiv (Routledge & Kegan Paul, New York, 1986). Braude uses harsh language for the 'intellectual community' and 'my colleagues in academia' to note the unscientific attitude of the scientifically minded. This is despite academically rigorous studies proposing to revamp 'humanities' by taking paranormal and supernatural phenomenon seriously. See Jefferey J. Kripal, *The Superhumanities: Historical Precedents, Moral Objections, New Realities* (Chicago University Press, Chicago, 2022). Kripal argues that the traces of another conception of humanities go way back to Friedrich Nitzsche, but despite the revival of interest in Nietzsche, this element of his work is not only neglected but copiously avoided. For Kripal's latest theorisation of the idea of religion as thinking the impossible, see Jefferey J. Kripal, *How to Think Impossibly: About Souls, UFOs, Time, Belief and Everything Else* (Chicago University Press, Chicago, 2024), Chs. 4, 5 and 6.

6 Derrida remarks: 'Only a theologian, only someone who understands the theological necessity of these concepts, can understand the law . . . One must be a thinking or informed theologian to understand modern politics, and therefore what sovereignty is, what the law is, what state is, what jurisprudence is.' Jacques Derrida, *The Death Penalty, Vol. I* 88 (Chicago University Press, Chicago, 2014).

7 Derrida, *Id.* at 1–27.

8 *Id.* at 26.

Derrida challenges any easy separation between theology and political sovereignty. This is indicated in his neologism 'theologico-political.' This diagnosis opens a possibility of 'another message' within religion and acknowledging an inseparable mesh between theological and political/legal interpretive work. The mystical rebellion against the established theology opens an alternative interpretation of religion, another religion, beyond the confines of religious orthodoxy or the dominant *doxa*. My argument opposing separation of 'religious' from the law is premised on the fact that such cleansing would amount to compulsory blindfolding towards this alternative message or alter voice from within religion. Though Derrida limits his analysis to the Abrahamic context, one can find equally forceful references of mystical tradition in India disrupting, truncating and rebelling against the dominant caste and ritual orthodoxy. Mirabai, the devotee of Lord Krishna and devotional (*bhakti*) poet of North India, was condemned for abandoning her official family and 'shamelessly' dancing in the streets, caring little for her upper-caste modesty. Kabir and his songs openly mock the hierarchical rituals in Hinduism. They constitute only a few of many voices from what is known as the Bhakti tradition in Hinduism, which offered another message from within the religious tradition.[9]

Also pertinent to mention is an almost-forgotten figure of syncretic identity, a naked Jewish-Muslim-Hindu sage, Sarmad Kashani, who was beheaded in 1661 in the reign of Aurangzeb outside Jama Masjid in Delhi for heresy and his association with Aurangzeb's brother Dara Shikoh.[10] Shikoh, the eldest son of Emperor Shah Jahan and grandson of Emperor Akbar, was himself an illustrious example of allowing religion of the *other* within the sphere of the political. He is known for a confluence of Islam and Upanishads in the political sphere, provocatively calling out the Upanishadic Hindu texts as possessing the 'secret doctrine' professed in the Quran. Further, he promoted religious plurality by officially producing translations of various Upanishads in European languages under his patronage. This is another example of political and theological confluence opening dialogues against sectarian religious identity and challenging fixed and rigid religious identities.[11] Jeffery J. Kripal situates this episode of Dara Shikoh as an instance of a call for 'Superhumanities.'[12] He forcefully argues

9 See John Stratton Hawley, *Three Bhakti Voices: Mirabai, Surdas, and Kabir in Their Times and Ours* (Oxford University Press, New Delhi, 2012).

10 See Nathan Katz, 'The Identity of a Mystic: The Case of Sa'id Sarmad, a Jewish-Yogi-Sufi Courtier of the Mughals' 47(2) *Numen* 142–160 (2000).

11 For a philosophical overview syncretism of religions in India during Mughal reign, see Jonardon Ganeri, 'Dārā Shukoh and the Transmission of the Upaniṣads to Islam' in William Sweet (ed.), *Migrating Texts and Traditions* 177–188 (University of Ottawa Press, Ottawa, 2012).

12 See Jeffery J. Kripal, *The Superhumanities: Historical Precedents, Moral Objections, New Realities* 50–52 (Chicago University Press, Chicago, 2022).

against a binary opposition of the immanence of humanities studies from transcendental thinking:[13]

> I continue to believe that we can actualize human potential in richer, more complex, more effective and *other* ways. I think it is time to look into the future and foretell the approaching horizon of what I am calling the superhumanities, which would deepen and celebrate the prophetic moral functions of the humanities but not deny the transcendental dimensions one more time for the sake of some perfectly just reservation or accurate criticism.

In the same vein, the argument proposed in this book continues to believe in the openings possible in engaging with what is crudely called religious. This is the only way to deepen the discursive realms of legal thinking of and for the future to come. Following Derrida, this may be *another* law which dares to see the religious ruse: a law which is not inimical to opening the doors of interpretive realms of the yet unknown. Undoubtedly, this would pose unimaginable challenges which need not align with our heart's desire. Nevertheless, shutting down this dimension of the unknown does not show any better alternatives in the contemporary world. I want to be clear: by no means do I propose that taking the margins seriously would make one follow the right path. By no means do I romanticise or underestimate the rotten core of organised religious morality which has relegated women, homosexuals and the laity or ordinary persons to a subhuman status. But the plea of the superhuman also emerges, phoenix-like, from the ashes of the same religion. Remarkably, even within the liberal tradition there are voices, as noted in the introduction, which would not accept obliteration of religion.

Margaret Davies proposes inclusion of the religious as 'feminist and with a view to promoting the interests of women and sexual minorities.' Arguing that religion cannot be reduced to the private sphere and 'participatory secularism is in the interests of promoting diversity, and allowing dissent to emerge both within and beyond religious communities,'[14] she states that leaving religion to the community of religious believers is to stifle dissenting voices and consolidate the orthodox dogmatism to have the final word. For it is 'arguably not religion per se which is problematic for women, but rather religiously based promotion of insularity and dogmatism.'[15] Davies' argument is relatively limited as she highlights a few 'dissenting voices' to subvert the dogmatic religious frame. Derrida, on the other hand, proposes that these margins are both revolutionary and foundational to religion, possessing the potential to

13 *Id.* at 27 (emphasis in original).

14 Margaret Davies, 'The Future of Secularism: A Critique' in Nadirsyah Hosen and Richard Mohr (eds.), *Law and Religion in Public Life* 53 (Routledge, 2011).

15 *Id.* at 58.

unsettle the foundations of all that is rotten in religion. Still, Davies's argument presents an important plea against the exclusion of religious voices from the public sphere as undemocratic and unequal and therefore unsettling liberal constitutionalism from within.

Ratna Kapur has proposed an alternative reading of the Advait (non-dual) Vedanta tradition of Hinduism as opening a deeper understanding of 'freedom' useful for feminists, 'sexual subaltern' and even religious minorities.[16] However, Kapur's reading erases the complex genealogy of the Advait tradition and borders on denial of the bodily erotic in favour of some exotic transcendental freedom. To add to this, her recurrent fear of appropriation by the 'Hindu Right' presents her argument in a strangely defensive tone. However, that is precisely the point, to open debate on registers of readings or paradoxical possible meanings within a religious tradition. Given the fact that an acute deconstructionist philosopher, a political scientist and law professor see the importance of theology, Kripal's quip of 'looking into the future and foretell[ing] the approaching horizon' does not appear merely rhetorical.

It is about time to face the question of religion without hiding the face (ostrich-like) or the proverbial *washing of hands* from *quaestio religiosa* (the question of religion) or *quaestio fidei* (the question of faith). Ganeri has described Upanishads as a *Trojan text*: 'a false gift that will blow up in the mind of its recipient, destroying the error of which it too is a part. It is a false vehicle with a true content.'[17] It is a compelling invitation to closely work through, rather than escape, the text to excavate the potential which can 'blow up' the *mind forged manacles*. Of course, this may sound impossible. But as Kripal has usefully articulated, if politics is the art of the possible, then religion is the art of the impossible. Even if this impossible is not attainable in our lifetimes, it is a pursuit certainly worth giving a try.

16 Ratna Kapur, *Gender, Alterity and Human Rights: Freedom in a Fishbowl* (Edward Elgar Publishing, 2018).

17 Jonardon Ganeri, *The Concealed Art of The Soul: Theories of Self and Practices of Truth in Indian Ethics and Epistemology* 4 (Oxford University Press, New York, 2007).

Author Index

Adcock, C. 25–27, 75–76, 94, 173
Adorno, T.W. 2
Ahmed, F. 20
Amin, S. 22
Anderson, G.W. 21
Anderson, M.R. 4, 19
Ankit, R. 3
Asad, T. 109
Austin, G. 77, 91

Bapu, P. 76
Baxi, U. 2, 10–15, 18, 20, 25, 84, 126, 166
Bhatia, G. 69, 70
Bindal, A. 30, 52, 105
Braude, S.E. 183
Brown, W. 102
Brown, W.N. 72
Butalia, U. 179–180
Butler, J. 176

Caputo, J. 126
Casanova, J. 1
Chatterjee, P. 21–22, 26, 34, 37
Cohn, B.S. 15, 17
Cossman, B. 101

Davies, M. 28–29, 185–186
De, R. 74, 85–86
Derrett, J.D. 14, 57, 71
Derrida, J. 3–4, 6, 183–184
Deshpande, P. 25
Dhavan, R. 34–35, 146
Douzinas, D. 15

Eire, C. 182

Felman, S. 32
Fitzpatrick, P. 2–3, 8, 71–72, 99
Freitag, S. 76

Ganeri, J. 5, 13, 17, 100, 184, 186
Gautam, K. 41
Goodrich, P. 4, 6–9, 23, 71, 140
Gordon, R. 76
Gould, H.A. 138–139
Guha, R. 22, 24
Guha, S. 4, 73
Gupta, A. 140, 149

Hailey, J. 67–68
Hamilton, C. 85
Hawley, J.S. 184
Hirsche, R. 2
Horkheimer, M. 2

Jacobson, G.J. 102–103, 119, 125
Jha, D.K. 137–138
Jha, K. 137–138
John, M. 101

Kant, I. 9
Kapoor, S. 99, 173
Kapur, R. 29, 109, 186
Katz, N. 184
Kelsen, H. 9
Kishwar, M. 21
Kolsky, E. 21
Kotiswaran, P. 67–68
Kripal, J.J. 183–185
Krishna, D. 13

Legrand, P. 20
Levinson, S. 28
Lingat, R. 14

Macaulay, T.B. 21
Macleod, J.M. 21
Mani, L. 21
Marx, K. 11

Menon, N. 12
Millett, F. 21

Naik, A. 175
Nair, J. 18, 65
Narain, A. 101
Nariman, F.S. 34
Nauriya, A. 101
Newbigin, E. 21
Noorani, A.G. 123, 138, 142, 146, 148–149, 165

Olivelle, P. 110

Pandey, G. 76, 177–178
Parel, A. 76
Parker, K. 17

Rai, A. 79
Ranade, R.D. 111
Rao, A. 21, 44
Rawls, J. 103
Rekhi, V.S. 108, 109
Robb, P. 76
Rose, J. 32, 179

Sarkar, S. 22–23
Sathe, S.P. 125
Savarkar, V.D. 149
Saxena, S. 101
Schmitt, C. 16
Schroeder, J. 6
Scott, D. 27
Scott, S.D. 2
Seervai, H.M. 51, 66, 90
Sen, R. 35, 42, 71, 101, 123
Sethi, A. 176–177
Singh, M.P. 64, 90
Singh, P. 79
Singha, R. 19
Skinner, Q. 5
Smith, G. 2
Smith, W.C. 26
Sood, J.D. 9
Staples, J. 97, 173
Suresh, S. 79–80

Taylor, C. 1, 28
Tayob, S. 177
Tejani, S. 26, 73–74, 174
Tellis, A. 32
Thomas, T. 16
Thursby, G.S. 75
Tripathy, P.K. 36, 40–42, 48, 71, 119

Vashist, L. 9, 24, 32

Warrington, R. 15
Watt, G. 6

Yang, A. 76

Zavos, J. 75

Thematic Index

Abdul Hakim Qureshi Case 88, 89
abstract: formulation 19; legality 24; universalism 94
Advait Vedanta 186
ambivalence: in law 10; of love 97
another religion 181–186
anthropocene 96, 174–177
anti-exclusion principle 68–69
'anti-search' of legal traditions 14
Ashutosh Lahiri Case 91, 92
Ayodhya: addendum 162–164; Allahabad high court judgment 130–132, 140–143; Archaeological Survey of India (ASI) Report 147; change in sovereignty 144–145; and constituent assembly 129; faith and belief 143, 145–147, 159, 162–164, 178; idol installation 137–139; *namaz* by Muslims 136; perpetual minor 131–132, 160; principle of (natural) justice buried 142–143; property of idol versus property of individual 54; review petition 168–169; the suit of 1885 148–150; worship at mosque during Mughal period 145–147

Bhagavad-Gita 119
biological determinism 65, 68
Bohra Muslims 49–52
Bukhari Case 116, 123
butchers: caste and class of 85–86

Chandogya Upanishad 110, 113
class antagonism 12
Classical Hindu Law 14–15
codification: and caste 21; and gender 21; and translation 16; uniformity and precision in 21
colonial: adjudication and interpretative techniques 17; anxiety 101, 126; modernity 13–14; subjectivity 15
communal identity formation 115
community determination 29–30, 46, 55, 68–70
Constitution Assembly Debates 79–82
Constitution of India: complete justice 143, 160, 162, 164–165, 168; cow protection clause 74, 78, 91–92, 94; free exercise clause 35, 85; right to equality 85; right to freedom to practice trade and business 85, 88
constitutional: hierarchy 36; morality 64–66, 68–69, 171–172
constitutionalism 84, 91; and religion 2; transformative 10
cow: age and usefulness test 87; Arya Samaj and the dual idiom 27; dung as Kohinoor diamond 97; and eco-law 96; as an ideological symbol 75–77; as mother 79, 83; protection 74, 78, 80–81, 172–173; and reversal of constitutional logic 91–92; sectarian discourse of cow protection 75–77; and self-determination 81
cultural nationalism 72, 77

Dara Shikoh 184
Debutter property 152–153, 155–156
denominational autonomy 55, 57, 63
despotism 16
dharma 14
Dharmashastras 14
Dhruva Case 111
doctrine: of constitutional interpretation 72–73; of essential practices 33, 42–43, 46, 48, 55, 85, 91; of

presumption of constitutionality 86, 89, 91, 95, 172
double marginalization of native women 21
Durgah Committee Case 46
Dvija and *Sudra* 14

East India Company 15
economic: base 11; utilitarianism 80–82, 84, 87
Excommunication Case 49

Faruk Case 90–91, 95
First Anand Margi Case 57, 59

governance feminism 67

Haji Usmanbhai Qureshi Case 93–94
Hanif Qureshi Case 84–87
Hashmatullah Case 92–93
Hindu identity: before courts 119, 126; formation 76; as a militant project 100
Hinduism: as religion 109, 118–119; as a 'way of life' 109, 117–118
Hindutva: eros/thanatos 126–127; judgments 101, 104, 120, 124–125; meaning 120, 122

ideological infrastructure of British rule 15
Indian political history 102–103
indigenous dispute settlement system 15
internal resistances 13
Islamic law and the colonial encounter 18–20
Ismail Faruqui Judgment 133, 135–137

Jallikattu Judgment 176–177
judicial: faith 172; unconscious 32, 162
juristic person: *Guru Granth Sahib* as 157–158; Hindu idol as 150–162; land as 158–159

K.K.K. Nair 138–142
Kultar Singh Case 114

language question 79
law: deafness of 8; emancipatory force 3; fixity and certainty of 20–22; instrumentalist approach 11; judge-made versus jurist-made 20; Marxist tradition 10–11; materialist approach 11; mythic self-enclosure of 4; mythologization 73; positivist understanding 4; reject proposal 10; relative autonomy of 12; return proposal 9; and subaltern 22–25; as superstructure 11–12; system of language and interpretation 10; textual and customary 14
liberal paradox 34, 37, 51
'living law' 3, 10
Lutherian reformation 182

Mahant Raghubar Das 148–149
marginalization of legal subjects 21
mask of secularization 28
mimamsa 14
mind forged manacles 182
Mirzapur Case 94, 96, 97
moderate contextualism 5
modernity: binary of myth and 25; as profound reorientation of past 13; project of 3; or rationality 72, 78
modern law: denial of the 'other' in 7; a gift from the west 2; habitual logic of 7; judges as theologians in 13, 17; mythology of 4
Muslim Personal Law 116
mystical: construction 7; efficacy 111; symbolism 110, 113

narrative: or language of faith 9; of mystification 83–84
Nathdwara Temple Case 52, 56–57
non-legal vocabulary: annihilation and erasure of 7, 23; dress 6

Occidental property 8
Om Judgment 110, 111
Orientalist tradition 17

partition 102
permanent rape 179
pious purpose 153–159, 161
Platonic guardians 15
political: liberalism 27, 103; speech as corrupt speech 102–103
politics of translation 26
President's rule 134
public: character of private temple 44; order 36, 41, 57–59, 61; versus private divide 103

Queen Victoria's Proclamation 25–26
Quran 16

Ratilal Premchand Gandhi vs State of Bombay 43
religion: doctrinal tenets of 41–42; essential versus non-essential facets of 38; as a European historical category 26; high versus popular 42; as the 'other' of modern law 1; as a 'private' affair 27; rationalist or modernist 42
religious: administration of the shrine 47–48; appeal 104, 107, 113, 120; autonomy 33; denomination 46; discrimination 52; essential versus 91; institutionalized practices 52; symbol versus myth 112; symbolism 11, 107, 100; systematic appeal 105
Representation of Peoples Act, 1951: section 123(3) 100, 104, 121; section 124(5) 105
reversal of transcendence 8
rule of: harmonious construction 45–46; law 3, 9, 26, 133, 157, 159, 164; primogeniture 53–54

S.R. Bommai Case 124–125, 133–137
Sabarimala: judgment 62, 65, 68–69; review petition 169–171
sacrifice 80
sati 21, 68
Satsangi Judgment 118, 122
Second Ananda Margi Case 60, 61
secular: constitutionalism 73; mythology 3, 72, 74, 94–96, 98, 172; versus mythological 72–73
secularism 124, 126–127; ameliorative 119; basic structure 134; governance-oriented 103; rethinking 27–29; separation of church and state 37
Shakuntala Nair 138
Shashtric law 14
Shebaits 131, 152–157, 159–160
Shirur Matt Case 33, 38–42, 47, 49, 55, 69–70
Shubhnath Deogram Case 106–107, 109
silencing of multiple significations 24
social: constructivism 5; order 12; welfare and/versus reform 34, 36
Sri Venkataramana Devaru Case 36, 44–46
superstructure 11

temple entry legislation 38, 44–46, 117–119
theocratic state 16
translatability 19
Trojan text 186
typological metaphor 12

untouchability 45–46, 66–67, 119

vulgar instrumentalism 11

Warren Hastings 15–16
Western Enlightenment tradition 1

Yousuf Rawther vs Sowramma 20

FSC
www.fsc.org
MIX
Papier | Fördert gute Waldnutzung
FSC® C083411

Kolibri 360 GmbH
Ferdinand-Jühlke-Straße 7
99095 Erfurt, Deutschland
produktsicherheit@kolibri360.de